Galley Guru

EFFORTLESS GOURMET COOKING AFLOAT

BY

Lisa Hayden-Miller

D1417887

Paradise Cay Publications, Inc.
Arcata, California

Cover design by Rob Johnson, www.johnsondesign.org
Editing and book design by Linda Morehouse, www.webuildbooks.com

Illustrations by Joanna Betts, www.joannabetts.com

Cover photo by Ingrid Misner, www.aiphotography.com
Galley photo aboard *Solitude,* owned by Gayle and Boyd Halliwell

Printed in the United States of America
First Edition
ISBN 978-0-939837-79-X

Published by Paradise Cay Publications, Inc.
P. O. Box 29
Arcata, CA 95518-0029
800-736-4509
707-822-9163 Fax
paracay@humboldt1.com

For Lesley. Towards a wilder shore...

Table of Contents

Acknowledgments

Each book is, in its own way, a voyage. There are so many people to thank for their help and support along the odyssey that has become this manuscript that I could truly fill another volume with gratitude. But needs must and so I have chosen not all, but the most significant in what is almost an embarrassment of riches.

Towards the end of this crossing I ran into an unexpected tempest and would never have come through but for the assistance of one very unique person and special friend, Allan Nimmo. Thank you, Allan, for your generosity, your innate kindness, inexhaustible patience (though you must admit, I tried) and, incredibly, for being "my eyes" in the darkness. It is a remarkable person who will put the needs of others above his own. If I suspected this of you before, I know it now with certainty. You do it all with laughter. You do not give up just because it would be easier to do so. The world, Allan, is a much better place because you're in it. This is but a small token of "my wonderment of you." Without you the *Galley Guru* would still be at sea.

Equally, this project might have run aground many times were it not for Peter Betts, my stepfather, who is also my indefatigable agent, good friend, and staunch supporter; and Pat Silver-Lasky Betts, my mother, who is also a writer, teacher, and my best critic. Thanks to both of you for innumerable good times, fabulous dinners, and for giving me shelter. (That makes twice that I've learned how to walk!) Thanks, too, for the best test kitchen in London. Thank you to Stephen Johnson, for teaching me to distinguish stem from stern and for encouraging me to write about the journey. Merci mille fois to the lovely Colette Lotti-Purta. We didn't use the pictures but we had fine adventures, didn't we? Merci aussi to Jacques Martin for sailing off into the sunset, leaving Sunset Charters in my hands. Thanks to Dick and Barbara de Kew, wherever you are, for the islands, for Greece, and for not knowing how to cook. Thank you to my vegan connection: Richard, Aylin and Alexander Niles for just the opposite.

My publisher, Matt Morehouse, thank you for providing safe harbor. And an abundance of thanks to my talented editor of infallible taste, Linda Morehouse. You are an absolute joy to work with.

To the amazing and beautiful Joanna Betts, a very heartfelt thank you. Your illustrations are wonderful and elegant and have brought these pages to life. We will do another soon again I vow...

Finally, to all the fascinating and warm people whom I have had the great good fortune to meet no matter how near or far, thank you for educating me, welcoming me as a guest at your table and for sharing the good life with me. This book is also for you.

About the Author

Lisa Hayden-Miller adores sailing and has a passion for food and far horizons. In the Greek Islands, she ran a gourmet's galley for Celebrity Charters, serving up the bounties of the Mediterranean in rough seas or calm.

In Spain she was concurrently chef/co-owner of Marbella's popular dining spot El Pozo Viejo as well as the exclusive "Upstairs" Restaurant. On Sunday mornings, she co-hosted *The Good Life*, a two-hour English language radio magazine program. In spare moments she gave cooking classes to residents and tourists alike, both in English and Spanish.

After El Pozo, she created Hasty Pudding, an exceptional catering business, featuring uncommon cuisine from all over the globe. Subsequently she took Hasty Pudding from the Costa del Sol on to London, New York, Santa Barbara, and Los Angeles.

In all her travels, with countless experiences of cruising the Caribbean, crossing the Atlantic to sail the Mediterranean, as well as writing numerous articles and collecting a wonderful stock-in-trade of authentic and delicious international recipes, she has learned what works and what doesn't work in the galley.

Her last book, *Fondue with Friends*, was published in London by Powerfresh Ltd.

Introduction

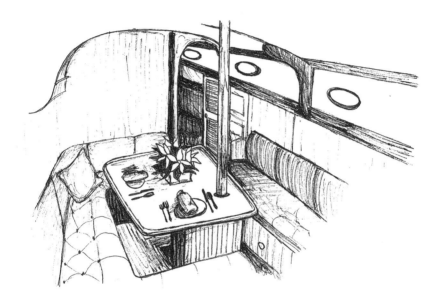

*"Sharing food with another human being is an intimate act
that should not be indulged in lightly."*

—MFK Fisher

Truly Great Food

The galley of a sailboat is a doll's house kitchen pared down to the barest necessities. How on earth—or sea—will you manage? A toy pantry, how quaint! The merest suggestion of counter space . . . .

The demands of a tiny postage stamp galley are utterly different from those of terra firma kitchens with ample pantries, broad central islands, and unlimited conveniences. In a galley you may have gas or electricity—but not always. And then there will be the times when you will find it difficult just to stand upright. How can you propose to produce extraordinary cuisine in conditions like that? Dinner? Somebody send out, please. Ah, but what if you are in the middle of the Atlantic?

Let us not give up the ship so soon. Where is it written that to acquire the art of sailing you must also surrender the art of eating? One can find romance on the high seas without having to forgo the sensual pleasures of the palate. The secret? Well, there are only two, really.

First: Truly great food does not always have to be a production number.
Second, and most important: Everything depends on your pantry.

On a sailing boat that means prudent choices about what to bring aboard and what to leave behind. And then you have to learn how to organize it once you've got it. In a kitchen, you must be comfortable. But in a galley, you must above all be organized. It requires planning.

You will need to plan for the most inclement weather, when setting foot below decks may become impossible for more than moments at a time. At times like these, you will be more concerned with oilskins than olive oil. Nourishment will need to be simple, sustaining, and stowed firmly yet within easy reach.

But when the winds blow fairer and the waves are gentle upon the bow, a sailor can venture again to the galley for something more than nutrition. There are those who set to sea content to merely subsist on stews from cans whatever the weather, either from lack of imagination or just because it seems easy. I call this giving up. With a little forethought and with almost the same ease, you can feed your spirit as well as your body. You can create real cuisine. From a tiny galley!

This life, and the nourishment thereof, is about more than just survival. It is, or should be, about good company and sharing and all the pleasures that enrich and restore us as human beings. We thrive on this at home. How much more so should we thrive, then, where water's edge meets wind and sky?

Setting sail for far-off lands, you will do well to be armed with a plan and a pantry full of useful ingredients. This book will help facilitate the plan. The *Galley Guru* makes good use of shortcuts and has specific techniques for the extraction of every bit of flavor from as few ingredients as possible. With its help you will find more time to be above decks enjoying the sail, fueled with real food from which you will derive pleasure as well as plenty of strength for battening down the hatches.

Later, when the sun sinks splendidly over the yardarm, those with an appetite for life may squeeze the last drop of lime in the coconut, survey the horizon, and welcome the end of another splendid day at sea.

Whether winds are calm or foul, sailing is a learning experience. Eating habits afloat change of necessity, since you work and live in a small space and haven't a whole lot of time to prepare dazzling meals created from ingredients that neither spoil easily nor, hopefully, sink the ship. Landing in a foreign port, your culinary horizon expands again, as you are able to add the freshest, most delicate, often most unusual foods to your menu.

For me, from the first landfall one of the most rewarding aspects of the cruising life has been the fun of hopping off the boat, mixing and mingling in foreign markets, learning what fresh food is available, and hauling it back to the galley to start the cooking pots sizzling. Often the mingling process brings fascinating new friends who are eager to share their stories along with local recipes, "the way the people really do it in my country." This will add to your repertoire and reputation, as it has mine, as a multifarious cook with a flair for the exotic.

I am continually surprised at the number of sailing memoirs written by people who, intoxicated with the excitement of traveling rough round the globe, and thinking nothing of the possible dangers or discomforts of a life at sea, pale in enthusiasm when faced with the prospect of having to change their eating habits. Nevertheless, if you'd wanted to stay home and eat what you were used to, you would be on that couch right now with the rest of the tubers. Since you are reading this book and contemplating the victuals you will need to prepare onboard an oceangoing vessel, you are obviously the adventurous type. Renounce the hamburger. Relinquish the french-fry. Fill your table with rare fruits and vegetables. Reward yourself.

Many of the recipes I've included can be made without refrigeration. I have taken the tack that you will not have (or perhaps not for very long have) the use of a refrigerator. On a boat, the motto is, "better safe than sorry." The best equipment can go wrong. The use of any electrical or otherwise powered equipment is a luxury you might just as well not count on. If you have a fridge and a good working freezer, it will ensure that you have a supply of fresh bread (that you don't have to bake with your own hands), a chicken for your pot, and plenty of fish to fry. You will ice your drinks, crunch into crisp Caesar salad, and follow with a luscious slice of chilled chocolate pie. If all these things are a dream of shore leave, make up a bowl of linguine with clam sauce, raise a glass to the stars, and consider yourself a fortunate being in the scheme of things.

Definition of Symbols

All the recipes in this book are categorized (quite loosely) according to practicality of preparation depending on weather conditions and other variables. Symbols refer to the following rather arbitrary states of affairs. Use them as a guide only. If you feel like making pizza in heavy seas, be my guest.

Shore Power

Remote Anchorage

Beam Reach, Trade Winds, Beautiful Weather

Under Way

Heavy Seas

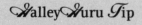 Valley Guru Tip

The secret to cooking in a small space, especially one that won't stay still, is to be very organized. Use a plastic shoebox for the spices you need for the meal. You can put spice bottles in it and put it in the sink so it doesn't slide around as you are cooking. Always put your utensils and ingredients back where they came from after use. Never, ever, leave a knife lying around.

What You Will Find in This Book:

✳ Top secret chef's techniques for quickly and easily getting the utmost flavor into food.

✳ Delicious and easy recipes created around galley staples and loads of tricks to preserve them.

✳ One classic and classy cooking method that works wonders at sea.

✳ How to keep it simple, sailor.

✳ How to live your dream and eat like royalty doing it.

 Galley Guru Tip

Believe this: It is no more difficult to bathe a few vegetables in extra virgin olive oil and garlic and fling them on the barbecue or under the grill than it is to open and cook a tin of readymade beef stew.

Servings

All of the recipes in this book serve four people quite generously unless otherwise specified.

So, sails set for adventure, it's off to see the world and bring the world to your table!

Survival in the Galley

Tips and tricks on the art of preservation, self and otherwise . . .

Help! I've Lost My Measuring Cup

Measuring is not rocket science. Get out your trusty wineglass. It may be smaller or larger, but it will do for most liquids, not the least of which is wine. The measurements in this book are suggested as a guideline only. They are never meant to be exact. For our purposes, a cup is a cup is a cup. As long as you have a measure that you are comfortable with, and you are consistent, you can make these recipes your own.

When you read a pinch of something, it might mean ¼ teaspoon or ½ teaspoon. Just go by feeling. Remember you can always go back and put in more, but it is difficult to take something out if you have put in too much. If you run across an ingredient you just don't like, leave it out entirely or substitute for it something you do like.

A pat of butter: Remember those little individual slices of butter that you get at coffee shops? That is what we are calling a pat. Use this to garnish soups to make them creamier or to top a fish before serving.

The following is a conversion guide you might find useful. It is the basis for the measurements in this book, because a cup of water weighs more than a cup of feathers but less than a cup of lead.

Conversion Chart

¼ teaspoon =1.25 ml	1 ounce = 28.3g
½ teaspoon = 2.5 ml	2 ounces = 56g
¾ teaspoon = 3.75 ml	3 ounces = 85g
1 teaspoon = 5 ml	4 ounces = 115g
½ tablespoon = 7.5 ml	5 ounces = 140g
1 tablespoon = 15 ml	6 ounces = 170g
2 tablespoons = 30 ml	7 ounces = 200g
3 tablespoons = 45 ml	8 ounces = 225g
4 tablespoons = 60 ml	9 ounces = 255g
5 tablespoons = 75 ml	10 ounces = 285g
6 tablespoons = 90 ml	11 ounces = 310g
4 tablespoons = ¼ cup	12 ounces = 240g
8 tablespoons = ½ cup	13 ounces = 370g
16 tablespoons = 1 cup	14 ounces = 400g
1 cup = ½ pint	15 ounces = 425g
2 pints = 1 quart	16 ounces = 455g
4 quart = 1 gallon	1 pound = 455g
¼ cup = 60 ml	2 pounds = 910g
½ cup = 125 ml	1 kg = 2.2 lb
¾ cup = 185 ml	Butter
1 cup = 250 ml	1 cup = 225g = ½ lb
⅓ cup = 85 ml	½ cup = 115g = ¼ lb
⅔ cup = 170 ml	¼ cup = 56g = ¼ lb = 4 tablespoons

Liquor

The sun is over the yardarm. I don't have to tell you what to drink. I trust you will have figured that one out for yourself. You may prefer beer to wine, rum to gin, mint tea to mint juleps. Don't worry, apart from offering a selection of my favorite cocktails for you to choose from, I wouldn't dream of entering into this discussion. Should you come to visit, I would make every attempt to have a glass or two of your favorite for you.

When it comes to food preparation, however, I have an opinion that I will share with any passing stranger. I didn't invent it. It has been passed down through an illustrious line of French chefs, who, let us be honest, are qualified to pass down whatever they like when it comes to food.

So here it is: Alcohol, of late a much-maligned substance, enhances many a goodly pot. In other words, with nothing more innovative than a splash of the grape or grain, humble food is transformed into something finer. And since it is something that cannot spoil, your precious grog, navy or otherwise, is worth setting aside a shelf for. Not only for its contribution to the flavor of your dishes, but also for its ability to preserve foods that might otherwise spoil, liquor is nearly indispensable in a gourmet's galley.

The master chef throws together a joyous concoction of butter and oil, wine and herbs, sets it to bubble furiously for a few raucous seconds, and, with the grand gesture of a magician pulling Coquilles Saint Jacques from a beach hat, pours the mixture over an attendant fish. Et voilà! Heaven in a soupspoon. This trick would be hard to pull off without the wine. All of this can be done in the smallest galley.

For white wine, you can, and I often do, substitute dry vermouth. It packs more punch than wine and has an herby taste that adds a certain *je ne sais quoi* to food. If you have nothing more than a sausage and a bottle of red, well, that's dinner and a good one—particularly if you remember to cook the sausage in some of the wine before you drink the rest with the meal.

Apart from such delights, in galley-speak, generosity of spirit means that any spirits you have on hand could, with benefit, be shared with your dinner. And as those of a culinary bent know, "many a slip between the cup and the lip" often refers to complete accidents that have developed into the great *Méthode* of classic French cuisine.

Consequently, when the boat rocks, you needn't hold that hand too steady. If some little something spills into the pot, it will lend flavor if not fervor to a meal.

 Galley Guru Tip

I probably don't have to say it, but you never know: The galley is no place to try out your amazing Cherries Jubilee, Steak Diane, or any other flambéed dish. Even in port, there is just too much that could go wrong with a flare-up, so leave your recipe card for Café Brulot at home where it belongs.

Chocolate

Theobroma cacao, chocolate's scientific name,
literally translates as "food of the gods."

The benefits of chocolate have long been known. Substances in chocolate named anandamides (ananda is the Sanskrit word for bliss) act on specific receptors in the brain called bliss receptors. As well as being a natural analgesic, or pain-killer, chocolate is also mildly stimulating because of the presence of theobromine, an alkaloid that is closely related to caffeine.

For all these cheerful reasons and because cocoa has a superlatively high food value, is high in antioxidants, and contains as much as 20 percent protein, chocolate can help us feel better and function more efficiently. It is exceptional for quickly replenishing stores of physical and mental energy lost in such strenuous and energetic activities as mountain climbing, for instance, or sailing in any weather. Full of magnesium, which feeds our nerves, chocolate may even restore mental clarity needed for quick thinking in times of stress. In any case, it is delicious, it keeps, and it doesn't take up much room on a shelf. Unless you just have an aversion to chocolate, here is a case where indulgence might be a good thing.

All of the benefits apply, of course, only to high quality dark chocolate such as Belgian, French, or Swiss that contains at least 70 percent cocoa solids produced only with cocoa butter. A little of this divine chocolate goes a long way. The gooey stuff from the confectionery counter overladen with sugar and ersatz ingredients is not helpful for anybody.

You will find that as well as sweet chocolate recipes, I have included a recipe for a quick and delicious Chicken Mole (pronounced Mo-lay), a delightful Mexican dish that uses chocolate in a way that might surprise.

Tofu: The Other White Sauce
or
What To Do Until A Cow Comes Aboard

Cream is nice. Ice cream, yummy. Sour cream converts a virtuous baked potato into something sinful. Butter is better with everything—unless, of course, it's rancid, separated, or just plain off your diet. Of all the food tricks I have learned on land or sea, the one that involves tofu will truly make you a galley guru!

There are plenty of people who do not think they like tofu. These are conservatives who peer with distrust at those—let's face it—rather tasteless little white cubes they encounter in their stir-fry or floating listlessly in their miso soup. Some might have ventured as far as the health food store to try one of those savory packets of barbecued tofu creations in the hope that they will encounter something that tastes like something recognizable. Unfortunately, tofu prepared in that way just tastes like tofu with some sauce helplessly clinging to it like a drowning person to a life raft. Personally, in this form, I can take it or leave it.

OK. But, if you live in the modern world you may have come across the notion that dairy products, while promoted as healthful by some, are entirely repudiated by others. In any case, I don't think there are many (save, perhaps, the dairy association) who would not agree that overdoing dairy fat can be bad for you. So even if you could preserve the necessary ingredients for the duration of your trip, an overindulgence in cheese soufflés or generous lashings of cream sauce could elevate your cholesterol into the reaches where it is time to call in the medics. I have nothing at all against butterfat. You will see real cream in these recipes when it is simply the only thing that will taste just right. Cheese of every shape and variety is wonderful to grace a humble sandwich or to set to bubble in an excellent fondue. But by eating these foods in moderation you can enjoy them without remorse. Sailing builds health, but it also requires health. So why live on a consistent diet of foods that are taxing for our digestion and at the same time make it increasingly arduous to hoist the main?

Tofu to the rescue, where east has at long last met west! The very blandness of tofu makes it take on the surrounding flavors of a dish, but especially if it is blended into a cream. A certain kind of tofu, called silken, which is readily available in many supermarkets and all health food stores, has a sort of custard-like texture and is actually produced inside little stackable airtight boxes. **It never sees light or air until you open it, which makes it just about indispensable on a boat.** In other words, it keeps. And the things it can do!

How would you like to have all the lusciousness of a perfect cream sauce with little effort, no cholesterol, and an end result that is not fattening? Or perhaps a rich chocolate pie would take your fancy, especially if it didn't pile on a lot of extra pounds that would keep you from all the really fun things—such as climbing the mast.

Ounce for ounce, replacing tofu for cream in a recipe does two important things. It removes fat and adds protein. This makes it an excellent dietary choice for the rigors of the cruising life. This, you may argue, is not enough of a reason to wax lyrical. But consider. Handled with a little care, tofu can do anything cream can do. It can admirably blanket a lasagne or stuff a cannelloni. You can produce a beautiful vegetarian stroganoff rich with wild mushrooms, or a creamy fettuccine that you could serve without apology to Alfredo himself.

The scrap of effort required in preparation is hardly worth mentioning (mostly, opening a box and whirling a few ingredients around in a bowl.) You might be forgiven for thinking you were doing a bit of magic. With tofu as your new best friend, you'll be a culinary star and nutritional savior all at the same time.

In this book I show you ways to use tofu for sauces, soups, or desserts. Do so and you'll be out of the galley and up on deck before anyone can whisper seasick.

Stocking the Galley Pantry
or…
I have a little list

You know the old pirate adage: a ship is only as good as the loot in her hold. Which brings me to loot of a culinary nature: ingredients—and you should take care to make them the best that they can possibly be.

While I've listed a few ingredients you might not be familiar with, I don't expect you to journey to a secret garden hidden in the mists atop the most sacred mountain in Tibet to hand-pluck the rarest bud that flowers only one night of the year just before moonrise. That having been said, there are some things that are worth taking the trouble to find because, and repeat this to yourself at regular intervals as a litany:

You can't make good food with bad ingredients.

In an ideal world, we would be provisioned to the hilt with spices from Samarkand and thus be able to whip up a steady stream of impeccable meals, to the deathless admiration of all our friends. At the time of this writing, from my home computer I have only to pull up one of a dozen websites to have Maine lobster delivered fresh to my door. Tomorrow night could find me indulging in black truffles from France or Beluga caviar from the Caspian Sea. Whatever floats my boat.

At sea, it's all very tricky. I have at my disposal only what I have been able to bring with me, or if in port, whatever I am lucky enough to find in the local markets. While faraway places can offer unexpected gastronomic pleasures, there may come a day when scarcity will stare you straight in the shopping bag. What to do?

I make my case for the careful choosing of staple ingredients from something as simple as the salt to season your meals to those little tins of lobster pâté that you might tuck away for that rainy (or worse) day. You will do well to buy the best from the start. The best occasionally means the most expensive, but not always. It's what tastes best. In the case of a galley, the best not only has to be delicious but should also save your time and your health as well as be able to be stored without spoiling for long periods. It should be compact enough to stow without having to jettison the engine to create space. It's a tall order, growing taller with every requirement.

With only honey, money, and a small guitar, the owl and the pussycat set out on a perilous sea journey. You will take more. When you are wondering where in the world you are going to procure some of what might be the more unfamiliar items, please see Where in the World? This special section (pages 293-298) is full to brimming with information on how to shop for these things. So, to the list.

Sea Salt

You might think it unwarranted to enter into a discussion about something so ordinary as salt, especially when you are planning to be surrounded by seawater. You would be mistaken, however, because the trace elements of seawater, present in sea salt but not in the commercial brands of salt found in supermarkets, not only enhance the flavor of foods, but most importantly provide vital nutrients we cannot get any other way. Vitamins are only important; minerals are essential.

There are many varieties of naturally harvested sea salt: The French grey salt from Brittany, Maldon salt from England, and Celtic salt are a few. In the Hawaiian Islands you can get a sea salt that has a distinctive pink color from a natural mineral called *alaea*, which is actually a volcanic red clay. Any of these has seriously healthful properties and adds something to the taste of your food. Perhaps the finest salt of all is Fleur de Sel (France) or Flor de Sal (Portugal or Mallorca). It may seem expensive, but how much salt in the scheme of things does one use, really? Carefully harvested in only the purest areas where the Atlantic currents run cleaner, Fleur de Sel is not processed or refined in any way and is free of toxic substances. Pollution is one reason I do not recommend simply lowering a bucket over the side of the boat to get your minerals from the salt water you find there.

Salt and Air Cured Meats, Including Prosciutto di Parma, Jamon Serrano, Pata Negra, Virginia Ham

Cured in nothing but salt and fresh air for as long as two years, real Italian prosciutto, prosciutto di Parma, or Spanish jamon serrano is delicious and has the added advantage of already being preserved for you. Find the real thing, though, produced in its country of origin and boasting no added preservatives such as sodium nitrate or nitrites. Apart from producing an inferior tasting product and being questionable for your health, oddly enough these "preservatives" will ensure that your ham actually spoils far quicker than the real thing.

Finally, and perhaps most importantly, there is no comparison in the taste. Slice it or cube it with eggs for breakfast in the morning, make paper-thin slices for sandwiches, add it to steamed clams, serve it wrapped around cold melon or grilled figs for a scrumptious little bite. The Spanish add chunks of jamon serrano to vegetables, which definitely kicks them up a notch. Virginia ham, also called country or Smithfield ham, is dry-cured to an old recipe. It is very good and makes lovely sandwiches but it has a saltier taste than the European hams. You can soak the meat in water to remove some of the salt.

If you purchase a half or entire ham on the bone you can do as a friend of mine did and keep it hanging in the locker with the foul weather gear, slicing off just what you need. You might become so friendly with your ham you'd give it a name. My friend nicknamed his Sam the Ham. With or without pseudonym, for long or short journeys, cured ham is indispensable, a highly prized gourmet food that can be used in many ways, will nourish you well, and will keep for months without refrigeration as long as you control the moisture.

Bresaola

Air-cured beef—almost as delicious as cured ham.

Salt Cod

Along with air-cured ham, salt cod is the staple that will not let you down. Practically the first food ever to sustain a sailor on his way in ancient times, it still does its job. It stores easily and, though it needs reconstituting, can be made into lovely chowder. It also makes one of the most scrumptious dips ever to come from Provence, **Brandade de Morue**.

Tuna (Canned)

Another ingredient that bears rethinking. Forget the tasteless water-packed stuff served up in children's sandwiches and dine instead on beautiful, velvety-rich Mediterranean tuna packed in pure olive oil. Use this fine tuna to elevate a salad to heights divine as they do in the humblest Spanish taverna, or turn it over straight from the can or bottle, with its oil, to produce an instant and remarkably delicious sauce for pasta. In the States, you can order Bonito del Norte and Atun Claro from La Tienda: www.tienda.com

Dried Wild Mushrooms

Now, this is real value for your money! For a start, nothing could be easier to store. The bang you get for your buck is a powerhouse of concentrated flavor. They go a lot further than fresh. One ounce of dried mushrooms reconstitutes into 3 or 4 ounces. Reconstitute them in water, but wine or broth is even better. Or grind them in a coffee grinder or mill and use small spoonfuls of the powder to flavor sauces. The best are easy to come by: morels, chanterelle, porcini, portobello are all wonderful varieties that can be used on their own or in combination with fresh mushrooms to create deep, intense sauces and fillings.

Sun-Dried Tomatoes

Similarly, the dry version of these shriveled-up little powerhouses of flavor are easy to store, take up little room, and, reconstituted (pour boiling water over them), have many uses from sauces to flavoring all sorts of foods and making sandwiches. Sun dried tomato makes a lovely sandwich with cream cheese. You can also carry the version that needs no rehydration, packed in olive oil. While not space-saving, these are delightful and instantly gratifying.

Nuts

Nuts are a near perfect food. Stock up on an assortment to eat for quick sustainable energy and to cook with: cashews, pecans, walnuts, hazelnuts, almonds, macadamias, pine nuts. You can experiment with them. Use pistachios in pesto, pecans in Romesco, hazelnuts to robe a fish, macadamias to top a salad or stuff into a chicken. The oils in nuts do go rancid, and for this reason they are at their very best kept in the freezer or at least under refrigeration, but if you wish to extend their life in jars on your pantry shelf, throw in a pack of the ingredient that I consider a nautical necessity: Silica Gel Pak desiccant.

Marigold Bouillon Powder

I would not be without it at home. Aboard, it's indispensable. It obviates the need to make stock from bones and vegetables, which, while ambitious on land, at sea would be preposterous.

Renowned English cook and television personality Delia Smith quite unabashedly uses it for no other reason than that she likes it. She has stated, "This is without doubt an ingredient that has revolutionized modern cooking. Before Marigold you had to either make your own stock or resort to the dreaded chemically flavored cube. If there were good ingredient awards, this would win first prize."

It makes salad dressings great; flavors soups, rice, pasta, couscous; gives that "all-day" taste to sauces; and does so much more. You can use Marigold in place of salt in almost any recipe calling for salt. After opening the large cardboard container, place a desiccant packet inside to keep out moisture. Bugs seem to be particularly fond of bouillon, so throw in a few bay leaves to foil their plans. For a long trip, empty the contents into an airtight plastic canister.

* If you can't get Marigold, substitute your favorite bouillon powder, but remember that the flavor will be different. Also, the commercial brands tend to be so much higher in salt that you will need to use less than these recipes call for. Exercise caution.

Liquid Aminos (Marigold, Braggs)

This is a tremendous flavoring agent. It is made from liquid soy protein and is richly concentrated in flavor. You can get it at any health food store. It bears a faint resemblance to, but is more versatile than, soy sauce. It comes in an unbreakable bottle and is virtually unaffected by the passage of time. Use it in salad dressings, soups, and sauces; it's great in mushrooms. Together with Marigold bouillon powder, I consider this flavoring short-cut indispensable in a galley.

Mori-nu Silken Tofu

A galley star. In an unassuming little box, with a little help from you, it transforms itself into rich-tasting sauces, a fine vegan "egg" salad, and many desserts. Four dozen boxes would not be too many in my pantry for a two-month journey. You can toss them anywhere you have room, for as long as the boxes remain intact, they are indestructible. Mori-nu Silken Tofu comes in soft, firm, and extra firm. They are all non-GMO and you can also find organic. You can use any of them. The soft tofu makes blender drinks and sauces, but so do the others, and I am happy using the firm or extra firm most of the time. Extra firm is also a bit denser and can be frozen to make meat-like patties, but this process brings us back to the tedious and is not necessary nor recommended for boat life.

Boston Brown Bread
The Staff of Life in a Can?

Yes, folks, there is an answer for the bread challenged amongst us, and it is a rather sweet one. Boston Brown Bread—a moist, dense, and sweet molasses-tasting treat—can be found at virtually any supermarket. It can be served right out of the can or toasted or even nuked to warm it in the microwave. It is a natural with cream cheese, fantastic with peanut butter, or makes a fine little sandwich wrapped around ham or chicken. Or serve it with baked beans. Be creative and be sure to salt away some tins of this delicious bread.

Coconut Milk

Bring along several cans of this delicious creamy liquid coconut for use in all sorts of dishes and drinks. Look for the pure coconut milk, not the sweetened one that is "loco" with sugar. This is used in Thai mussels, soups, Indian as well as many island recipes, and a very special Brazilian fish stew called **Moqueca**.

Canned Foods

There are a variety of canned foods you should add according to your own preferences: **Olives, Roasted Red Peppers, Crab**, and

Clams, to name a few. Use clams chopped or whole, for linguine, for chowder, and for incredible **clam dip** (horseradish and lemon with crumbled bacon).

Capers

Capers packed in salt are best, since the ones packed in brine tend to have no taste other than the brine. They are Mediterranean, so buy Spanish or Italian ones.

Anchovies

Like capers, anchovies are best packed in salt, which you rinse off the outside of the filets before use.

Garbanzo Beans

They make the best addition to a salad. Without lettuce, you can improvise a salad only with them. Make hummus, make soup; don't leave home without them.

Kidney Beans

Part of that three-bean salad.

White (Canellini) Beans

With tuna . . . some onion . . . some dinner.

Black Beans

Black Eyed Peas

Baked Beans

In fact, any beans at all.

Hearts of Palm

Once upon a time, when all our hi-tech systems aboard failed us, this was all we had to eat. Cases and cases of it. Turned out rather well, actually.

Artichoke Hearts

Salad in a tin, topping for pasta for a start. Stuffing for a fish, stir fry with shrimp . . . I could go on, but there's hardly room.

Onions, Garlic

Onions and garlic last a fairly long time without refrigeration. To preserve garlic, peel cloves and store in a jar of olive oil in the refrigerator. The oil will keep mold from forming on the garlic, which otherwise will happen very quickly to peeled garlic, even in the fridge. Then use the garlic oil to cook with, remembering to top up the olive oil to keep the garlic covered. Otherwise, make **Onion Confit** and **Garlic Confit** for even more shelf life as well as a head start in many recipes.

Ginger Root

Ginger root is one of those things that goes bad very quickly. Dried ginger (not powdered) can be found in whole fingers and also in slices. Use to flavor **Gløgg** or in recipes by soaking in liquid before using. You can also buy preserved ginger in syrup, which makes lovely topping for desserts and is used in some recipes.

 Galley Guru Tip

> To store ginger, peel ginger root and cover it with sherry wine or vodka before refrigeration. If you can't refrigerate it, it will still keep for a month under the alcohol. Ginger flavored alcohols make some fine drinks. See **Ginger Sunset**.

Fresh Fruit

Lemon, lime, orange, grapefruit will last from one to four weeks, which will take you a long way on your voyaging. Of all the citrus fruits, limes spoil quickest. Keep apples as cool as possible. The most difficult thing about keeping fresh fruit on a boat is the little gnat-like bugs that it attracts. Be sure you don't bring any on board from the open markets. Wash well and try wrapping individual pieces in aluminum foil if you are planning a long cruise.

Canned Fruit

Some fruit is quite lovely in cans, some not. Pineapple, mango, lychee, almost any tropical fruit is very good. Peaches are a personal taste. I don't find them anything to sing arias about unless you make a sauce out of them. Cherries can do wonderful things in desserts. Also consider taking some cherry or apple pie filling. This with some prepared custard and a nice cookie makes an instant dessert.

Eggs

OK. Here is my feeling. Petroleum products and food to be consumed by humans just don't mix. So my eggs will never be slathered with crank case oil or Vaseline in this lifetime. Eggs keep quite well for two to four weeks without refrigeration. If you want to keep them longer you can rub them with a food oil, vegetable oil, or olive oil. This will seal the tiny air holes on the eggshell, thus preserving the egg inside from oxidation. Otherwise there is the brining method that has been done from time immemorial, because, well, don't tell me you don't know the answer to the question, "Which came first, the chicken or the refrigerator?"

To Brine Eggs

Get a large mason jar. Fill with water. Pour the water into a pot on a stove and bring to a boil. Add some sea salt, stirring until it dissolves. Continue to add salt until the water will dissolve no more. Allow this liquid to cool. Place as many washed and dried eggs in the jar as it will hold. Pour the cooled brine over the eggs. Store, remembering to keep eggs completely covered in brine at all times. These eggs keep for months. As they continually absorb salt from the brine, you may grow tired of them, but they will not spoil. After all, how long do you really want to keep eggs? I have tried a hundred-year-old Chinese egg. I was not impressed.

Bottled Chestnuts

Chestnuts are perhaps an unusual choice for the galley pantry, but they are great, and if you have some in bottles you can make one of the most delicious soups ever in just minutes. Sweetened, they make fantastic impromptu desserts. Try the sweet kind on ice cream if you haven't before and you'll see what I mean.

Cakes

There are some fine and very inexpensive German liqueur cakes in boxes wrapped up in aluminum foil that will keep until you open them. Dutch ginger cake, eaten for breakfast in Holland, has real pieces of ginger inside. One or two of these would be nice to have around for a special occasion—for instance, when a neighboring crew comes aboard for tea.

Crackers/Biscuits

Whatever your heart desires. Provides the crunch. Lasts longer than bread. Store in plastic containers. Desiccant packet, please. Crackers go mealy very fast on board ship.

Rice

If you are Asian or Spanish, you will not need to be told this. Rice is very nice.

Pasta

First and foremost, it keeps on a boat and is easy to store. Spaghetti, penne, linguine, capellini, and so forth: bring several varieties with you. It cooks quickly and practically nothing makes an impromptu meal better. Pasta has been reported to be good for queasiness, which can strike the best of us.

Couscous

Really just a tiny form of pasta and keeps equally well. Another blessing in the galley, it doesn't even require cooking. You simply put it in a serving bowl or thermos with an equal amount of boiling water. Cover for 10 to 15 minutes and toss with a fork to separate the grains. It can be used anywhere rice or pasta is used and is obligatory for many Middle Eastern as well as Brazilian dishes.

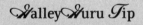

Galley Guru Tip

Store dry ingredients out of their packages and put into stackable airtight clear plastic containers along with a trusty desiccant packet. Cut the label neatly off the box of crackers or couscous and place it inside so it is visible. This way you never end up with a curious collection of boxes filled with strange contents, the true identity of which you have long forgotten.

Canned and Preserved Meats

Confit

On or off the water, I am a great fan of confit, which is often erroneously thought to apply only to duck or to meats cooked in duck fat. The French word confit, however, simply translates as preserved or conserved, so the term confit can equally apply to marmalade or jams made with fruit or vegetables.

This technique with meats is thousands of years old (clearly predating the refrigerator), making it, for our purposes, excellent. I present it here to you for its historical value and because you may want to try it sometime. The duck or goose is rubbed with salt and spices, then covered in salt to cure for 24 hours. It is then simmered (a minimum of 2½ hours) in its own fat and stored in earthenware crocks with the hot fat poured over. Sealing the meat with fat this way excludes oxygen, thus preserving it. Properly made, confit will keep in a cool place for many months without refrigeration. The meat is mellow, tender, almost buttery, and quite exquisite.

Duck confit makes a wonderful traveling companion. It requires nothing more than heating so is truly fast food, though I daresay it will never make the menu at Mickey D's. In the modern age you can buy this wonderful traditional product surrounded by its fat packaged in vacuum-sealed plastic bags. You can open a packet of one or two duck legs, perhaps dig out a fine claret. Spoilage will not be a problem. Nothing will be left over.

Spam

You may think that we have hurtled recklessly from the sublime to the ridiculous, but there are a multitude of Spam aficionados out there and you know who you are (you will find others of your stripe at http://www.spam.com). If you like Spam, you like it. It could be a blessing on a boat if you do, as it comes out of its little can, substitutes for bacon with your egg, and makes pretty fair sandwiches with the leftovers. You can chop it for a salad spread, wrap it up in egg rolls, adorn tacos. You can even (forgive the redundancy) make meat loaf from your meat loaf. Spam is trustworthy, solid fare when all else fails. Just ask Monty Python.

Canned Meat: Ham, Bacon, Chicken, et cetera

Take small enough cans so that you don't have to worry about leftovers. Plumrose makes excellent hams. Plumrose canned Danish bacon was phenomenally good but it has been out of production for some time. It has many fans—including me—who all hope fervently that Plumrose will reconsider production of this product.

Vegetarian Meat Substitutes
Textured Vegetable Protein (TVP)

Whether you are vegetarian or not, you might think about meat substitutes while cruising. Though the best ones on the market are probably the frozen ones, and there are quite acceptable varieties in cans from health food stores and some supermarkets, TVP, textured vegetable protein, could be a godsend. It is soy granules that come dry in a bag (rather like kibble) and it keeps in that dry state just about forever. When you need "meat" for your Bolognese sauce or your Moussaka, you need only reconstitute with some hot broth (and don't forget the touch of liquid aminos—Marigold, Braggs) and use as ground beef in your recipe. TVP comes in flavors as well, so you can get bacon, sausage, or ham flavors if you want. Store it in sealed containers with a desiccant packet to ensure that it stays dry. Throw some bay leaves in with the TVP to deter bugs.

Nestlé Canned Cream

This comes in little 6-ounce cans and is indispensable when you want real cream and are nowhere near land. It is much better than canned evaporated milk, which tastes more like a can than it does milk. Again, though it is found all over Britain and in far-flung island paradises, it has been difficult to find in the States, unless your market stocks British or Hispanic products. It is sold online, though, through British food shops.

Clam Juice, Bottled

Whips up a quick sauce for fish and shellfish. Necessary in clam chowder.

Beef Broth or Consommé, Canned

Consommé and canned beef broth can be quite useful short cuts in sauces and soups. They usually add some depth of flavor but need a bit of wine to offset the intense tinny quality of the taste. Be very careful, because you will be adding a great deal of salt with most of these.

Boxed: Needs No Refrigeration Until Opened

These are perfect for voyaging and you can find small ones so that you don't have to use it up so fast.

Milk (UHT)

Soy Milk (UHT)

Chai

Juices

Mori-Nu Tofu (See Tofu Section)

Stock (Beef, Chicken, Vegetable)

These are better in a box than canned; they store more easily, and I prefer them. They have a purer flavor and most brands have less salt. Try the organic versions.

Velveeta Cheese

Smooth and creamy, Velveeta is that famous processed cheese that is barely cheese at all but that makes the American Mac 'n Cheese...well, American. It does not need to be refrigerated until it is opened. As much as I love cheeses both exotic and authentic, there is room in my heart for Velveeta too. On the Kraft website you can find a recipe for a cheese dip that is nothing more than Velveeta melted in the microwave together with a can of Rotel diced tomatoes and green chilis. It seems pretty foolproof.

Oats

Use old-fashioned rolled oats to make hearty porridge as well as quick toppings both sweet and savory.

Popcorn

All you need to make great popcorn is a heavy covered pot, a little oil, and some popcorn. You throw the popcorn in when the oil is hot and shake the covered pot around a little till the popcorn is done. Tip into bowls, sprinkle with butter and salt, and enjoy a low-fat treat. A lot of pleasure for a little pot-watching.

Peanut Butter

Smooth or crunchy, this is full of nourishment. Spread on toast. Use in recipes to make thick creamy sauces. Enjoy. Also try almond butter and cashew butter. Luscious.

Honey

Here is something worth knowing: Honey has a nearly infinite shelf life, probably because of the abundance of a compound known as phenolics, a natural antimicrobial agent. The darker honeys, such as buckwheat, are higher in phenolics and antioxidants than common lighter honeys. Honey has been used since ancient times for its medicinal and antimicrobial properties; it can heal rashes and wounds of the skin. It has been used in ancient Ayurvedic and Chinese medicine as a tonic, as well as for many conditions from upset stomachs to ulcers to sore throats, because it stops the growth of bacteria. Clover honey is the most common honey on supermarket shelves because it is bland, sweet, and nearly tasteless, but it has the least amount of medicinal compounds. The darker, raw, unprocessed honey not only tastes better but is better for you than its poorer cousin. As an example, Greek wild thyme honey is so good as not to be believed.

One caveat: Honey contains a substance that is toxic to infants under the age of one year because of their undeveloped digestive systems. This applies even to cooked honey. So be safe. Do not give honey to babies and ask your pediatrician.

Tea, Coffee, and Spices

Here's a list of basics that I would take for my kitchen. Your personal favorites and the amount of space you can make will affect the final look of your spice racks. Spices need to be really fresh to be good. Once open, they start deteriorating, even on land. You should place small desiccant packets inside the little bottles to get more life out of them.

Tea
Coffee
Cocoa Powder
Allspice
Basil
Bay leaves
Butter flavored salt
Caraway seeds

Cardamom

Cayenne pepper

Cilantro

Cinnamon, ground

Cinnamon sticks

Cloves, ground

Cloves, whole

Cumin

Curry powder

Dill weed

Dry mustard

Fennel seeds

Garlic, minced dried

Garlic powder

Ginger, ground

Mace, ground

Marjoram

Mustard seed

Nutmeg, ground

Nutmeg, whole

Onions, minced dried

Onion powder

Oregano

Paprika

Spanish paprika is smoked. It is the principal flavoring in chorizo and the defining ingredient in paella. Its complex depth of flavor makes it another secret ingredient that should be sought out. It is dark, rich, and earthy, in contrast to the bland, commercial type of paprika you find in the U.S. market. There are three: sweet (dulce), medium (agridulce), and hot (picante). You can get both the paprika and the chorizo as well as many other little treasures at **http://tienda.com**.

Parsley

Peppercorns

Rosemary

Rubbed sage

Tarragon

Thyme

Turmeric, ground

Bottled Sauces and Other Goodies

Olive Oil (Extra Virgin)

Arguably the most important bottle in your larder. There are no substitutes for the fruity, pleasantly rich taste of extra virgin olive oil in salads, in pasta, to drizzle on a fish or steak, or just for dipping your bread in. It fries a perfect egg. When I do popcorn with it, the popcorn somehow comes out more tender and buttery. It is easy to find good extra virgin olive oil in supermarkets now that doesn't cost the earth, and everything you touch with it will taste better, believe me.

Wine vinegar

Balsamic vinegar

Cider vinegar

Liquid aminos seasoning (Marigold, Braggs)

Bragg Liquid Aminos is a Certified Non-GMO liquid protein concentrate, derived from soybeans, having essential and nonessential amino acids in naturally occurring amounts. It is similar to soy sauce; however, it is not as salty and is more versatile. It is one of the seasonings that I recommend that is essential for making foods have that "cooked all day" flavor.

Marmite

Nothing beats this little taste sensation in a jar; so say the British and so say I. Toast and butter with a careful spreading of Marmite along with a lovely cup of tea turns a dull day fair again. Or to induce a glow of pleasure you can make a cockle-warming and quite passably nourishing cup of broth out of your Marmite. I'm a fan. Can you tell?

Worcestershire

Hot Sauce

Sriracha Hot Chili Sauce

This is a hot chili sauce par excellence. Sun ripened chili makes it taste of tomato, though there is no tomato in it. It is garlicky and sweet and hot and sort of incomparable. Use it anywhere you need some spice. Great on eggs, in **Avocado Prawn Cocktail**, on hamburgers, in Chinese and Mexican food.

Soy Sauce

To my mind, there is no comparison to the quality of tamari soy sauce with other types. Tamari is aged and has a delicacy and a mellowness and far less salty taste than other commercial brands found in the supermarkets today. There are several different types of tamari, which you can find at most health food stores and some enlightened supermarkets, usually in the health foods section.

Horseradish

Wasabi Powder

Mustard (Dijon or Meaux, Yellow)

Mayonnaise/Miracle Whip

There are aficionados of one and not the other. Personally, I like both and use them for different things. Bottled mayonnaise keeps a long time. The new plastic squeeze jars keep bacteria out. If it's in a jar, take out what you need with a clean spoon and put the lid back. And then there's...

Kewpie Mayonnaise

A new staple in my kitchen. It comes in a smaller squeeze bottle so no worries about its going bad. It is sushi mayonnaise from Japan and absolutely the best commercial mayonnaise I have ever encountered. It's priceless for that extra punch of flavor we are always looking for.

Curry Paste (Thai)

Red, yellow, and green all have different flavors and different heat levels. Available in Asian markets and supermarkets, this comes in jars, tubes, and little packets. It is very concentrated. A couple of teaspoons of this make a great base for a spicy sauce instantly.

Hoisin Sauce

This unique, sweet Chinese soybean paste makes wonderful sauces and marinades for fish or chicken.

Dried Rice Paper Sheets

Available from Asian food shops and many supermarkets, these Vietnamese summer roll skins keep forever, dry, and are made edible merely by dipping them in some water for a few seconds to soften. You do not have to cook them. As well as using them to make traditional Asian food, you can put two together to make them a bit stronger and roll them with some turkey or ham slices or sautéed veggies and cheese and have instant sandwich roll-ups.

Protein Powder

Take along a supply of whatever brand you like. As well as other electrical kitchen equipment, bring an individual battery-operated blender. This will ensure that you get adequate nutrition for all those times when you are stuck at the helm or aren't able to prepare food in the galley. Protein powders also make good breakfast fare and are easy to drink for energy in times of stress when even chewing seems beyond you.

Silica Gel Pak Desiccant

Damp is the enemy of food. I cannot extol the virtues of anything you can bring aboard any more than these nifty little packets. Ranging in size from the very small, which fit into a spice jar, to large enough to discourage moisture and mold in storage compartments as large as 40 cubic feet, your desiccant will ensure that your food's shelf life is as long as possible. Place a desiccant in all food containers that open: flour, sugar, spices, cookies, crackers, the lot. With these little miracles you can have your cake and eat it too.

Batterie de Galley

Call it assault with a friendly weapon—batterie de cuisine (pronounced: batu-ree du- kwee-zeen') is the French term for the range of precise tools used in a serious professional kitchen. It involves knives of every ilk, skillets, bakeware, graters, shapemakers, and an indiscriminate number of otherwise inexplicable instruments. While a huge array of earnest kitchen utensils is de rigueur for a chef with both feet on the ground, over the bounding main, wedged in your galley with barely enough space to turn around, such folderol is completely unfeasible. Still, we must eat, mustn't we?

The batterie de galley means having the cooking utensils you actually need ready to hand at the moment when you need them. It signifies a seamless cooking experience and the difference between a cheerful ocean-going gastronomy and haphazardly gouging open a few cans, tipping them into a pot, and hoping for the best.

While this by no means pretends to be a comprehensive list, here are a few items for the galley that make light work. They are, for the most part, unacquainted with electricity:

A manual food mill

Turn the handle and make purees of all your ingredients, thus rendering beautiful fresh vegetable soup not an unthinkable project. You may do mashed potatoes with this or you may use . . .

A potato ricer

The *finest* mashed potatoes come not from beating the hell out of them with an electric beater but from this superb item, which looks something like an overgrown garlic press. You simply put the hot potato inside and press it through the sieve end. Then all you have to do is stir the potato purée gently with your butter or cream. They will be smooth (not a lump in sight) and heavenly, not glutinous and flimsy. All without that infernal whirring.

A food processor

Surprise! It does not have to be electric. There is a perfectly serviceable smallish manually operated one with a cutting blade and whipping attachment that can be had for less than $20.00. I use it for everything from emulsified salad dressings to pâtés and sandwich fillings.

A traditional mandoline (expensive) or a V-slicer (inexpensive)

Either will quickly slice potatoes and other vegetables with razor-sharp precision, thereby cutting not only the odd zucchini but galley time as well. There are different blades that will make chips (French fries) and other pleasing shapes. A manual item that is often neglected but well worth its weight and the space of storage (both negligible).

Vegetable peeler

While the peels of the majority of vegetables harbor most of the vitamins and are often better left on, there are times when you need this instrument—for that long, curly lemon peel for your vodka, for instance.

Can opener

Of course. To get at that lobster pâté you were sage enough to bring.

Balloon whisk

Well, only if you want perfect omelets and get a kick out of beating egg whites into submission.

Wok

A wok can be used to stir-fry or steam food in a short time and is a sensational cooking utensil on a boat. The round-bottomed shape produces a small, very hot area at the bottom and uses less fuel than other pans. Stir-frying in a wok seals in flavor and is fast and easy once you have all your ingredients cut up and ready.

Carbon steel woks need to be seasoned before use. That means they need to be scrubbed and then rubbed with cooking oil (peanut oil is preferable) and heated to an intense heat. You may choose a Teflon coated wok that will not need this first step. However, I use and I suggest an anodized metal wok, which never rusts, is virtually nonstick, and can be heated to much higher temperatures than Teflon.

Pressure Cooker

The pressure cooker is an item that has no equal for making hearty meals fast. You can transform dried beans into soups in a mere 20 minutes and cut hours off the time it would take to make rich, satisfying stews. If you are going to invest in one, buy a good quality stainless steel version, as eating from aluminum changes the taste of food and has been linked to many health problems. Super-fast cooking means saving on fuel. A pressure cooker can save up to 70 percent of the fuel normally used in cooking, so even if you are not in the habit of cooking under pressure, it is worth thinking about for this reason. There are many cookbooks solely dedicated to the many things you can do with a pressure cooker and a new cooker will generally be accompanied by a very nice cookbook.

Knives

Buy professional-quality knives, I pray you. They are easy to use, easy to maintain (they stay sharp longer), and last a very long time. For these reasons always choose them over the cheap versions if you can. Cut on a wooden board or a plastic one to keep from dulling the knife. Believe it or not, a sharp knife is safer to use than a dull one because you don't need to use force in cutting with it. The chef's knife with a scalloped edge can be excellent. You need at least a 7-inch and a 5-inch chef's knife as well as a long boning knife for fish. Knives should be stored very carefully—horizontally or sharp side up, to preserve sharpness—in slots made for them and never left carelessly where they can fall or fly about the cabin. Don't forget the steel to keep your edge.

Strainers

Colander

Garlic Press

Grater

You may opt not to get a box grater if you have a mandoline with enough different blades. What you should get, though, is a Microplane Grater. A narrow flat grater that is as easy to store as a knife, the microplane has found its way from the hardware store to the kitchen via top chefs who have snuck it into the kitchen, discovering in it a little miracle. Grate cheese with it or whole nutmeg; it has a very fine grater and also zests citrus fruit. I love mine and find it truly indispensable.

Coffee Grinder or Mill

The idea is that you will be able to grind whole coffee beans, which will keep your coffee fresher than buying pre-ground. These are mostly electric but take little time and energy from the 110v. If you have room, you may want to keep a second one of these to grind fresh spices. This may seem like a waste of time, but once you have become used to the taste of freshly ground spices in your food, you will be loath to give them up. Spices, which go stale on the kitchen shelf, are even more of a challenge on a boat. By all means put desiccant in them to help.

Immersion Blender

Yes, this also requires electricity. So if we are not condemned to live our lives in the Stone Age, an immersion blender would be amongst my first choices for a high-tech power tool. You can plunge it into a pot of soup ingredients with a certain unbridled sensuality and produce a marvelous velvet soup (or, more correctly, a potage, but let us not get inextricably tangled in semantics). You can also make puréed cauliflower to rival the mashed spud of your dreams, and if you like that, you will find other roots and tubers that respond with a will to its ministrations. Carrots, parsnips, celery root, even the odd turnip make a mash-lover's mash. Add some salt. Some pepper. Now, plunk a bit of butter on top and you will likely *like* this piece of equipment. Likely, you will like it a lot.

Flexible plastic chopping boards

Don't leave home without them. Carry several. They have many advantages. They are thin as paper and so store easily. After chopping, pick your board up and bend it to form a spout to transfer food from the counter to the pot. You can stack them in layers to give you more space in the galley as you chop and prepare food on them.

Marine Refrigerators

Even though they are hardly one-third the size of your home refrigerator, most top-loading marine refrigerators have too much space. That is, they have empty space at the bottom where things easily fall down but never seem to come up again. Even if you don't mind turning yourself ankle over elbow rummaging around in tight spaces all the time, overloading the refrigerator will cause loss of energy. A good idea to properly store foods with space for air circulation is to cut a piece of insulating Styrofoam to fit in the bottom of the refrigerator. Because the bottom is hard to reach, you will not be losing any usable space but will be adding to the efficiency of the equipment. With proper air circulation, the refrigerator will stay colder on less power.

A helpful thing to solve the lost-forever-in-the-refrigerator syndrome is to purchase a set of plastic stacking boxes about the size of shoe boxes, preferably with clear plastic tops. Each box stacks neatly on top of another. Put meats, cheeses, vegetables, even small bottles away in separate boxes and label them too. That way you have everything neatly to hand and you can see what is in each box.

Those plastic boxes are also useful to stand bottles in, inside the pantry. While a holding bungee cord in front of shelves keeps most things from toppling out under normal conditions, in a good sized sea this is not enough. Fit the plastic boxes one behind the other in as many rows as fit your shelves. Then store bottles, boxes, cans in rows inside the boxes. The sides of the shoe boxes are high enough to further discourage tipping over, especially if you fit soft packages like soup mixes or grains in any extra space so that everything is held firmly against each other.

If you have room, it is nice to have spice racks fitted inside the pantry door and/or along one galley wall in easy reach. The bottles are fitted in behind a thin wooden retaining strip, allowing you to see each label. Stow spices in alphabetical order. That way, you have everything to hand and are not using up otherwise valuable space.

Stove

Fuel and stove choices are personal. There are safety considerations with any kind of liquid fuel, which includes alcohol, compressed natural gas, kerosene, and propane. Such considerations are beyond the scope of this book. I have personally always used propane stoves and have been very happy with their efficiency and safety when handled properly. Suffice it to say that extreme care must be taken with any of these fuels. Learn the proper procedure and stick to it religiously every time you use your stove. As for other safety issues in the rock-and-roll environment that is a galley, gimballing keeps the stove rocking free and level no matter what angle the boat may be. The one exception might be when you open your oven. Take especial care that you don't let your beautiful dinner slide right out.

Using fiddles—clamps that hold your cooking pots in place on the stove—will prevent pots from tipping over.

First Aid from the Galley

'Let your food be your medicine and your medicine be your food.'
—Hippocrates

If you are seized by a headache or caught by a cold, if you cut your finger or burn your hand while cooking, or if you find it difficult to sleep at night, you would probably run to the nearest supermarket or pharmacy to purchase a commercial product in a box, bottle, or tube to relieve your symptoms. If you are cruising off shore, you don't have that option. Therefore, you must without question carry a first aid kit—and they are becoming astonishingly expensive. Even so, it is awfully tempting to buy the biggest one to try to take care of any eventuality that could strike at sea. Though it is difficult to know just how many bandages, painkillers, and antibiotics are too many, there is always the hope that none will be needed. Everyday ailments, however, may find remedies as close as your galley and you won't have to mortgage the boat for their purchase. While I don't advocate their complete substitution for the remedies of modern medicine, it is remarkable how effective they can sometimes be.

Hippocrates, generally considered the Father of Medicine, compiled a list of over four hundred herbs and their uses. Herbs, spices and other nutritional substances are the oldest form of medicine known to man. The practice of using nature as a pharmacy can be traced back to the most ancient of civilizations. For many centuries, plants have offered a vast storehouse of natural medicines capable of healing many ailments, usually without the harmful side effects of drugs.

Many of the plant-based substances that our ancestors used as preventative and curative measures can be used to wonderful advantage at sea. If you have taken only a little extra thought when stocking your galley you will already have an abundance of herbs, spices, and essential oils, a virtual natural pharmacopoeia of first defense for everything from sore throat to the dreaded and truly debilitating seasickness that can strike sailors of every age, no matter how experienced. I list only a few here, but I suggest, alongside your first aid kit, you carry with you a book on natural herbal medicine.

Ginger

For an all-around star in the galley, think ginger. Ginger, apart from containing nearly a dozen antiviral compounds, relieves pain, in addition to being an antiseptic and antioxidant. It is valuable for preventing and treating colds, sore throats, and inflammation of mucus membranes. It reduces fever and also has a mild sedative effect. And ginger, an ancient ayurvedic nausea remedy, has been proven to be more effective at relieving motion sickness symptoms than Dramamine, an over-the-counter drug that carries some unpleasant side effects such as drowsiness and confusion... even addiction.

As an aid to digestion you can take a tea, or, for more medicinal effect, make tea from fresh ginger in hot water. You can take it as a tincture and, of course, include this delicious spice liberally in your food.

For seasickness:

Take 1 to 2 capsules of powdered ginger every 15 minutes until symptoms abate.

To prevent motion sickness:

Take 6 to 8 capsules of powdered ginger about 45 minutes before setting off shore.

Echinacea

It is an old saying that "the time to treat a cold is before you get it." At the first sign of a cold, echinacea is a wonderful remedy. Used by American Indians for hundreds of years to ward off illness, it is now available as a tincture in little bottles. Mix and drink in water to increase levels of properdin, a chemical that activates the immune system, increasing defense mechanisms against virus and bacteria attacks. Echinacea is harmless to the human body even at several times the recommended dose.

Lemon/Lime

Lemons and limes are rich sources of vitamin C. Taken hot in a hot lemon and honey drink, lemon juice is a traditional remedy for colds and sore throats. Mix ¼ teaspoon cayenne pepper with the juice of a lemon and a teaspoon of honey to loosen mucous secretions and increase blood flow in the sinus cavity to reduce congestion. This is said to help with sinus headache as well.

Miso

A delicious, high protein, fermented soybean paste that has been used for centuries in Asian cuisine, miso has many healing properties. Many Japanese studies have identified miso as a potent medicinal food. Western doctors are now realizing the benefits of this simple ingredient, thanks to incontrovertible clinical evidence connecting miso to healing of such disparate conditions as high cholesterol, high blood pressure, cancer, chronic pain, and radiation poisoning, as well as bad digestion and food allergies.

Unpasteurized miso is a "living food" containing a combination of soybeans, grain, and sea salt. It has been revered in Japanese cuisine. It is said that a bowl of miso soup can cancel the poisoning effects of large amounts of nicotine and other mutagens. On a more quotidian level, due to its purifying effect on the liver, a nice bowl of miso soup is a welcome restorative for everything from fatigue to a hangover. Remember that to retain the healthful properties of the micro-organisms in miso, it must not be boiled, but hot water may be added to it. To store it, a refrigerator is best. Otherwise it holds for a couple of weeks if you keep it cool.

Garlic

Garlic's curative powers have been known from the days of the early Egyptians. The Romans (who still feed upon it daily) fed it to their soldiers before battle. Garlic has antibacterial properties that help the immune system to fight infection, containing several helpful compounds, including allicin, one of the plant kingdom's most potent antibiotics.

For a general health tonic and to bolster the immune system against a cold, miso soup with garlic is easily made.

Garlic Miso Soup

Simmer a head of garlic in a litre (2 pints) vegetable broth (you can use Marigold bouillon powder for this). Allow garlic to soften, about 15 minutes. For each cup of miso soup, add 1 or 2 tablespoons miso to the bottom of a cup. Pour over the hot broth, mixing well. Drink the warming liquid several times a day for a cold.

A Word about Insects

My theory is that anyone who comes aboard should be prepared to pay their passage or work their passage. This disallows room for any uninvited creatures, including insects. However, without malice aforethought on our part, they tend to get into places where we don't want them, not the least of which is our food.

To kill all wheat and other larvae before you sail so you will not have vile stowaways on board, there are several well-documented solutions. You could try putting a small piece of dry ice in the bottom of a large plastic container, then pouring in the flour or other dried foods you plan to carry, such as beans and grains. Leave the lid a little ajar to allow the dry ice to work. The whole process takes a couple of hours. The cold CO_2 will displace the regular air, killing the beasties.

If it's hard to get the dry ice, and you have use of a microwave, you can nuke your flour and other dry goods for a few seconds before tipping them into scrupulously clean storage containers. This method will bump off whatever fugitives the flour is harboring (you did know they were in there from the store didn't you?).

A pleasant natural remedy against bugs and vermin that for some mysterious reason really works is to put a few bay leaves, or other fragrant dried herbs in your canisters. Buy more leaves than you will ever need for cooking. Throw them in flour, sugar, whatever you are storing. Hang a few bunches of fragrant dried herbs such as sage, bay leaves, lavender in your cupboards as well. Humans like these herbs. Bugs, bless them, don't.

Whatever method you choose, make sure to store your flour in airtight containers, throw in your desiccant (silica gel pak) and you will have fresh, dry, and wholesome food for the whole trip.

As for the dreaded cockroach: They come from the dock, not thin air, and are particularly problematical in the warmer climes where the balmy breezes blow. Be scrupulous about what you stock. Never, ever bring cardboard boxes (roach sanctuaries) on board. Wash all fruits and vegetables in a weak bleach solution of a tablespoon of ordinary bleach to a half gallon of water. Dip them in quickly; you don't want the bleach soaking into your fruit. Get into the habit of inspecting everything before it comes on the boat. If you see little fruit flies making frenetic circles around those bananas in the market, you will see them again onboard the boat unless you do the bleach wash. At the very least, dunk the bananas in sea water before bringing onboard.

If you see roaches, boric acid, nature's insecticide, is the happy answer that will not also poison the people aboard. It is safe enough to use around children as well as animals. There is advice out there to mix this boric acid with honey or sugar or other stuff, and this may be the way to entice the ants, but boric acid is tempting enough to cockroaches on its own and utterly poisonous and can be put in little piles in strategic places. Or make your own roach motels out of little wooden matchboxes half full of boric acid and left half open in nooks and crannies of the boat.

Peppermint essential oil is healthful for humans but not for ants and it is easy to make an environmentally friendly ant deterrent spray by putting a teaspoon or two of peppermint oil into a spray bottle and filling with water. Shake well and spray the oil anywhere food is stored as well as on countertops and in corners along the baseboards of the sole.

Before You Set Sail . . .

If you pick up the clues and enjoy the cruising concoctions in this book along with your own wonderful ideas, you will find you have a gourmet's galley, conjuring an infinite variety of meals that will please all who sail with you.

Enjoy a gorgeous galley experience, but above all, enjoy the sail.

I wish you fair winds and following seas.

For a Start

. . . Being a Ship's Record of Hors D'oeuvres,
Pâtés, Dips, Spreads,
and Appetizers

Artichoke Stuffed Mushrooms

Serve just one or two of these to guests as a first course. Or serve more for a light little dinner for you and crew.

   8 large, flat mushrooms
   olive oil
   2 tins artichoke hearts
   4 tablespoons (60ml) mayonnaise
   2 tablespoons (30ml) sherry
   8 cheddar slices to cover
   16–24 cooked tiger prawns, 2–3 per mushroom

In a food processor, blend artichoke hearts with mayonnaise and sherry. Wash and de-stem mushrooms, then sprinkle them with a little olive oil. Grill them round side up. Turn. Grill until done, about 10 minutes. Fill with artichoke puree and cover with cheese. Put the mushroom caps back under the grill until cheese is melted. Top with prawns and serve with crusty bread.

Mushrooms Stuffed with Shrimp

Another way to stuff mushrooms that is a snap. You will love how simple and good these are to pass around with a drink or to start a meal.

   1 pound (about ½ kilo) large mushrooms
   8 ounces (225g) cooked shrimp (you can use canned)
   ½ cup (125ml) Ritz crackers, crushed
   4 ounces (115g) cream cheese, room temperature
   3½ ounces (100g) shredded sharp cheddar cheese

Preheat oven to hot. Lightly grease a baking pan. Remove stems from mushrooms. Finely chop stems and put in a large bowl with the cooked shrimp, crackers, and cream cheese. Mix well. Mound the filling into the mushroom cavities and place stuffed mushrooms in the baking dish. Top each one with shredded cheddar. Place in the oven and cook until cheese is melted and bubbly, about 8–10 minutes.

Parmesan Crisps

These unbelievably easy, lacy little Parmesan crisps are sensational for hors d'oeuvres or as a clever topping for a great Caesar salad. With only one ingredient, the quality of the Parmesan is everything here, so use the best. Be warned: These little treats are addictive—once you start eating them, it is pretty hard to stop. If you want any left for yourself, you might want to double or triple the recipe

½ cup (125ml) Parmigiano Reggiano or best Parmesan, grated

Preheat oven to fairly hot (400 degrees F). Put heaping tablespoons of Parmesan onto a silicone* or parchment paper lined baking sheet and lightly pat down. Repeat with the remaining cheese, spacing the spoonfuls about a half-inch apart. Bake for 3 to 5 minutes or until golden and crisp. (Ovens vary; yours may cook faster or slower.) Cool.

* There are several silicone baking mats on the market, a Silpat being one of them. They provide a completely nonstick surface and are indispensable if you like to bake cookies and such, which cook evenly on them and don't burn. They are flexible, thin as a piece of paper, and so take up virtually no storage space.

Artichoke Pâté

This is really simple to throw together when a few guests are coming.

2 tins water-packed artichoke bottoms (artichoke hearts work as
well)
1 cup (250ml) Parmesan cheese, grated
1 cup (250ml) mayonnaise

Heat oven to medium. Rinse and drain artichokes. Blend all
ingredients in food processor until smooth. Turn out mixture in
a flat oven dish or cake pan. Bake 25 minutes or until top begins
to turn golden and is bubbly. Serve hot or cold with fresh bread,
biscuits, or crackers.

Brandied Mackerel Pâté

Any smoked fish will do here, but mackerel or mullet are the best kind as they are full of good fats and thus are richer than, say, a trout.

3 skinless smoked mackerel filets
10½ ounces (300g) cream cheese
1 tablespoon (15ml) creamed horseradish
1 tablespoon (15ml) brandy
1 teaspoon (5ml) paprika
handful chopped chives
juice of 1 lemon

Put all ingredients in a food processor and blend, leaving the pâté a bit coarse. Serve with toast or crusty French bread.

Tuna Pâté

This tuna pâté is very pleasing in a delicate way for a handful of reasons, not the least of which is that its elusive flavor is rather hard to identify as tuna. This is for tarragon lovers, and you can be generous with it here. It is to be served chilled where the bit of butter, cooling, draws up the ingredients to a smooth, buttery, firm texture. It is fine on crackers but warms to warm bread. Try it on Irish Soda Bread (see following page).

6 eggs, hard-boiled (still warm)
1 12-oz can tuna, drained
4 ounces (56g) butter, softened
handful fresh tarragon, chopped
juice of ½ lemon (or more to taste)

Put all ingredients in a food processor and whiz until smooth. Put into a mold and refrigerate until ready to serve.

Irish Soda Bread

There is a great deal of advice about baking bread on board ship. Perhaps some people enjoy such things. If you, like myself, are not awfully attracted by the idea of kneading bread and finding places for the dough to rise as an alternative to taking the helm, this authentic delicious soda bread is a great alternative. It is so easy and is sure to delight all who get a whiff of the lovely smells coming from the oven.

4 cups (1 litre) whole wheat flour

2 cups (500ml) plain white flour

1 cup (250ml) buttermilk

or fresh milk and 1 teaspoon [5ml] cream of tartar)

2 ounces (56g) butter

pinch salt

2 teaspoons (10ml) brown (or Demerara) sugar

1 teaspoon (5ml) baking soda

Grease and flour large baking sheet. Set oven to medium high. Rub butter into flour and salt in a large bowl. Add sugar. In another bowl dissolve bicarbonate of soda into milk. (It bubbles and expands, so use large bowl). Add it to flour mixture, stirring with fork. When absorbed, knead lightly. Flatten into 1 large or 2 small round flat loaves. Cut a criss-cross on top with a floured knife. Prick with fork. Bake for 35 minutes, on middle shelf. Eat warm, or wrap in tea towel to keep soft and slightly moist. Does not keep well, but if you have a freezer it can be frozen and reheated in the oven or, unlike yeast breads, in the microwave.

Taramosalata

Here is another pâté made of smoked fish roe that is ubiquitous in Greece. Sometimes known as poor man's caviar, Taramosalata is fun to dip and makes a delicious addition to the ample burden of the Greek table of appetizers called Meze. Its taste is rustic, creamy and sharp with lemon, suffused with more than enough garlic to discourage stray vampires from stowing away in the lazarette. Start with smoked cod or carp roe that you can find in jars in Greek and specialty shops. These are nice to have on board if you like Taramosalata, as I do. It is often served with pita bread to dip in it. This is the Turkish style bread but you can use any peasant bread with it. The Greek peasant bread has a particularly soft crumb and is equally good.

There are two schools of thought about Taramosalata. One insists upon garlic as the flavoring and one upon onion. I am a graduate of the garlic school, so here is my recipe. It is dead easy.

1 (7–8 oz/200–225g) jar smoked cod roe
2 slices crustless bread, moistened and squeezed of excess water
2–3 cloves garlic, crushed
½–¾ cup (125–185ml) good olive oil
juice of 1 or 2 lemons

Place cod roe, garlic, and crumbled bread in a food processor. Mix well. Add the olive oil a little at a time and blend until you have a light fluffy mixture. Add the lemon juice to taste. Serve cold.

Tomato Pesto Cream Cheese

A crowd-pleasing combination.

>   8 ounces (225g) of cream cheese
>   ¾ cup (185ml) pesto (prepared or homemade)
>   1–2 tablespoons (7.5-15ml) olive oil
>   1 tablespoon (15ml) balsamic vinegar
>   chopped fresh tomatoes (vine ripened or Roma)
>   (3–4, depending on size)
>   ½ cup (125ml) pine nuts
>   salt and pepper to taste

Mix pesto and olive oil in a bowl. Add balsamic vinegar; consistency should be somewhat pourable but not runny. Add salt and pepper to taste. Spoon over cream cheese. Top with chopped tomatoes and pine nuts. Serve with toast, favorite crackers, or pita chips.

Bacon Clam Dip

This clam dip is a classic, reinvented with the addition of crispy bacon and horseradish. Serve with potato chips, crackers, or crispy celery.

>   6 slices bacon, cooked and crumbled
>   8 ounces (225g) cream cheese, softened
>   ½ cup (120ml) sour cream
>   2 (6½ oz/185g) cans minced clams
>   3 tablespoons (45ml) minced green onion or chives
>   1 clove garlic, minced
>   few drops Worcestershire
>   1 teaspoon (5ml) prepared horseradish
>   lemon juice to taste
>   few dashes Tabasco (to taste)

In a skillet cook bacon over moderate heat, stirring until golden and crisp. Drain and crumble bacon. Drain clams, reserving clam juice. Whisk together cream cheese and sour cream. Add clams, bacon, and remaining ingredients to the mixture, adding enough of the reserved clam juice to make a smooth dip.

Hummus

This is the best, very authentic, and spicier version of this Middle Eastern appetizer. Greek olive oil tends to be full-fruited and taste of the olive. Get the darkest green color, as fragrant of olives as possible.

8 ounces (225g) chick peas (garbanzo beans), cooked or canned
2 cloves garlic, minced
¼ cup (60ml) lemon juice
⅓ cup (85ml) tahini (sesame paste)
¼ cup (60ml) water
½ teaspoon (2.5ml) cumin
1 teaspoon (5ml) ground coriander
½ teaspoon (2.5ml) ground red chili pepper or paprika
sea salt
extra virgin olive oil (Greek if available)

Place chick peas in the food processor along with the garlic, lemon juice, and water. Process until smooth. If too thick, add more water. Stir in tahini and spices. Taste for seasoning. Serve surrounded with pita or other bread or crackers. Drizzle with olive oil, sprinkle lightly with hot red pepper, and garnish with black olives and minced parsley.

Guacamole

Well, you will be in port some of the time. That means you will sometimes get to enjoy that perishable of perishables, that epitome of evanescence: the avocado.

To do it justice, guacamole should start with the nuttiest, butteriest avocados you can find. This avocado is the rough, dark, almost black-skinned kind like the Haas variety with green, tender flesh that is grown in California, Mexico, Chile, New Zealand, and the Dominican Republic, as well as southern Spain. They are far superior in richness and food value to the insipid if larger smooth, green-skinned kind that abound in subtropical places like Florida.

An avocado that is perfectly ripe responds like a lover by yielding slightly to gentle pressure of the fingers. Any more yielding than this and you may be assured they are "past it," so do not be fooled into buying a soft, squishy avocado thinking it will be perfectly good and ripe for mashing. Ripe is a pinnacle of perfection that, once reached, vanishes in a day or a few short beats of the heart, whichever comes first. Immediately put your ripe avocados in the refrigerator where they can keep for a couple of extra days, since the cold will somewhat retard the ripening process.

Next, you must not turn this guacamole thing into a purée. The avocado is a subtle fruit with an exquisite texture that is destroyed by such insensitive handling. Instead, fold the ingredients gingerly in a bowl, just to mix, starting with chunks cut from the avocado halves, as in the recipe that follows. Always take care that the avocado flesh stays plump and as intact as possible. The stirring will make quite enough of a purée out of the soft, silky avocado.

There is no gentle way to say this: Guacamole should not have tomatoes in it. The particular acid of the tomato in no way complements this beautiful concoction and neither is the resultant color particularly pleasing. Keep your guacamole green. You can, however, if you find them, use tomatillos, which resemble small tomatoes (the name means little tomatoes) but are actually a large green berry related to a gooseberry. Otherwise, leave the whole thing out. Guacamole is just wonderful with very little fussing and is ruined with "improvements."

> 2 large just-ripe avocados
> juice of 1 lime
> 2 tomatillos, chopped fine (optional)
> 1 small onion, chopped fine (optional)
> 1 small jalapeño or green chili, chopped fine
> 1–2 cloves garlic, crushed
> ½ cup (125ml) cilantro (fresh coriander), chopped fine
> 1 tablespoon (15ml) sour cream (optional)
> salt and ground red chili pepper

Cut avocados in half and remove stones. Using a sharp knife, make a cross-hatch pattern right through the flesh just to the skin. Using a large spoon, scoop out squares of avocado into a bowl. Mix all ingredients together (except sour cream), turning the avocado lightly as you go. Guacamole should be smooth and satiny, but chunky. Season with salt and chili pepper to taste. Serve immediately.

Though the guacamole can be kept for about an hour if covered and kept cold, it is very delicate and prone to rapid oxygenation, which turns avocado black and ruins the flavor. The lime in the mixture helps to prevent this but only to a certain extent. If you must keep the guacamole a little longer (only a few hours) without its discoloring, you can stir in 1 tablespoon (no more) sour cream (strictly speaking, this is not authentic and not my first choice) and store covered in refrigerator. Take plastic wrap and press it down over the entire surface of the guacamole to prevent any air from getting to it. Pressing a stone into the dip may look attractive but it has little effect on oxygenation and you will do better with the plastic wrap. The sour cream will slightly mask the avocado flavor but should be all right if you don't add too much.

Beer Cheese

Here is the perfect cheese to eat with your beer—or your wine, for that matter. Like all the best Galley Guru *recipes, it is good and simple and it keeps for ages. You will always have something on hand to serve to guests who drop by from neighboring boats. You can also use it as a topping for a hamburger or spread on a BLT. Use whatever beer you have, or some ale would be nice. Use any cheddar-type cheese. It's all good. Spread on crackers. Enjoy.*

    1 pound (455g) sharp cheddar cheese
    2 cloves garlic
    1 teaspoon (5ml) Tabasco sauce
    1 tablespoon (15ml) Worcestershire sauce
    ½ teaspoon (2.5ml) salt
    ½ teaspoon (2.5ml) pepper
    1 teaspoon (5ml) paprika
    1 teaspoon (5ml) dry mustard
    ½ cup (125ml) beer

Use a food processor to combine all ingredients, then put in a small crock and, if you can, keep in the fridge for a day or two before serving, because it gets better with age.

Baba Ganouj

Baba Ganouj translates to something like "Sugar Daddy," though the reasons for the name seem lost in the mists of time. This smoky, savory mixture of roasted eggplant and garlic appears as a dip, sauce, or spread on Middle Eastern tables. Though Baba Ganouj is traditionally served with warm pita bread, you can pair it with almost any bread at all or use it as a condiment for grilled meats or fish. Authentic Baba Ganouj gets its characteristic taste from char-roasting the eggplant over an open fire, thus imparting to the vegetables an earthy smokiness that is indescribably delicious. If you can't do this step, add a few drops of liquid smoke to approximate the taste.

> 2 medium eggplants
> 2 tablespoons (30ml) olive oil
> ½ cup (125ml) lemon juice
> ¼ teaspoon (1.25ml) coriander
> ¼ teaspoon (1.25ml) cumin
> dash Cayenne pepper
> 2 garlic cloves, minced
> ⅓ cup (85ml) tahini
> liquid smoke (optional)
> salt to taste

Prick the eggplant all over with a fork. Place in oven. Roast at 450 degrees for 30–40 minutes or until the flesh of the eggplant is soft. Remove from the oven, spoon the eggplant out of its skin into a food processor. Process the eggplant until it is smooth. Add the remaining ingredients and process again to combine. This is one of those dishes that seems to need a lot of salt. You can serve it at room temperature or cold as a dip, in a bowl, swirled with a little more olive oil on top and perhaps some parsley, for color.

Imam Bayildi Pâté
Caviar of the Desert

Another Mediterranean hors-d'oeuvre, a starter, or part of a meze. This is an adaptation of one of my mother's dishes that she adapted from one she was served in an elegant hotel in Fez. It's a different take on the eponymous dish that caused the Imam of legend to swoon when he tasted it. In this one, the ingredients are made into a rich dark pâté that is spicy but not too hot. The Imam must have known that this dish is great with a drink. The original requires you, the chef, to stand, stirring until dizzy. My version is simply pressed into a pan, cooked in the oven, then left to be served at room temperature or put in the refrigerator, where it can store and lasts for days. I have given all the names I know for an eggplant, but a rose by any other name.

4 medium aubergine (eggplant, berenjena, melanzana, melitza'na ...)
1 large onion
3 cloves garlic, chopped or pressed
2 cups (500ml) walnuts, finely chopped
1 teaspoon (5ml) coriander (seeds or ground)
1 teaspoon (5ml) ground cumin
8 cardamom seeds, shelled (or 1 teaspoon [5ml] ground)
good pinch nutmeg
1 teaspoon (5ml) cinnamon
1 tablespoon (15ml) sweet paprika
1 tablespoon (15ml) hot paprika
pinch turmeric
2 tablespoons (30ml) honey or brown sugar
1 teaspoon (5ml) white wine vinegar
1 teaspoon (5ml) dried tarragon or fresh leaves
3 tablespoons (45ml) tomato paste
5 tablespoons (75ml) extra virgin olive oil

2 teaspoons (10ml) Marigold bouillon powder (if substituting,
    see * p. 19)
salt to taste

Discard the ends of the eggplants, but do not peel. Cut eggplant
and onion in pieces and put in a food processor. Add the remaining
ingredients and 1 tablespoon of the olive oil. Blend the mixture into
a slightly chunky paste. Press into a baking dish. Drizzle some olive
oil over the top. Bake at medium heat, covered, for 15 minutes.
Uncover dish and bake for another 15–20 minutes, until nice and
brown and top becomes crusty. Allow to cool.

This is excellent cold or at room temperature with thin strips of
pita or peasant bread for dipping. Top with yet another little drizzle
of olive oil and a handful of Spanish olives tossed about, perhaps
with some sprigs of basil and another sprinkle of paprika. Cut into
this like a cake or serve with a spoon.

Avocado Prawn Cocktail

This is the simplest of starters but that doesn't make it ordinary. The sauce that dresses the prawns, called salsa rosa in Spain, is customarily made with brandy, which certainly kicks it up a notch. I sometimes substitute Drambuie, which only makes it sensational. You can use tiny canned shrimp (drained) here or large prawns, which are usually more flavorful. Any of them will work and any of them can be swathed in this sauce more or less with your eyes closed. It is of prime importance to have good mayonnaise. When I don't make my own (which, I hasten to add, translates to just about never on board a boat), I use Kewpie, a Japanese mayonnaise that is readily available and the best commercial mayonnaise I have ever tasted. Start with your ingredients chilled if you can.

    2 just-ripe avocados
    14 ounces (400g) cooked prawns
    ½ cup (12 ml) high-quality mayonnaise
    2 tablespoons (30ml) Sriracha hot chili sauce,
    or ketchup and a few drops Tabasco
    2 tablespoons (30ml) brandy or Drambuie (or to taste)
    good splash of Worcestershire sauce
    cayenne pepper
    salt and freshly ground pepper
    limes, quartered

Dump the prawns into a bowl. Stir in the mayonnaise, ketchup, Worcestershire sauce, and brandy or Drambuie. Season to taste with cayenne, salt, and a lot of freshly ground pepper.

Simple serving method: Open the avocados and remove the pits. Pile the prawns into the avocado.

Best serving method: For an elegant presentation, which this really deserves, the salad should be served nestled into the bottom half of large Martini glasses. For this you need to be in port or in dead calm. Put chunks of avocado in the bottom of each glass and pour the prawns with their sauce over top. Garnish with chopped chives and serve with quartered limes.

You can sprinkle this with chopped fresh dill, parsley, or chopped chives, if you have them.

Steamed Artichokes

1 artichoke per person

Cut off the bottom stems flat so that the artichokes can stand upright. Pluck off one or two rows of the bottom leaves around the base, then lay the artichoke on its side and cut off the top third of it with a serrated knife. Pull the leaves outward to expose the choke. Pull out any sharp leaves that may be directly over the choke. Cut the sharp tops of the leaves off with a scissors. With your thumbs in the center of the artichoke, pull the leaves slightly outward to loosen them and make the flower a bit bigger. This will ensure that the artichoke cooks evenly.

As you finish each artichoke, plunge it into a bowl of water with the juice of a lemon squeezed into it, to prevent it from turning brown. When the artichokes are ready, put them into a big pot about one-third full of water. Cover and bring to a boil. Turn down heat. Simmer artichokes for 55 minutes, or until leaves come out easily when pulled. Serve with melted butter.

Deviled Eggs with Crab

I like my stuffed eggs really stuffed, so I will sacrifice a white or two to make this happen. If you feel that you can't bear to throw food away, you could always eat them while you prepare these. Your conscience would then be clear as you scoop the filling into the cavity of the remaining eggs, continuing the mound right to the edge of the egg surface and smoothing it with a spoon.

8 hard-boiled eggs
½ pound (227g) crab meat, picked over
½ (125ml) cup high-quality mayonnaise

1 teaspoon Dijon mustard

two or three dashes Worcestershire sauce

good pinch of cayenne (to taste)

1 teaspoon (5ml) dry sherry

1 teaspoon (5ml) fresh chives, snipped (optional)

paprika

salt and freshly ground black pepper

Cut the eggs in half lengthwise. Carefully remove the hard yolks from the eggs. Discard four halves of the whites. Pass the yolks through a sieve or a rotary cheese grater into a bowl. Stir in the mayonnaise, mustard, Worcestershire sauce, cayenne, and sherry. Blend well until the mixture is smooth. Fold in the crab meat and chives, if using, keeping the crab pieces as intact as possible. Season with salt and black pepper to taste. Divide the crab meat mixture among the 12 halves of hard-boiled egg whites, scooping the mixture into the cavity with a spoon. Sprinkle decoratively with paprika and serve.

Prosciutto-Wrapped Melon

Prosciutto wrapped around cold melon slices is a meltingly delicious blend of salty and sweet flavors. It takes seconds to prepare this wonderful first course.

16 slices Prosciutto di Parma (about 4 per person)

16 slices of chilled sweet honeydew melon or cantaloupe

Take each slice of prosciutto and wrap it around a slice of melon. Lay these out attractively on a serving dish, allowing about 4 slices per person as an appetizer.

Ceviche

Sail southward and you'll find that almost any South American country has a version of Ceviche. Some of Peru's finest attractions can be found in abundance on her tables: divine fruits and vegetables, unutterably perfect avocados, and endless variations of this splendid appetizer. Undoubtedly, here is justice done to the catch of the day. Ceviche requires no cooking but does require perfectly fresh, perfectly firm-fleshed white fish. Mahi Mahi, sea bass, swordfish, halibut are all good choices. Snapper is also used, and if you are lucky enough to find the yellowtail version of that fish you have found something very special. If you have shrimp and/or scallops, put them in. Any combination of acid citrus fruits will "cook" the raw fish in minutes. You will see the fish turn white and firm up in the marinade after the first 15 minutes to half an hour. The version I found the most sumptuous is served atop cubed avocado, whose silky smoothness creates a tender bass to the bright, tart notes of the spiced fish.

What you are basically making here is a salsa or pico de gallo, with which you mix the fish after it has marinated in the lemon or lime. There are versions that use bitter orange (Seville oranges) and if you have them, try substituting the juice of one orange for a couple of limes. In Peru they sometimes add a splash of Pisco, a traditional and very—let me repeat, very—potent liquor, to the mix. Pisco is distilled from grapes, as is brandy, but is more like Grappa or Eau de Vie. If you drink it and exhale, do not light a match. The national Peruvian drink is a Pisco Sour, which, though innocently masquerading as a sweet frothy drink, will leave you legless in no time.

1½ pounds (680g) fresh white fish filet

freshly squeezed juice of 1 lemon

freshly squeezed juice of 6 limes

2 tomatoes, diced finely

½ cup (120ml) tomato juice (or Clamato if such is on hand)

1 small red onion, finely diced or

2–3 green onions, minced finely

2 cloves garlic, pressed

large handful cilantro leaves, roughly chopped

1–2 hot green chiles, chopped (jalapeño or Serrano)

salt to taste

1 avocado, cut into cubes (optional)

Cube the fish filets into bite-sized pieces. Place fish in a ceramic bowl or plastic container with a lid. Pour the lemon and lime juice over, turning the fish gently to coat with the juice. Cover the container tightly and refrigerate for at least 1 but no more than 3 hours. Mix the remaining ingredients together. Drain the fish and toss with the salsa mixture. Taste for seasoning.

This is beautiful served over cubed avocado in "glass" (non-breakable, of course) bowls or martini glasses. If you are in a bit of a sea, get it to the table any way you can and it will be just wonderful too.

Brandade de Morue

Salt cod and hard tack: Those two items and little else sustained many a sailor of antiquity. For hundreds of years, fish has been dried and salted to preserve it for long periods of time. Soups and gruels were made of it by soaking it in water to reconstitute, then mixing it with hard tack, otherwise called ship's biscuit, similarly brought back to life.

Well, we are lucky. Everything old is new again. Brandade de Morue is a great Provençale dish whose simple and pungent story, like Pistou or Tapenade, is all about garlic and fruity olive oil. Though its preparation may perhaps appear unusual to most cooks unfamiliar with Mediterranean cooking, I include it here as it is actually quite straightforward and made entirely from items that will not go bad. You might like to try it sometime as an exercise, for there are a few steps to the process but they are pretty easy.

You must use your best olive oil. You can certainly use canned cream for it (media crema by Nestlé comes to mind). It is made with dried salt cod (bacala) which, though it needs reconstituting for a day or so in water in the refrigerator, repays this effort with a richness and an elusive depth of flavor that does not apply to the fresh fish of the same name. The subsequent cooking is nothing more than poaching the fish in an herby liquid for a few minutes. Then the Brandade is assembled. You make Brandade rather like a mayonnaise, incorporating the olive oil and cream to the base of fish until it becomes light, thick, and unctuous. As in taramosalata, this fish mixture can be mixed with potato or bread but I think the potato is more to the point here. (Today, we usually have more than the Spartan ship's biscuit hanging around in the galley.) Then dip some crusty bread into this mixture, grab a glass of wine, and enjoy. Mmmm. Brandade can be served just like that as an hors d'oeuvre to dip with bread, or as a casserole: bake it till it gets gorgeous and brown and bubbly, or use it as a filling for fish pies. It is even good stuffed into savory Basic Crepes.

Even though you must soak the fish in water for 24 to 36 hours, this recipe is quite easy, because you just tuck the container in the fridge and turn it once in a while whenever you think of it. The old methods of preserving food work fabulously well at sea and can be the basis for any number of wonderful, first-class recipes.

The standard recipe requires that you heat the olive oil and cream separately, then add them alternately to the fish. This process can be streamlined by heating the cream and olive oil together and adding the resultant mixture to the cod and potatoes. Simply stir the liquid frequently to keep it from separating. You then have the right proportion to add to the cod and potato mixture.

1½ pound (685g) piece salt cod

1 pound (455g) potatoes

2 bay leaves (or pinch of powdered bay)

½ teaspoon (2.5ml) dried thyme

4 cloves garlic, pressed

½ cup (125ml) extra virgin olive oil, warmed with

1 cup (250ml) light cream

Place the cod in a large plastic container with a fitted lid. Cover with cold water and put the lid on to seal. Put the box in your refrigerator to soak for about 36 hours, changing the water every 6 to 8 hours to remove salt. If you put the fish to soak in the morning and change the water every so often, it will be ready to prepare by the next afternoon for that night's supper.

Next day:

When fish is completely reconstituted you are ready to prepare the Brandade. Bake or boil potatoes until soft. While potatoes are cooking, poach the fish. Place the refreshed cod into a large saucepan and cover with water. Add the bay leaves and thyme. Bring to a boil and reduce the heat to medium low. Gently simmer for 10 minutes until the fish is flaky. Turn the heat off, cover the pot, and allow fish to stand for 10 more minutes. Drain water from fish. Flake the cod with your fingers, removing and discarding skin and any bones.

When potatoes are done, scoop out the flesh and mash it roughly or, if you want a smoother result, put it through a potato ricer or food mill. Season to taste.

Stir the cream with the olive oil in a small saucepan over medium heat, just to warm through. Gradually add it to the fish, a little at a time, stirring well to incorporate after each addition to make a smooth purée. Or you can put the fish into a food processor and add the oil and cream mixture a little at a time to get the right consistency. The Brandade should be light, creamy white, and fluffy, not runny. Taste for seasoning. Add salt, if necessary, and plenty of freshly ground pepper. If you prefer a piquant taste, you may add some lemon juice. Fold the fish into the seasoned mashed potatoes in a mixing bowl.

Gratinée method: Place Brandade in an ovenproof dish under the broiler part of the oven for 10 to 15 minutes or until the mixture is browned nicely.

Serve topped with **Garlic Confit** or **Persillade**.

 ## Pan Con Tomate (Pa Amb Tomaquet)

Garlic Toast with Tomatoes, Spanish Style

Pan con Tomate, originally from Catalonia, is found in every Spanish village tapa bar and restaurant. Crusty, earthy, gutsy with garlic, this dish is often enjoyed alongside a glass of sherry but surprisingly pops up as a breakfast—definitely not for the faint of heart! It is produced by toasting crusty country-style bread until golden over a wood fire, where it picks up a slightly smoky taste. You can do it on the barbecue grill, however, with great results, along with whatever fish or meat you are grilling that evening. You can also do the toast in a very hot oven or under the broiler the way the Italians prepare bruschetta. It is quick, easy, and crunchy—crunchier than conventional garlic toast—with the intense, assertive flavor typical of Spanish food. The bread goes to the flame dry. Rub the garlic and tomato over it when you serve it, or put it all on the table and let everyone make their own with as little or as much garlic as they like.

8 slices French, sourdough, or good peasant bread
4 garlic cloves, peeled and halved
4 ripe, juicy, halved tomatoes
fruity extra-virgin olive oil
sea salt to taste

Put bread slices on barbecue grill or under broiler. Allow to brown lightly, about 2 minutes on each side. Rub each slice with half a garlic clove and a piece of tomato, allowing juices and pulp to sink into bread. Discard any excess pulp and peels. Drizzle some olive oil over top. Season with salt and serve.

This will serve 4–8, depending upon what else you are serving.

Walk into any tapa bar in Spain, and you will find jars laden with garlicky olives alongside wonderful tender anchovies, as well as chunks of sausages and Manchego cheese in oil. A tapa of any of these is a pleasing addition atop your bread. Or thinly sliced Serrano ham or Prosciutto is lovely too, as the cured ham has a buttery texture and salty taste that is complemented by the crunch of the toast.

Another great appetizer is made by topping this bread with mounds of **Ratatouille** done in the oven quickly and with no fuss.

Awesome Brie

This recipe came from Joni, a great gal who can go into full dining mode at the drop of a sail. She has an unqualified love for entertaining and wherever her table, it is soon happily laden with miles of goodies such as these yummy and simple hors d'oeuvres. If you haven't got a microwave, you can do the cheese in a low oven just until it is soft in the middle. Do not allow it to melt completely or you will have a runny mess on your hands. You can also serve this as "afters," as it is not uncommon to serve cheese to follow a meal in Europe, and the sweetness of the brown sugar makes this one especially nice.

1 round of brie
4 ounces (115g) of butter
package portobello or crimini mushrooms
1-2 cups (250-500 ml) walnuts, chopped in chunks
4 cloves garlic, minced finely
½–1 tablespoon (7.5-15ml) of soy sauce (preferably Tamari)
and 1 tablespoon (15ml) of brown sugar
loaf of French bread, sliced in rounds

With a large knife, carefully slice the top completely off the round of brie, just under the crust. Discard. Place the cheese in a microwaveable dish and warm it slightly in the microwave (3–4 minutes on 30 percent power). Warm, do not melt the cheese.

Sauté butter with several minced garlic cloves to taste (I use 4 cloves), in saucepan over medium low heat. Chop mushrooms in bite-sized pieces and add to saucepan. Add walnuts and heat thoroughly. Add soy sauce and brown sugar. When sugar has melted into the soy sauce and coated the mushrooms well, it will begin to caramelize in the heat of the pan. Turn fire off. Pour sautéed mushrooms and nuts over the cheese. Serve with sliced French bread.

Soups

"The Mock Turtle sighed deeply, and began, in a voice sometimes choked with sobs, to sing
this:
'Beautiful Soup, so
rich and green, Waiting
in a hot tureen! Who
for such dainties would
not stoop? Soup of the
evening, beautiful Soup!
Soup of the evening,
beautiful Soup! Beau--
ootiful Soo-- oop! Beau--
ootiful Soo--oop! Soo--oop of
the e--e--evening, Beautiful,
beautiful Soup! Beautiful
Soup! Who cares for fish, Game, or any other dish? Who would not give all else for two pennyworth only of beautiful Soup?"

—John Tenniel, *Alice in Wonderland*

Echoing the Mock Turtle, sailors are quite inordinately partial to their soup. Whether it is the ease of boiling it or the pleasure of eating it, soup satisfies something deep within. From a potage based on ale to an enticing cream of chestnut that needs no cream, herewith is a sampling of restoratives that leave the chicken noodle flat at the gate.

Salmon Chowder

*Fragrant as spring and a very nice excuse to indulge in lovely tarragon.
In a wicked moment you might serve a glass of Pernod with this, since the
anise drink and the licorice tarragon are a match made in heaven.*

2 tablespoons (30ml) olive oil

1–2 stalks celery, diced fine

1 small onion, diced fine

1 clove garlic, minced

2 medium potatoes, diced

3 cups (750ml) broth (chicken or vegetable)

1–2 teaspoon (5-10ml) Marigold bouillon powder
   (if substituting, see * p. 19)

1 wineglass white wine

8 ounces (225g) cooked fresh salmon (or you can use canned)

1 wineglass cream

handful chopped fresh tarragon

or 2 teaspoons (10ml) dried tarragon

couple of dashes of hot sauce

salt and freshly ground black pepper to taste

Sauté celery and onion in the olive oil over medium low heat until
soft. Add garlic and continue to cook 2–3 minutes. Do not allow
garlic to color. Pour in white wine and scrape up any bits in bottom
of pan. Add potatoes, broth, and Marigold. Simmer 20 minutes or
until potatoes are tender. Add salmon, cream, and tarragon. Stir to
heat through. Season with hot sauce, salt, and pepper. Do not allow
to boil.

You can vary the flavors by changing the seasoning. Substitute
dill for the tarragon. Fresh (not dried) basil is also very nice with
salmon.

Leek and Potato Soup

This is the very essence of simplicity.

2 ounces (56g) unsalted butter

4 cups (1 liter) chicken or vegetable stock

6 large leeks, white parts only, sliced thinly

4 large potatoes, sliced

1 teaspoon (5ml) Marigold bouillon powder, or to taste (if
substituting, see * p. 19)

salt and pepper to taste

Heat butter in a large pot. Sauté leeks until transparent. Add the stock to the leeks with the Marigold powder, salt, and pepper. Bring to a boil, cover pan, reduce heat, and simmer 20 minutes. Add the sliced potato and continue cooking another 20 minutes, or until potatoes are tender.

You can pass this soup through a food mill, or serve it just as it is. You can swirl about a half a cup of cream in it at the end, which smoothes it out and makes it more elegant. You can garnish with dill or basil or parsley or any fresh chopped herbs you might have, but it is plenty good on its own.

Variation:

Leek and Potato Soup with Pesto

For a great Italian twist, swirl a couple of spoonfuls of homemade or store-bought pesto right into the center of this soup when you serve it. If you have some jars of pesto you are set. If you haven't, on the following page is a recipe for a classic pesto.

Classic Pesto

handful pine nuts or handful cashews and pine nuts

10 cloves garlic, peeled

enough fresh basil to fill food processor container (about two
   bunches)

1 teaspoon (5ml) salt

1 teaspoon (5ml) pepper

2 cups (500ml) olive oil

½ cup (125ml) Parmigiano Reggiano or best Parmesan, grated

Put all ingredients into a food processor except for the oil. Give a
good chop before you start to pour the oil in a steady stream into the
container. This pesto can be put in the freezer for later use, or, if
storing in the refrigerator, pour a little film of olive oil to keep pesto
from turning brown before you place plastic wrap on the surface and
put the top on it.

 Galley Guru Tip

Many herbs change taste dramatically when they are
dried. Prime among these are dill, chives, and basil. You
can buy these and many other herbs in jars, freeze-dried.
These taste very close to fresh and need no refrigeration
so they can stand on your shelves alongside your
conventional dried herbs.

Thai Green Curry Corn and Crab Chowder

Here is a luscious and exotic bowl that is made entirely from pantry ingredients. So-o-o velvety and warming. Marigold substitutes for a rich vegetable stock.

  1 onion, finely chopped
  1 tablespoon (15ml) peanut or vegetable oil
  2 cloves garlic, minced
  ½–2 teaspoons (2.5–10ml) green curry paste (to taste, this can be
      very hot)
  2 (14 oz/400 ml) cans rich coconut milk
  ¾–1 can water to dilute (to taste)
  2 (8oz/225g) canned sweet corn
  6 ounces (170g) or 1 can crab meat (use more if you like)
  juice of 1–2 limes, to desired sourness
  1 teaspoon (5ml) Marigold bouillon powder (or to taste) (see * p. 19)
  extra lime wedges for garnish

Sauté the onion in the oil over medium heat until wilted and translucent, about 5 minutes. Add the garlic and the curry paste. This is very hot, so add it carefully. One teaspoon will be quite spicy. Continue to sauté for another minute or two. Pour in the coconut milk. Add water. Bring to the boil. Stir in half the corn. Lower heat. With an immersion blender, puree the soup. Add the rest of the corn and leave whole. Cover pan. Simmer over low heat 5 minutes. Add the crab meat and half the lime juice and heat through. Serve hot with lime wedges to garnish.

Thai Corn Chowder (Vegetarian Style)

Follow directions for the above chowder, leaving out the crab. It, too, makes a beautiful soup.

Real New England Clam Chowder

"'Queequeg,' said I, 'do you think that we can make out a supper for us both on one clam?' However, a warm savoury steam from the kitchen served to belie the apparently cheerless prospect before us. But when that smoking chowder came in, the mystery was delightfully explained. Oh, sweet friends! hearken to me. It was made of small juicy clams, scarcely bigger than hazel nuts, mixed with ships biscuit, and salted pork cut up into little flakes; the whole enriched with butter, and plentifully seasoned with pepper and salt."

—Herman Melville, *Moby Dick*

An excellent chowder has moved more than one poet to wax lyrical. If you have perchance stumbled upon some lovely fresh clams and are overwhelmed with a sudden lust for soup, serve a steaming pot of this elixir born of necessity (and compulsion) somewhere along the brash North Atlantic coast of America. You can use canned clams (use the liquid in the can and add clams at the last minute) but please be warned that this is one of those times when nothing but real cream and butter will do.

Serves 4–6

4 dozen cherrystones (or other small clams)

¼ pound (115g) bacon, diced

1 large yellow onion, diced very small

2 ribs celery, diced very small

3 tablespoons (45ml) flour

3 large or 6 medium potatoes, peeled and cut into small dice

2 cups (500ml) heavy cream

bottled clam juice (if necessary)

3½ ounces (100g) (plus a few pats) unsalted butter

1 bay leaf

1 sprig thyme

1 pinch cayenne pepper (or Tabasco)

1 teaspoon (5ml) Marigold bouillon powder (if using a substitute, see * p. 19)

salt and white pepper to taste

handful chopped parsley

Place the clams in a large pot with enough water to cover by 2 inches. Cover, bring to a boil, and cook just until the shells open (about 10 minutes, depending on the size of clams). Allow to cool. Discard any clams that have not opened. Pour off and reserve the broth (strain to keep out any sand that may be at the bottom of pot.) Remove clams from their shells and cut in quarters. Set aside.

Cook the bacon in a large soup pot over medium heat until crispy. Remove bacon. Add the onion and celery to the pot and cook in bacon fat over medium low heat, stirring, until onion is tender and translucent. (Do not brown!) Pour off excess fat to leave about 3 tablespoons. Add the flour to the vegetables. Cook a few minutes, stirring around to coat well.

Add reserved clam broth (you should have about 6 cups; if not, add bottled clam broth) and the bay leaf and thyme. Bring to the boil and stir until it's thickened. Add the potatoes to the pot and stir well. Lower the heat, cover, and simmer until the potatoes are very tender, about 20 minutes.

Stir in the heavy cream. Season with Marigold, pepper, and cayenne. Add salt if necessary. Bring to the boil. Make sure the chowder base is the consistency you like. If it is too thin, boil it a bit more. If too thick, thin with a little milk or clam broth. When it is just right, add the clams and butter and immediately take it off the heat until you are ready to serve. To serve, just heat through; you do not need to cook the clams again. (Very important: Do not allow the soup to boil, or the clams will be tough!) Check for seasoning. Serve hot with oyster crackers and garnished with the parsley and extra pats of butter if desired.

As an alternative, try steaming the clams in a couple cups of white wine and use that liquid as the base for your soup. I am admonished that this is not strictly authentic but it tastes amazing, so no one should complain too bitterly.

 Galley Guru Tip

If you put the dishes you are working with on nonslip rubber mats, they will not tend to slide about. Put large bowls or pots as well as spices in the sink to keep them from flying around.

Gazpacho

Here are several variations of this wonderful salad soup of Spain. It is super cooling on hot days (when you have refrigeration and ice) and should be served as cold as humanly possible. I have given amounts of ingredients of vegetables, but these are to be used as very rough guidelines. If you have more pepper one day, use it. You may like more or less garlic. As long as you have the base of bread, oil, and tomatoes right, you can experiment.

½ loaf crustless French or Italian bread

1 wineglass olive oil

8–10 very ripe tomatoes, or 1 large can tomatoes, or a mixture of fresh and canned

1 cucumber, peeled and chopped

1 or 2 red peppers, chopped

¼ small onion, minced

12 cloves garlic, minced

2 teaspoons (10ml) white wine or sherry vinegar

1 wineglass water

lemon juice (to taste)

salt and pepper to taste

Soak the bread in cold water and squeeze out the excess. Place this bread into a blender with the olive oil. Process to form a paste. Blend in the tomatoes. When well blended, add the rest of the vegetables, water, sherry vinegar, and lemon juice. The bread and olive oil will make the mixture thick and creamy and it should be a lovely red orange color. Add salt and pepper. Straining this soup will make it smoother and is traditional, but it is not necessary. Keep it cold and serve chilled.

To garnish: Cube some bread, chop up red pepper, cucumber, onion into small dice, and serve to spoon over the soup. You can also vary this with cooked shrimp or cubed Spanish ham on top.

Gazpacho Almendras

This gazpacho uses no bread at all, but is thickened by almond butter. It is also sensational with cashew nut butter.

½ cup (125ml) almond butter
3–4 tablespoons (45–60ml) olive oil
1 large can tomatoes
1 cucumber, peeled and chopped
1 red pepper, chopped
¼ onion, minced
1–2 cloves garlic, minced
juice of 1–2 lemons
salt and pepper to taste

Mix all ingredients in a blender until smooth. Serve ice cold.

Mock Quick Gazpacho

2 (12oz/340ml) cans V8 juice (or tomato juice)
2 boxes silken tofu
juice of 2 lemons
1 teaspoon (5ml) Marigold bouillon powder (if using a substitute, see * p. 19)
1 tablespoon (15ml) olive oil
salt to taste

Put all ingredients in blender with 4 to 6 ice cubes. Blend until smooth. Serve immediately in bowls or mugs.

Mock Quick Gazpacho 2

2 (12oz/340ml) cans V8 juice (or tomato juice)

16 ounces (455g) yogurt

juice of 1 lemon

1 teaspoon (5ml) Marigold bouillon powder (if using a substitute, see * p. 19)

1 tablespoon (15ml) olive oil

salt to taste

Follow directions for Mock Quick Gazpacho.

Ajo Blanco

Ajo Blanco (literally "white garlic") is a delicious variation of gazpacho served all over Spain. It comes from the Malaga region in Andalusia in the south, where I lived happily, if not ever after, for quite a few years. It has nothing whatever to do with the other Spanish soup, Sopa de Ajo, which is a sort of garlic bread pudding of a soup. This one has wine in it but is light as a drifting breeze. As in many other dishes Spain inherited from the Arabs, almonds play a central role. My streamlined version uses almond butter instead of a mixture of breadcrumbs and almonds, which in the original you had to grind and make into paste anyway. It eliminates the breadcrumbs entirely. You can vary the white grapes with honeydew melon balls or slices of apple, according to what you have. The lusciousness of cold fruit is a perfect foil for the garlicky wine cream. Here is another occasion when, if you've got refrigeration, flaunt it.

> ¾ cup (185ml) almond butter
> 3 cloves garlic, chopped
> 1 cucumber, peeled and chopped
> 4 tablespoons (60ml) olive oil
> 1 glass white wine
> 1 tablespoon (15ml) chopped onion
> 2 cups (500ml) ice water
> 3 tablespoons (45ml) lemon juice or vinegar (sherry vinegar is most
>   authentic, if you have it)
> 2 teaspoons (10ml) Marigold bouillon powder (or to taste) (see p. 19)
> salt and pepper to taste
> cold seedless green grapes for garnish, peeled and halved lengthwise
> handful of flaked toasted almonds

Put all the ingredients except the grapes and flaked almonds in a food processor. Blend until smooth and creamy. Taste for salt. Chill until very cold. You can serve it in bowls, or it looks very nice in clear (unbreakable) glasses. Garnish with a few grapes and a sprinkle of almonds in each bowl. Add an ice cube to keep it very cold.

Jiffy Hot and Sour Soup

"You don't have to cook fancy or complicated masterpieces—just good food from fresh ingredients."

—Julia Child

Julia Child, who was known to illuminate folk in the arcane mysteries of some of the most time-intensive as well as intricate recipes, pronounced that soup made an excellent meal and that most soups are simple to make. If that is the case, this soup is the absolute quintessence of simplicity, while filling the rest of the bill dramatically.

> 2 pints (1.2Ltr) chicken stock, vegetable stock, or vegetable stock
> with clam juice
> 8 ounces (250g) white rice
> 1 cup (225g) peeled shrimps
> 1 cup (225g) boneless chicken breast meat, cut into thin strips, or
> use cooked chicken
> 1 can sliced water chestnuts (drained)
> 1 teaspoon (5ml) Marigold bouillon powder (or to taste) (see p. 19)
> 1 teaspoon five spice powder
> 1 tablespoon soy sauce
> 1 teaspoon (to taste) hot sauce (such as Sriracha)
> juice of a lime or lemon
> 1 glass medium dry sherry (Amontillado) or Sake
> large handful chopped green onions as a garnish

Bring the stock to a boil. Season with Marigold, salt, and pepper. Add the rice and the nutmeg. Let simmer gently 10 minutes. Add the ham and hard-boiled eggs. Cook 4 minutes. Add shrimp. Pour in the sherry. Continue to cook until the shrimp is done (3 minutes). Taste for seasonings. Serve garnished with fresh parsley.

Chilled Cucumber Soup
with Dill and Mint

This soup also makes fine use of your refrigerator and is an exceptionally refreshing way to begin lunch under a hot summer sun.

2 long cucumbers, peeled and cut into cubes

2 cups thick yogurt (Greek Total, for instance)

½ cup (125ml) cream

2 tablespoons (30ml) fresh dill, chopped

1 tablespoon (15ml) fresh mint, chopped

1 teaspoon (5ml) Marigold bouillon powder (if using a substitute, see * p. 19)

few drops liquid aminos (Marigold, Braggs) seasoning to taste

large pinch nutmeg

salt and white pepper to taste

Place all ingredients in a food processor and process until smooth (or pass cucumber through food mill and stir into yogurt). Check for seasoning. Refrigerate for at least one hour before serving. Garnish with a sprinkle of fresh snipped dill. Once chilled, can be kept cold in a thermos.

Thai Mussels with Rum in Coconut Broth

I love mussels. A big pot of steaming mussels in a fragrant broth can't be beat and is so simple and satisfying that everyone will think you worked really hard to create such a fine dish. Don't worry. I won't tell anyone.

Green-lipped mussels are nice in this beautifully aromatic soup but you can use black smaller ones too.

4½ pounds (2kg) fresh washed (and de-bearded) mussels

2 tablespoons (30ml) olive oil

3 minced shallots

2 cloves of garlic, finely sliced

1 tablespoon (15ml) Thai green chili paste (or to taste)

4 cups (1 liter) bottled clam juice

4 spring onions, sliced thin

4 teaspoons (20ml) minced fresh ginger

3 tablespoons (45ml) golden rum

juice of 2 limes

1–2 strips of lime zest

1 (14oz/400ml) can rich coconut milk

2 large handfuls of fresh coriander chopped finely

salt and freshly ground black pepper

lime wedges for garnish

In a large, heavy saucepan, heat the olive oil over medium heat. Add the shallots, ginger, and green chili paste. Stir and cook over low heat until the shallots are soft. Increase the heat. Add the clam juice, 2 tablespoons rum, lime juice, and zest. Bring to a boil and reduce liquid for 4–5 minutes. Taste for seasoning. Throw in the mussels and the spring onions, cover, and cook until all mussels have opened, shaking the pan frequently. Throw away any mussels that remain closed. Add the coconut milk, give it another shot of rum, and throw in the coriander. Bring to the boil again, taste for seasoning and serve immediately with lime wedges.

Mama Rose's Ukrainian Beet Borscht

Borsch or Borscht has its origins not in Russia but in the Ukraine. This is an easy method to make not just a good soup, but a fantastic, authentic Ukrainian beet borscht just like Mama Rose used to make. It cheats only in that it uses canned consommé rather than broth from boiling bones to make stock. What you get is a hearty, hot vegetable soup that would nourish a horde of Cossacks. It will amply reward the effort of opening a couple of cans with a bit of shredding and slicing thrown in. (Use your mandoline for this or the shredder/slicer blades of a food processor.) Full of character and satisfying, this is beet soup but it is not sickly sweet. Makes a fine, filling meal with rye or any good peasant bread.

2 cans (10oz/464ml) beef broth or consommé
2 cans water
5 or 6 beets, shredded
1 can stewing tomatoes
1 large or 2 medium onions
3–4 tablespoons (45–60ml) chopped fresh dill
    or 1 tablespoon (15ml) dried dill
1 bay leaf
salt and pepper
4 large carrots, sliced very thin
3 medium potatoes, cut in cubes
can of lima beans
4 tablespoons (60ml) vinegar (or to taste)
fresh cream or sour cream for garnish

Bring beef broth, water, beets, tomatoes, onion, and bay leaf to the boil in a large pot. Boil gently, uncovered, one hour. Add carrots, potatoes, dill, and lima beans. Cook till potatoes and carrots are done. Remove bay leaf. Stir in the vinegar. Ladle into bowls. Garnish with fresh or sour cream.

Curried Cauliflower Cream Soup

Vegetable soup is one place tofu shines as an ingredient. The resulting soup tastes so rich and creamy you will hardly care that it's also good for you.

- 1 medium head of cauliflower
- 1 box silken tofu, blended to a cream
- 1 medium onion, chopped
- 4 cloves garlic, minced
- a piece of fresh ginger, peeled and chopped
- 1 teaspoon (5ml) ground cumin
- 1 teaspoon (5ml) ground coriander
- ½ teaspoon (2.5ml) ground cinnamon
- ½ teaspoon (2.5ml) ground cardamom
- 1 teaspoon (5ml) curry powder
- 2 cups (500ml) water
- 1–2 teaspoons (5-10ml) Marigold bouillon powder (or to taste)
  (if using a substitute, see * p. 19)
- 2 teaspoons (10ml) liquid aminos (Marigold, Braggs)
- vegetable oil for frying

Heat oil in a soup pot. Sauté onion with ginger two to three minutes. Add garlic and cook gently a minute or two more. Add the cauliflower with the spices. Sauté gently until cauliflower just begins to color. Add bouillon powder, liquid aminos (Marigold, Braggs), spices, and water. Bring to a boil. Cover, turn heat down. Simmer on medium low heat, about 20 minutes, until cauliflower is soft. Add tofu to pot. With immersion blender, blend cauliflower mixture with tofu until smooth and creamy. Serve hot.

Delicious with a spoonful of mango chutney right in the center, as a garnish. This recipe works equally well with other vegetables: butternut squash or carrots, the sweetness of which gives the soup another dimension. Half carrot, half cauliflower is also nice.

Lebanese Lentil Soup

This is an easy and comforting soup full of exotic spices and the promise of the Orient.

2 cups (500ml) dried lentils

8 cups (2 liters) vegetable or chicken broth

4 tablespoons (60ml) butter

2 tablespoons (30ml) olive oil

1 medium onion, chopped

1 teaspoon (5ml) tomato paste

2–3 cloves garlic, minced

2 teaspoon (10ml) ground cumin

1 teaspoon (5ml) dried coriander

pinch or two of ground allspice

1 teaspoon (5ml) Marigold bouillon powder (or to taste) (see p. 19)

black pepper, freshly ground

2 tablespoons (30ml) finely chopped fresh parsley

lemon, cut into wedges

toasted pine nuts

Wash the lentils in a large sieve or colander set under cold running water, until the draining water runs clear. In a large pot, melt the butter in the olive oil over moderate heat. Add the chopped onions, stirring frequently. Cook gently for 15 minutes, or until they are soft and golden. Add the garlic. Cook on low 3 minutes. Do not brown them. Pour in the stock. Bring to a boil over high heat. Add the lentils and tomato paste, reduce the heat to low, and simmer partially covered for 45 minutes, or until the lentils are tender. Stir in the cumin, coriander, pinch of allspice, and Marigold bouillon. Taste for seasoning. Add salt and pepper to taste. Return the soup to the saucepan and stir and cook over low heat just to heat through.

Serve this soup peasant style. You can also purée the soup through a food mill or use an immersion blender to achieve a smooth soup. Serve garnished with parsley, toasted pine nuts, and lemon wedges.

I Don't Believe It's Not Cheese Soup
Cheeseless Cheese Soup

You can serve this soup to your vegan friends. But it's rich and satisfying for anybody, for it has no cholesterol and is low in fat.   As much as I love cheese, when I want to abstain I find I somehow don't want to completely abstain, so I fill in with soy cheese and I can be happy with that. Some soy cheeses melt better than others. They keep pretty much the same way that dairy cheese does. But the tofu is on hand anytime and it tastes great.

2 boxes silken tofu
2 or 3 tomatoes (from can or fresh)
⅓ cup (85ml) ale or water
1 teaspoon (5ml) Marigold bouillon powder (or to taste) (see * p. 19)
2 tablespoons (30ml) liquid aminos or liquid aminos seasoning
      (Marigold, Braggs)
1 cup (250ml) grated cheddar soy cheese
salt and pepper to taste

In a blender or with an immersion blender, blend tofu, ale (or water if you prefer), seasonings, and tomatoes until creamy. Over medium heat, bring the mixture to a simmer. Sprinkle in soy cheese. Stir until melted. Check for seasoning. Serve.

Variation:
Sauté some onions until golden and caramelized in a tablespoon or so of olive oil (or use prepared **Onion Confit**) before adding the tofu mixture to the pot. You could top with croutons, toasted slivered almonds, or crumbled soy bacon strips to keep it vegetarian.

Breadfruit Chowder

Breadfruit is a starchy fruit found from Jamaica to Polynesia. It can be sweet or savory. In the islands it is often paired with bacon and coconut.

1 large breadfruit
4 strips bacon, sliced
1 medium onion, chopped
3 stalks celery, chopped
2 carrots, diced
1½ cups (375ml) coconut milk
1 cup (250ml) corn kernels
1 teaspoon (5ml) Marigold bouillon powder (or to taste) (see * p. 19)
large pinch nutmeg
pinch allspice
salt and pepper to taste

Cook breadfruit in salted water. When tender, remove from water and reserve 2 cups of boiling liquid. Cool, peel and core breadfruit, and cut into cubes. Fry bacon until beginning to crisp. Add onions, celery, and carrots. Cook gently until tender. Add the breadfruit, boiling water, nutmeg, and allspice. Simmer until vegetables are soft. Add coconut milk, Marigold powder, and corn. Heat thoroughly. Add salt and pepper to taste.

What to Do with Callaloo Soup

When you are in the Caribbean you will not likely find spinach but you will find a spinach-like green leaf of the taro plant called callaloo. You can use it like spinach as long as you find the most tender, youngest leaves. In other latitudes use spinach in this soup or whatever greens you have.

1 large bunch callaloo leaves
3 tablespoons (45ml) butter
1 small onion, finely chopped
2 cloves garlic, minced
4 (10oz/284ml) cans vegetable broth (or chicken broth)
1 (14oz/400ml) can rich coconut milk
few gratings of nutmeg
pinch allspice
pinch cayenne
1 teaspoon (5ml) Marigold bouillon powder (or to taste) (see * p. 19)
2 tablespoons (30ml) liquid aminos seasoning (Marigold, Braggs)
¾ lb (340g) crab meat
salt and pepper to taste

Wash and trim the greens. Slice into shreds. Melt butter in a large pot over moderate heat. Add the onion and garlic and cook gently until wilted and translucent. Add the greens, tossing them until they are well coated with the butter and onions. Cook for two minutes. Add the stock, coconut milk, nutmeg, allspice, pinch of cayenne, and Marigold and liquid aminos seasoning (Marigold, Braggs). Simmer covered 10 minutes. Uncover. Add the crab meat and heat through. Season with salt and pepper. Serve hot.

Chestnut Soup

This is easy, smooth, and luxuriously rich, though it has no cream. It is a fine soup, particularly good at holiday season. On second thought, serve it whenever you like—make your own holiday.

    12 ounces (340g) bottled chestnuts
    2 tablespoons (30ml) extra virgin olive oil
    3 stalks celery, diced fine
    1 large carrot, diced
    1 medium onion, diced
    4 cups (1 liter) vegetable or chicken stock
    1 bouquet garni (1 sprig each of bay leaf, thyme, and parsley)
    ½–1 wineglass medium sherry
    few gratings nutmeg
    1 teaspoon (5ml) Marigold bouillon powder (or to taste) (see * p. 19)
    salt and freshly ground pepper to taste

Place olive oil in soup pot over medium heat. Add carrot. Cook for 5 minutes until it begins to caramelize. Add onion and celery. Cook until wilted and translucent, about 5–6 minutes. Add stock, sherry, and chestnuts. Add Marigold powder and nutmeg; bring to a boil. Lower heat, and simmer 20 minutes. Check for seasoning. Add salt if necessary. Remove bouquet garni. Purée with an immersion blender until creamy. Serve hot with a sprinkling of freshly ground pepper.

Beer Soup

A sustaining brew to enliven a chill night when you have some bottles of beer, a bit of bread and butter, and not much else. This soup can be made with any bread you have and any beer you have. Pumpernickel and Belgian ale will be rich, dark, and sour. French bread and lager will be light, dry, and creamy. But in any combination the outcome will be very satisfying. It really doesn't get much simpler than this. Work smarter, not harder.

    4 ounces (115g) unsalted butter
    6 slices bread (French, rye, or pumpernickel are all good)
    ¼ cup (60ml) all purpose flour
    4 cups (1 liter) chicken or vegetable stock
    4 cups (1 liter) beer or ale
    1 pinch sugar
    ¼ teaspoon (1.25ml) grated nutmeg
    salt and white pepper
    1 cup (250ml) heavy cream

In a large pot, melt half of the butter. Fry bread slices until crisped and lightly golden. Remove from pot. Add remaining butter to pot. Add flour and cook gently, stirring until it turns golden brown. Add stock, wine, and beer, stirring all the while, and bring to a boil. Season with the nutmeg, pinch of sugar, and salt and pepper to taste. Turn heat down to simmer for 20 minutes. Stir in cream. Allow to cook for 2 minutes more. Taste for seasoning. Add bread and push into soup until moistened. Ladle into bowls or mug.

Sweet Sweet Onion Soup

When you have sweet onions such as the ones that come from Hawaii, make this heady soup. It is so good you will not believe that you can prepare such a masterpiece so easily. The caramelization makes the already sweet onion sweeter, dense, and rich. That is all you need.

> 1 large carrot, 1 medium onion, 2 stalks celery, chopped into small dice (mirepoix)
> 4 tablespoons (60ml) butter
> olive oil
> 6 large sweet onions, sliced very thin
> 1 teaspoon (5ml) thyme
> 4 cups (1 liter) chicken (or vegetable) stock
> 2 glasses white wine
> 1 cup (250 ml) cream

Sauté mirepoix in butter and a little olive oil over low heat until beginning to caramelize, about 10 minutes. Add sliced onions and continue to cook over medium low about 20 minutes more until they have completely wilted and turned the color of golden apples. Throw in 2 tablespoons flour. Cook and stir over low heat 4–5 minutes, being careful not to burn flour. Add thyme, chicken stock and white wine. Cook uncovered, stirring occasionally for 25 minutes. Add the cream, bring to the boil, turn heat down and simmer 2–3 minutes, stirring. Soup should be thick and the color of light peanut butter. Serve hot.

Salads and Dressings

Salads are somewhat difficult at sea,
especially if you need to make them out of lettuce.
The lovely salads I have included here
do not rely too heavily on things that wilt,
but if you do have the freshest, coldest ingredients available,
then make one of these.
Try to use the best Parmigiano Reggiano
or best Parmesan you can find.

Perfect Italian Salad

crisp hearts of romaine (cos)
baby lettuces or arugula
1 can garbanzos (chick peas)
handful of pine nuts
small grape tomatoes
wedge of Parmigiano Reggiano cheese

Simple Dressing

cherry balsamic (or other good vinegar)
touch of olive oil

Drizzle with a light hand over salad. Enjoy.

Lemon Vinaigrette Dressing

1 part lemon juice
1 part vinegar
3 parts extra virgin olive oil
2 tablespoons (30ml) Dijon mustard
1–2 teaspoons (5–10ml) liquid aminos (Marigold, Braggs)
1 clove chopped garlic
1 minced shallot or
⅓ minced onion
sea salt
freshly ground pepper

Emulsify the dressing ingredients in a blender. Mix the lettuces in a serving platter or bowl. Top with garbanzos and tomatoes and toss with the dressing. Use vegetable peeler to slice off thin strips of Parmesan from a block of cheese. Top salad with these strips. Serve with garlic bread.

Green Green Salad

This green salad (no tomatoes) gets rave reviews. Though simple, it relies on the combination of lettuces and the finest of ingredients for its wonderful balance. It's the perfect light accompaniment to a great main course. Cherry balsamic vinegar is really fine and you should take the time to look for it. It makes a huge difference in the taste of your foods.

romaine lettuce

butter lettuce

pine nuts

garlic croutons

Parmigiano Reggiano

extra virgin olive oil

black cherry balsamic vinegar

Mix the romaine and the butter lettuce, using about half of each type of lettuce. Sprinkle with a good handful of pine nuts. Toss with olive oil and salt. Top with garlic croutons and thin strips of Parmesan from a block of cheese. Drizzle the cherry balsamic vinegar over the top with a deft hand.

Hearts of Palm Salad

Well, here's one that might make you forget lettuce.

Slice hearts of palm into rounds and arrange on plate. Scatter with a few halved black olives. Dress with lemon and olive oil or lemon vinaigrette.

Crab and Cucumber Salad
with Basil Dressing

When you peel the cucumber, cut it in half and take a teaspoon to core the center. This gets rid of all the seeds and makes the cucumber much dryer and crispier to go with the crab.

1 pound (454g) crab
1 large cucumber, peeled, seeded, and finely diced
2 tablespoons (30ml) extra virgin olive oil
juice of half a lemon
2 medium scallions, sliced thin
½ cup (125ml) fresh basil leaves, sliced thin (chiffonnade)
salt and pepper to taste

Put crab meat in a mixing bowl with cucumber and scallions. Toss gently with olive oil and lemon juice. Season with salt and pepper. Add the basil and toss well. Serve in lettuce cups or over toast.

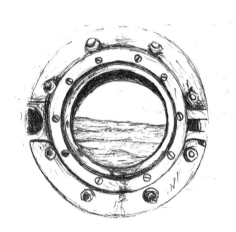

Green Grape Gorgonzola Salad

The sweetness of the grapes, the piquancy of the cheese, and the crunchy sugariness of the nuts make this a classic salad you can serve as a first course or as the main event.

1 head romaine (cos) lettuce, cut into bite-size pieces
4 ounces (115g) Gorgonzola, or other very good blue cheese (you can use Maytag, Stilton, or real Roquefort for this)
1 cup (250ml) iced green grapes, halved
¾ cup (185ml) Sugared Pecans
2 parts extra virgin olive oil
1 part balsamic vinegar (cherry balsamic is nice)
1 teaspoon (5ml) liquid aminos (Marigold, Braggs)
salt and freshly ground pepper

Mix the oil and balsamic vinegar, liquid aminos (Marigold, Braggs), salt, and pepper to an emulsion in food processor. Arrange a layer of lettuce on serving plate. Toss with some of the dressing to coat. Slice Gorgonzola as thinly as you can and lay over lettuce. Sprinkle over some pecans and decorate with the green grape halves. Drizzle a bit more of the dressing over all. Serve chilled.

Sugared Pecans

2 cups (500ml) pecans or walnuts
¼ cup (60ml) granulated sugar
¼ cup (60ml) water
salt

Allow sugar to melt in water in a heavy saucepan over medium heat. Pour over single layer of pecans placed on a large baking pan coated with cooking spray. Lightly sprinkle with salt. Bake in a preheated medium oven for 15 minutes. Turn nuts with a spatula and bake another 15 minutes. Cool and store in an airtight container.

Potato Salad with Walnut Pesto

Potato salad takes many forms other than coated with a plain mayonnaise dressing, which is the old standby. Try warm potato salad tossed with a simple vinaigrette. Or try this one that is so, so good and easy too. You can serve it warm or cold.

1½ pounds (680g) scrubbed gold or red potatoes (leave skins on)
¾ cup (185ml) (or to taste) Walnut Pesto
1 bunch chives, snipped

Cook the new potatoes in salted boiling water until very tender, then drain. Slice potatoes in half or quarters, depending on size. Add pesto to cover nicely and toss the potatoes. Check for seasoning and serve with some chives snipped on top.

 ## Walnut Pesto

1 handful fresh basil leaves
2 cloves garlic, minced
½ cup (125ml) walnuts
extra virgin olive oil
juice of half a lemon
salt and pepper
1 teaspoon (5g) Marigold bouillon powder (or to taste)
   (if using a substitute, see * p. 19)

Place the basil leaves, garlic, walnuts, and Marigold into a food processor and whiz until well mixed. Continue mixing as you add the olive oil in a steady stream until you have reached a lovely creamy pesto sauce. Add the lemon and salt and pepper to taste.

Grilled Tuna and Hearts of Palm Salad

A main course salad that is easy and quick to assemble, using tuna straight from the grill or the pantry.

1 head Boston or Bibb lettuce or favorite greens
2 Belgian endives, sliced
4 medium tuna steaks, grilled, or equivalent best tuna in olive oil
1 avocado, skinned, pitted, and sliced lengthwise into segments
1 handful grape tomatoes or 2 large or four small ripe tomatoes, cubed
1 can hearts of palm, sliced
1 can black olives, pitted
1 lemon, sliced into wedges
½ cup (125ml) extra virgin olive oil
3 tablespoons (45ml) sherry vinegar or lemon juice
1 teaspoon (5ml) Marigold bouillon powder (if using
  a substitute, see * p. 19)
salt and freshly ground pepper

Place the lettuce on each of four plates for the bottom layer. Add a layer of endive, then the hearts of palm. Make a ring around the outside of the plates with the tomatoes and olives. Slice the tuna into 4 pieces and place a piece on each plate in the center. Lay the avocado slices attractively over the top of the tuna. Mix the olive oil and vinegar with the Marigold and salt and pepper. Pour the resulting vinaigrette over the salad. Garnish with lemon wedges.

Panzanella
Tuscan Bread Salad

Here is what to do with French or Italian bread that has dried out before you got a chance to use it. From the Tuscan region of Italy comes Panzanella, an absolutely scrumptious salad that makes a thing of beauty out of stale bread with the addition of tomatoes, onions, and a few herbs. This comforting, filling salad, accompanied with a good red wine and followed by simple grapes for dessert, has made a wonderful dinner on many a warm balmy evening, proving again that splendid things can be made with modest ingredients. Do not try this dish, however, unless you have good authentic peasant bread to start with. Ordinary sliced stale white or wheat just won't do.

> 1 loaf stale rustic bread, about 4 cups cubed
> 2 cups (500ml) ripe tomatoes, seeded and diced (you can use very good canned tomatoes for this)
> 2 cloves garlic, minced
> 1 small sweet red onion, sliced very thin
> ⅓ wineglass red wine vinegar
> ½ wineglass extra virgin olive oil
> a handful whole fresh basil leaves, torn
> a handful minced parsley
> ¼ cup (60ml) Parmesan cheese, grated
> 1 teaspoon (5ml) Marigold bouillon powder (see * p. 19 for subs.)
> salt and freshly ground black pepper

Place the cubed bread into a bowl and sprinkle with water. Toss to moisten the cubes. Add the juicy tomatoes. Toss in the remaining ingredients. Before serving, let the panzanella rest at least 10 to 15 minutes to soak up the juices and all the flavors. Taste for seasoning. Sprinkle with Parmesan cheese before serving.

Variations:

This is a peasant salad and there are probably as many recipes for it as there are cooks that prepare it. To this salad you could add any or all of the following:

one can white canellini beans, rinsed and drained

a handful of Kalamata or Niçoise olives, pitted

a few anchovy filets, diced

a can of Italian tuna in olive oil

½ cup (125ml) roasted red peppers, diced

a can of hearts of palm, sliced thin

Tuna and White Bean Salad

A crusty bread, a plate of olives, and this classic Italian salad make a fine meal. Who said you have to live on cheese and crackers?

2 (6 oz/170g) cans tuna, packed in olive oil

1 (10 oz/280g) can white canellini beans, rinsed well

small handful of capers, drained, rinsed, and chopped

2 tablespoons (30ml) extra-virgin olive oil (if needed)

juice of a whole lemon

2 tablespoons (30ml) red wine vinegar

salt and freshly ground black pepper

1 small red onion, thinly sliced

1 jar roasted red pepper, sliced into strips

fresh basil or parsley

In a small bowl, add the tuna, reserving the olive oil for the dressing. Shred tuna between two forks or with your fingers until it is fine, with no lumps. Stir in the beans and capers. Add olive oil from tuna, adding extra olive oil if needed just to get a nice consistency. Add the lemon juice and vinegar. Season with salt and pepper. Allow to stand a few minutes to marry flavors. Form a circle around a serving plate with the red pepper strips. Place the tuna and white bean salad in the center. Spread a thin layer of onion over the top. Garnish with a handful of torn fresh basil leaves, chopped parsley, or other fresh herbs.

Waldorf Salad, an Homage

The following four salads are sweet and refreshing in the summer. You can make Waldorf salad with mayonnaise, or the ubiquitous (in England) salad cream (notably missing from the table on "Gourmet Night" at Fawlty Towers). Or you might like to try the more streamlined version with tofu cream. This is a brilliantly crunchy mixture containing ingredients that we don't seem to be out of.

½ cup (125ml) cinnamon tofu cream* or
½ cup (125ml) mayonnaise with 1 teaspoon (5ml) cinnamon
juice of 1 fresh lemon or lime with zest
2 sweet, crispy apples (Galas, Fujis, or McIntosh)
½ cup (125ml) pecans or walnuts
⅓ cup (85ml) dried cherries or golden raisins
2 celery stalks
sea salt, pepper

Whisk half the lemon or lime juice with zest into the tofu. You can reconstitute the cherries in boiling water for a few minutes for a softer consistency, but this isn't necessary if you chop them fairly finely.

Cut apple into cubes. Toss with lemon juice to prevent cubes from turning brown. Slice celery into thin julienne strips. Toss together the apple, nuts, celery, and cherries or raisins with the dressing.

Waldorf salad is often served over crisp lettuce. If you have lettuce and it is crisp, you are in luck. If not, this Waldorf will still be crispy, chewy, and delicious served on its own.

* See recipe page 271.

Lunch in a Melon Salad

*Here is a tantalizing summer main course salad with an amazing
dressing. It can be done whenever you get a nice ripe melon and you have
a little grilled chicken on hand.*

> 1 large ripe honeydew melon
> ¼ cup (60ml) cashew butter
> ½ cup (125ml) pineapple or orange juice
> 2 tablespoons (30ml) rum (optional)
> ½ pound (225g) cashews or pecan halves
> 2 skinless chicken breasts, cut into bite-size pieces

Slice melon in half. Cut a small slice off the bottom of each half so
it lies flat on a plate. Remove seeds and scoop out the inside with a
melon-baller.

Mix the cashew butter with the juice and the rum to a
mayonnaise-like consistency to make a dressing. Toss the melon
balls with the pecans or cashews and chicken. Refill the melon
shells with this mixture. Top with dressing and a few cashews or
pecan halves.

Chicken Salad Veronique

Here is another chicken fruit salad that is light and sweet but makes a fine main course.

> 2 cooked chicken breasts, cut into bite-size chunks
> 1 bunch (1 cup/250ml) seedless green grapes
> ½ cup (125ml) cashews
> ⅓ cup (85ml) mayonnaise
> ⅓ cup (85ml) yogurt
> juice and zest of half a lemon
> 3 tablespoons (45ml) honey
> small handful fresh chopped tarragon
> lettuce leaves (butter lettuce is perfect for this)
> smoked paprika
> grape clusters for garnish

Mix the mayonnaise with the yogurt and honey, lemon with its zest, and tarragon in a food processor. Mix the chicken, grapes, and cashews with the dressing. Lay a couple of large lettuce leaves out attractively on top of a salad plate and place a scoop of the salad on top. Sprinkle with a little smoked paprika. Garnish with grape clusters.

Salad of Sweet Delight

There are upwards of 7,000 islands in the Philippine Archipelago. At one time or another they have been colonized by Japan, the United States, and Spain. Malaysian traders, as well as traders from China, India, and Arabia, have come and gone, leaving a melting-pot heritage reflected in a diverse cuisine.

This Philippine salad, usually served as a dessert salad, is ridiculously good. If you are lucky enough to be cruising in a tropical paradise, it is rather easy to make. The canned cream that you can find more easily outside the United States is perfect for this and is authentic to this dish.

Use any or all of these fruits that you can find, in a combination that pleases you.

mango
papaya
cherries
fresh grapes
lychees
jackfruit
banana
nata de coco (cream of coconut) or macapuno coconut
1 cup (250ml) cashews
1 cup (250ml) heavy cream
1 (14 oz/400ml) can coconut milk (or condensed milk)

The day before:

Soak cashews in the cream overnight in the refrigerator.
Slice the mango and papaya; toss with the cherries, grapes, lychees, whatever you have. There are no proportions here. It is according to what you have and what you like. When cashews are nicely softened from soaking in the cream, mix them, along with their soaking cream and the coconut milk, with your other fruits. Be sure to use the soft coconut strings—you will find these all over the Pacific islands as well as in specialty shops. They make a huge contribution to the taste and provide an amazing texture. The texture is a unique part of this enchanting salad. If you have a lot of fruit and it is not liquid enough, you could add more cream or a little fruit juice. Set aside to chill for a few hours (if you can wait that long to eat it), as it is best cold.

Coconut plantations abound in the Philippines. Buko or macapuno (young coconut strings) or nata de coco (a kind of coconut jelly treat) are Philippine delicacies that can be found in Asian markets and should be sought out. They will make this dish sensational.

Langka (jackfruit) can be found fresh or in cans in the Philippines and Polynesia as well as the Caribbean.

This is sometimes made with canned fruit salad—the kind that has cherries in it—and it is still wonderful, so you can see that you have room to experiment. A perfectly delicious vegan version can be made substituting **tofu cream** for the dairy cream in the recipe.

110

Sandwiches, Melts, and Such

One of the lessons I have learned at sea?
You can't have tuna sandwiches every day.
Here are some great ideas that lift the humble sandwich
from innocent bystander to major player.

Mushroom Sandwich

The mushrooms on page 164 are killer just as they are in a sandwich with lots of ground pepper, but for an extra treat, combine them with some sliced sun-dried tomatoes. Spread some nice crusty bread with mayonnaise on one side of the bread and the juice from the mushrooms on the other. Fill with the mushroom mixture and press the top down firmly before cutting. Vegetarian delight.

Tartine

*A Tartine is a wonderfully easy French sandwich that makes a quick, satisfying, and rather impressive lunch. Tartiner means to spread, lending the name to these clever open-faced sandwiches, which are first spread, then layered, and usually finished under the grill to get them hot and bubbly. As you might complement a pâté with an excellent bread to make a delicious meal, next time you need to use up some (compatible) leftover meats and vegetables, whip up a Tartine. A **Welsh Rarebit** might qualify as a Tartine if you, perhaps, spread ham paste on the bread before covering with a cheese mixture.*

For your Tartine, start by layering a slice of bread with a spread: tapenade, hummus, pesto, et cetera. This acts as the paste that holds the rest of the ingredients. The following are a few ideas, but once you get the hang of it, making up your own is part of the fun. Thus, I do not give exact amounts. The proportions are very loose, according to your taste and how much of each ingredient you have, but as a general rule, don't skimp on the spreadable part of the recipe.

Tartine Provençale

4 large or 8 smaller slices of good bread

black olive tapenade

8 thin slices of prosciutto or other good ham

8 slices Fontina cheese

sun-dried tomatoes

4 sliced artichoke hearts

Preheat the oven to medium high (420°F). Lightly toast the bread slices on a cookie sheet for a few minutes. Remove from oven. On each slice, spread a good thick layer of tapenade, then place the ham over it. Cover with the slices of cheese and decorate with pieces of sun-dried tomatoes and artichoke hearts. Grill sandwiches until warm and the cheese starts to melt.

Serve with a green salad with a good vinaigrette. This same method can be used with the following toppings, or make up your own.

Greek Tartine

hummus

grilled vegetables (leftover aubergine and courgettes with some
    carrot would be nice)

8 ounces (225g) good feta cheese

½ head roasted garlic

Spread hummus on toasted bread and layer with vegetables. Top with feta cheese and a few slices roasted garlic. Place sandwiches under grill until top begins to brown and bubble.

Scampi Tartine

½–1 cup (125ml–250ml) pesto
20 large prawns, sliced in half lengthwise
mayonnaise
paprika
Parmesan cheese

Preheat grill. Spread bread with pesto. Cover with sliced grilled prawns. Spread a thin layer of mayonnaise over the prawns and sprinkle with paprika and Parmesan cheese. Place sandwiches under grill until top begins to brown and bubble.

 # Smoked Salmon Tartine with Bacon

This is a kicked-up version of smoked salmon and cream cheese. It is served cold, since smoked salmon is not improved at all by cooking it. The bacon, which should be quite crispy, makes a scintillating contrast to the smoothness of the salmon. It would be wonderful if you had some exotic bread like walnut bread or olive bread.

cream cheese
12 ounces (340g) smoked salmon
8 slices bacon, cooked crisp
capers
red onion, sliced thin

Spread bread or toast with cream cheese. Sprinkle with capers and sliced red onion. Lay slices of salmon on each slice and garnish with crispy bacon. Serve.

Cuban Sandwich

This feast in a crust is a Cuban version of a Panini. A great textured crunchy sandwich, grilled or toasted on the outside, it is pressed down so that the bread is flattened and the ingredients are happily squished together on the inside. To make this traditional flattened Cuban sandwich without a panini maker or other toys, use a griddle or a large frying pan and flatten the sandwich with another skillet or heavy plate while you toast each side.

> sliced crusty French/Italian/Cuban bread
> butter, softened
> mayonnaise
> ¾ pound (340g) ham, sliced
> ¾ pound (340g) sliced roast pork
> ½ pound (225g) Fontina, Havarti, or Baby Swiss cheese, sliced
> sliced dill pickles

Preheat a griddle or large fry pan. Cut the bread into sections about 8 inches long. Cut these in half and spread butter on one half and mayonnaise on the other. Pile each sandwich high with pickles, roast pork, ham, and cheese. Lightly butter the hot griddle or fry pan. Place sandwich on the pan. Place a heavy skillet or plate on top of the sandwich to flatten. You can also use a saucepan lid that is smaller than the size of your pan so that you can push the sandwich down to really flatten it. Grill the sandwiches for two to three minutes on each side, until the cheese is melted and the bread is golden. Slice the sandwich in half diagonally and serve.

If roast pork is not readily available, this might be the most opportune time to use that Spam you have rattling around in the hold.

Muffaletta Sandwich

Here is a recipe for the ultimate deli sandwich. Hailing from New Orleans, it is of Sicilian origin and is a classic. I had my first bite of this sandwich, washed down with jolly swigs of a Pimms Cup, at the Napoleon House in the French Quarter. Down the road, in Bourbon Street, my friend had just lost a bet with a street boy. "I bet you a dollar I know where you got them shoes," the boy had said. My friend smiled and shook his head. "OK. I'll bite. Tell me where I got these shoes." The boy replied with a smile, "Why, you got them shoes on Bourbon Street!" He stuck out his hand for his well earned dollar.

My friend and I took somewhat shamed refuge in a shared lunch of a perfect Muffaletta. I never saw it much outside of New Orleans but I've introduced it to friends in many a corner of the world. The secret ingredient in this delightful mixture is the olive salad, though you will see a lot of recipes for this that have only ham and salami. The pastrami is what clinches this Muffaletta's authenticity, so don't leave it out if you can get it. By the way, the way they pronounced it was "muff-a-lotta" (lotta, not letta), a fact not as important as the taste of this scrumptious, completely satisfying sandwich. You can slightly toast it as I have done here, or just serve as is if you have nice crusty bread.

Olive Salad

4 cloves garlic, finely minced

½ cup (125ml) chopped green stuffed olives, slightly crushed

1 cup (250ml) chopped black olives, (Greek or Italian pitted)

1 stalk celery sliced lengthwise and then into thin slices

4–5 pepperoncini, minced

4 tablespoons (60ml) capers

4 ounces (115g) roasted red peppers, sliced

½ cup (125ml) olive oil

3 tablespoons (45ml) parsley

red pepper flakes, to taste

½ teaspoon (2.5ml) each oregano and basil

2 tablespoons (30ml) wine or balsamic vinegar

Sandwich

1 large loaf Italian bread (round is traditional)

6 ounces (170g) ham, thinly sliced

6 ounces (170g) pastrami (or roast beef)

6 ounces (170g) Sopressata or other salami, thinly sliced

¼ pound (115g) Mozzarella cheese, sliced

¼ pound (115g) Provolone cheese, sliced

1 cup (250ml) Olive Salad with oil

Combine ingredients for salad and allow to stand 4 hours or overnight to marry flavors. Slice the bread in half, slicing off the top portion (like a cap). Scrape out some of the bread from inside loaf. Drizzle oil from salad on both top and bottom halves. Lay the olive salad, cold cuts, and cheeses in layers until all ingredients are used. Cover with bread top.

Serve cold or place loaf in hot frying pan with smaller top or dish to weight down. Cook two minutes. Turn loaf over and cook two minutes on other side. Cut into wedges. Serve.

Valley Guru Tip

When anticipating heavy weather, premake bland sandwiches, cut them in half, wrap them, and have them ready to hand up when the need arises.

Pan Bagnat

Pan Bagnat, (pronounced "pan-ban-ya") means bathed bread (bathed with olive oil and vinegar dressing). This is another original from Nice. Actually a sort of salad (Niçoise) in a sandwich, it is big on crust, full of flavor, and (you guessed it) ideal for cruising. It makes an excellent picnic since it actually improves from standing and is so loved that it is found for sale on every street corner in Provence. You might need to double the quantities. These sandwiches are addictive.

    1 large loaf of crusty French (or Italian) bread
    2 tablespoons (30ml) red wine vinegar
    ½ cup (125ml) extra virgin olive oil
    1 garlic clove, halved
    2 (6 oz/170ml) cans tuna packed in olive oil
    6 anchovy filets packed in olive oil
    1 small red onion, sliced thinly (or use 1 or 2 spring green onions)
    4 hard-boiled eggs, thinly sliced
    8 ounces (225g) Kalamata or Niçoise olives, pitted and sliced
    4 teaspoons (20ml) capers, drained
    2 tomatoes, thinly sliced
    handful chopped flat leaf parsley or fresh basil
    salt and freshly ground pepper

Slice the bread in half horizontally. Remove some of the soft inside of the bread to make a hollow. Rub each half with garlic.
Drizzle the inside of the bread with olive oil and vinegar. Sprinkle with salt and pepper. Begin to layer the bottom slice of bread with tomato, olive oil, fresh herbs. Sift the tuna in your fingers until it is very fine. Make a layer of tuna followed by onion and black olives. Sprinkle some capers over this. Lay the anchovies over the top neatly. Now make a layer of sliced egg. Finish with the rest of the sliced tomato and more fresh herbs. Drizzle with remaining oil and vinegar. Place the top half of the bread on the sandwich and press down.

GALLEY GURU

Wrap in aluminum foil and allow to stand at room temperature until ready to eat. You can let stand for one to two hours. The sandwich will absorb the juices and become more delicious as it stands.

Irie Burgers
Happy Burgers

It was a raggedy Jamaican burger shack perched improbably alone on a beautiful expanse of beach lovingly caressed by a turquoise sea. In the Caribbean, everybody tries to outdo each other with their special version of rum punch guaranteed to be the best—and the strongest. We survived one (was it one?) of those rum punches while munching Irie Burgers. And a pretty irie way to stretch ground beef it is too. They are excellent: spicy, succulent, and delicious. This is my version of them. I serve them smothered with spoonfuls of **Onion Confit** *and just some mayonnaise. I do not give exact measurements for the spices because this is all about how you feel at the moment.*

1 pound (455g) ground beef
1 small onion, chopped
cayenne pepper (to taste)
pinch allspice
pinch dried ginger
good pinch curry powder
pinch dried thyme
3 ounces (85g) fresh or dried breadcrumbs
1 tablespoon (15ml) tomato paste
1 teaspoon (5ml) Worcestershire sauce
1–2 beaten eggs (to bind together)
salt and pepper to taste

Mix all ingredients. Form into patties. Grill or broil 7 minutes on each side for medium or until desired doneness.

Welsh Rarebit

Welsh Rarebit is an old standby in the U.K. Welsh Rarebit (pronounced rabbit) is one of those cuddly, homey dishes that are somehow cuddlier on a boat. If you like, you can make Buck Rarebit, which would involve putting a slice of ham or back bacon on the top, or turn it into a Tartine by spreading the bread with ham paste or even liver pâté before you cover it with the cheese sauce, but the "just cheese" version is the classic and is so good it needs not much else.

4 slices of bread

2 tablespoons (30ml) butter

2 tablespoons (30ml) all-purpose flour

1 teaspoon (5ml) Dijon or wholegrain mustard

1 teaspoon (5ml) mustard powder

1– 2 teaspoon (5-10ml) Worcestershire sauce

½ cup (125 ml) brown ale

1 cup (225ml) Cheddar cheese, grated

Preheat grill or broiler. In a medium saucepan over low heat, melt the butter and whisk in the flour. Cook gently, whisking constantly for 2 to 3 minutes. Whisk in mustard. Add beer, Worcestershire sauce, salt, and pepper to taste. Continue to whisk until smooth. Gradually add cheese, stirring constantly, until cheese melts and sauce is smooth. Pour cheese mixture over toast and put under hot grill until bubbling and golden brown. Serve hot. Garnish with sliced tomatoes if desired.

Greek Roasted Vegetable Sandwich with Aioli

This is the vegetarian sandwich. It makes a great lunch or supper when you can get Mediterranean vegetables.

¼ cup (60ml) mayonnaise

1–3 cloves garlic, minced

2 tablespoons (30ml) lemon or lime juice

4 tablespoons (60ml) extra virgin olive oil

1 eggplant, peeled leaving part of the skin, then sliced into rings

2 red bell peppers, sliced

1 zucchini, sliced

1 red onion, sliced

2 cloves garlic, sliced

salt and pepper

thyme

rosemary

loaf of French bread

4 ounces (115g) feta cheese, sliced thin

To make the aioli, mix the mayonnaise, as much minced garlic as you like, and lemon juice. Set aside.

Turn oven to high. Toss vegetables with garlic, olive oil, salt and pepper, and herbs on a baking tray lined with foil. Cook until all the vegetables have caramelized, about 30–40 minutes (oven temperatures vary). Alternatively, place the vegetables on a hot grill for 3 or 4 minutes a side, until they are done.

Spread aioli on the bread. Layer with the veggies and feta cheese.

Tuna Melt
and Good Old Tuna on Toast

Well, it had to be in here somewhere. For those of you who can't see any reason to eschew tuna just yet . . . .

SJ's Tuna Salad

one 6-ounce (170g) can good tuna in olive oil
mayonnaise or Miracle Whip
handful chopped almonds
two stalks celery, chopped fine
small bunch chives, chopped (or handful chopped green onions)
salt and pepper to taste
best bread you can find

Mix up tuna with two forks. The secret to good tuna salad is not to leave any chunks of tuna. It all has to be smooth. Add a couple of spoonfuls mayonnaise. Mix well. Then add the rest of the ingredients. Spread generously on bread.

For Tuna Melt

Place a slice of good melting cheese inside the tuna sandwich, spread the outside with butter, and toast in a heavy skillet on both sides until golden.

Pasta, Rice, and Potatoes

Pasta, to an Italian, is a primary food group.
How wonderful that it is also inexpensive and easy to keep, cook, and eat.
Leftovers can be reinvented the second day in a casserole.
To those of us of a mind to forage around refrigerators in the mornings,
leftover pasta makes a surprisingly respectable breakfast.
In civilized circles, at supper, one pound of pasta
amply serves four people with moderate appetites.

Home Is Where The Pasta Is

When preparing pasta, do as the Italians do and add the pasta to the sauce and not the sauce to the pasta. Cook pasta in lots of boiling water until it is al dente. Al dente translates to "to the tooth," which means the pasta is still slightly chewy. It will finish cooking when it hangs around in the sauce for a minute or two before serving. Add it to just enough sauce in the pan to coat the pasta well but no more. Continue to cook and toss for a minute so that the pasta and sauce can cohabit briefly, during which time the pasta absorbs some of the sauce. If you have extra sauce, when you serve, put a touch on top with a restrained hand. Never drown the plate with it.

Mythbuster:

You do not need to add oil to the pot of boiling water to keep the pasta from sticking together. What you must do, however, is stand over the pot and stir the pasta frequently during the cooking. If you do not do this, even with the addition of unnecessary oil the pasta will more than likely clump into unseemly shapes as if you had purposefully glued them for a school project. As for salt, do add it to the boiling water. There is no way to make unsalted cooked pasta absorb salt after it is cooked. The flavors never marry, but leave a curious too-salty and not-salty-enough taste on the palate.

To rinse or not to rinse:

That is not a question at all. Don't—unless you want to lose all the natural starches that help your beautiful sauce adhere to the pasta. The one exception is when you are making a cold pasta salad, for which there are no recipes in this book only because they are not particularly Italian and they are one of the things for which I never acquired a taste.

Last note:

I know it has been proposed that pasta can be cooked in sea water. I am of the conviction that just because a thing can be done does not necessarily indicate that it should be done, and here is a perfect example. The attempt to create a harmonious meal using such a discordant ingredient as the briny, should not be attempted even in jest. You will end with nothing but chagrin and an inedible meal. There is too much salt (and a profundity of other mysteries that would require at least a second volume) in the sea to cook anything respectably.

I know of a clever sailor who decided he could make some pasta with salt water, thinking he would save the water onboard. He went below in a rolling, pitching sea and spent an hour, half seasick, putting this grand feast together, then delivered it to the deck, where it looked and smelled great. From the first bite all the diners knew it was simply awful, but no one wanted to be the one to say anything. Finally the chef gave up and deep-sixed his meal, followed closely by the other crewmembers' dumping theirs with sighs of relief heard all round.

If you have run out of fresh water, do, please, find something else to dine upon. At sea as at home, treat your noodle with a modicum of respect. From a crusty macaroni and cheddar to the sensuously sophisticated (yet simple) Fettuccine Alfredo, pasta, in its endlessly varied forms, is the quintessential comfort food and indispensable galley staple.

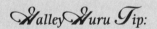
Galley Guru Tip:

Fill the pot for boiling pasta no more than three-quarters full of water. It will come to the boil faster if you put a top on the pot as it boils. This makes sense from the point of view of safety, since you have less chance of any water spilling out over the pot. When you add the pasta to the water, however, take the top off. The starch in the pasta will make the water boil over if it is covered. This is when to watch the pot carefully and stir frequently. Angel hair pasta only takes about three minutes to cook; regular varieties take from 8 to 12 minutes, depending on how thick they are. This is certainly not too long to stand over your pot to see that all is well.

Pasta with Tuna

The secret to managing cuisine on a boat is to think creatively, use staples that need no refrigeration, and then, when in port, hop off the boat and buy whatever is fresh and looks great to you. This dish will certainly prove to the skeptic that it is possible to go to sea without going hungry.

Boil a pound (455g) of pasta in salted water according to package directions (angel hair only takes 3 minutes). It should be al dente. Strain and slip back into pot, reserving half a cup of the pasta water.

Open a can (or two, if you're feeling flush) of finest tuna packed in olive oil and pour the tuna with its oil over the pasta, taking care to break up the tuna with two forks or sift it through your fingers over the pot. You may add a touch more olive oil if you wish. Remove from heat. Spoon in the reserved pasta water. Toss till heated through. Pull out the pepper mill and give a few twists over the pasta.

Eat.

No kidding. That's it. This is a deceptively simple pasta they make in Italy every day. On land. That's because it is so good. If you have any fresh herbs, like parsley or basil, by all means chop some and throw in the cooked pasta to enhance the flavor. If you are drinking wine (white this time) that night, you can tip half a glass or so into the pasta with tuna while you are tossing. However, none of this is necessary and will not alter the fact that in this sublimely simple dish you have the comfort food of the ages . . . and you can live on it!

✓ Fast Marinara

This recipe is amazingly simple but works because of the way you cook it. The sauce will be rich and mellow and sweet, with a characteristic piquant flavor. This sauce takes about 30 minutes from start to finish, most of which time is spent in slowly cooking the onions until caramelized. Use a good skillet with high sides or, if you are making more sauce, a large, heavy soup pot.

1 large onion, chopped fine.
4–6 good-size cloves of garlic, finely minced
1–2 large cans best quality chopped tomatoes
½–1 can tomato paste
extra virgin olive oil
red chili pepper flakes
salt
pepper

Pour olive oil into a large skillet to cover the bottom of the pan. Heat oil over medium-high heat. Add onion, which should sizzle when it hits the oil. Stir onion around so it does not pick up any black sides. Immediately turn heat down to medium. Keep stirring onions; cook until they have turned color. They are ready for the addition of garlic when they are looking yellow but not quite golden. The entire process takes anywhere from 10 to 20 minutes and must not be rushed.

Add the garlic and red pepper. Cook 1–2 minutes until the garlic becomes golden. Add the tomatoes to the pan and stir in the tomato paste. Turn up the heat and bring the sauce to a boil. Turn down heat to medium, allowing sauce to boil gently to reduce liquid content. Turn flame to low and continue cooking sauce about 10 minutes.

This sauce is somewhat chunky. For a smooth sauce, simply add to blender or insert handheld blender and process a few seconds. Salt and pepper to taste.

At this point you may add chopped fresh parsley and/or basil or any fresh herbs you have on hand. Serve over pasta.

Pasta alla Carbonara

Here is something else to do with your bacon and eggs. It is delicious and nearly effortless. Carbonara as the Romans do it is traditionally prepared with cured, not smoked, bacon, known as pancetta. You can, by all means, make it with a good standard streaky bacon or even prosciutto, which is not bacon at all but ham. For that matter, a nice country ham will produce a great result. As cured meats are a galley guru's secret weapon, you are bound to have something that will do nicely. Use the best you have.

I have proposed two versions. The first is fairly light, if you consider bacon and eggs light. The second is richer with the addition of cream. A cup or so of fresh (or frozen) green peas, added at the last minute, makes a lovely addition. You can be flexible with any combination of ingredients from either recipe.

As always, do not overcook the pasta, for you will be cooking it a little longer in the pan with the sauce. The eggs must be added off the heat; they will cook just enough from the heat of the pasta.

> 1 pound (455g) fettuccine, linguine, or spaghetti
> 1 pound (455g) pancetta or diced bacon or ham
> 2 tablespoons (30ml) olive oil
> ¾ cup (185ml) grated Parmesan or Romano cheese (or a mixture)
> 4 eggs or 6 egg yolks
> pinch hot red chili flakes
> salt and freshly ground black pepper

Heat a large frying pan over medium heat. Add olive oil and pancetta or bacon. Cook until pancetta browns. (If using ordinary bacon, it will render quite a bit of fat. Pour off all but 2 or 3 tablespoons of it.) Meanwhile, bring salted water to a boil. Cook the pasta according to package directions, stirring to separate, until al dente. Drain, reserving ½ cup of the cooking water. Toss the pasta with the browned bacon and heat through about a minute, adding a few tablespoons of the pasta cooking water to the pan to get a nice coating. Remove from heat. Beat eggs with the grated cheese and enough of the cooking water to make a glistening sauce. Add this to the warm pasta, tossing until fully incorporated. Divide the pasta among 4 warmed serving bowls. Season with freshly ground black pepper and grate additional cheese over the top. Serve immediately.

Carbonara II

1 pound (455 grams) fettuccine, linguine, or spaghetti

¼ cup (60ml) extra-virgin olive oil

1 yellow onion, minced

2 cloves garlic, minced

8 ounces (225g) bacon (or pancetta or prosciutto), diced

4 eggs or 6 egg yolks

½ cup (125ml) heavy cream, at room temperature

sprinkle of nutmeg

¾ cup (185ml) freshly grated Parmesan

2 tablespoons (30ml) fresh parsley, chopped

salt and pepper to taste

Heat oil in a large frying pan over medium heat. Add the onion and garlic and cook until translucent. Remove. Add the bacon or pancetta to pan. Cook until crisp. Drain all but one teaspoon of fat. Return onion to pan. At the same time, bring a large pot of salted water to a boil. Cook the pasta, stirring to separate, according to package directions until al dente. When pasta is done, drain (reserve a few tablespoons of the cooking liquid) and add with the liquid to the pan with the onion and bacon mixture. Toss pasta over medium heat until well coated. Remove. Place in serving bowl.

In a bowl or large measuring cup, whisk together the eggs and heavy cream with the sprinkle of nutmeg and fresh parsley. Add to pasta. Add the Parmesan and toss all together until well coated. Season with salt and freshly ground black pepper, to taste. Serve hot with more Parmesan.

Linguine With White Clam Sauce

This is truly the best clam sauce and dead easy. From a time-honored family recipe, it's an old standby of mine on land. Of course, when the sea is all around, the stores are down, and the appetite is keen, this dish, made entirely from pantry ingredients, could be just the grace to save an evening.

Whether you prepare the pantry version of this linguine or the alternative, which takes advantage of the day you stumble upon gorgeous fresh clams, the excellent sauce in which the clams are cloaked depends entirely upon the precise method of the sautéing of the garlic and your handling of the reduction of the wine. It isn't hard, just specific, and is well worth it.

The Marigold powder has just enough salt not to require the addition of any more. It takes the place of my (or your) grandmama's homemade stock, which might be unavailable to you while cruising the Southern latitudes. If not using Marigold, add a touch of salt to taste.

1 pound (455 grams) linguine

2–3 small dried red chilis, crumbled, or

a few sprinkles of red pepper flakes

4–6 good-sized cloves of garlic, minced

¼–½ cup (60–125ml) extra virgin olive oil

2 tablespoons (30ml) butter

2 cans chopped clams, drained, reserve juice

2 glasses dry white vermouth or white wine (or some of each, who's
    counting?)

1 teaspoon (5ml) Marigold bouillon powder (for substitutes, see * p. 19)

freshly ground pepper

2 or 3 large handfuls of chopped fresh flat leaf parsley

or 2 tablespoons (30ml) dried parsley, rubbed between the fingers

a little finely grated zest of lemon and

a few torn leaves of fresh basil (optional)

freshly grated Parmesan cheese (optional)

Bring a large pot of salted water to a boil. Cook the pasta according to package directions, stirring to separate, until al dente.

Meanwhile, in a large sauté pan, heat the oil over a medium-high flame. Add the chilis and the minced garlic to the oil. Sauté until the garlic is lightly golden brown. In the moment before the garlic seems as if it will burn, throw in the wine. Timing is crucial. Turn the heat to high and allow the wine and garlic mixture to boil down a minute or two. The browned garlic will magically begin to turn white again. Add the juice from the clams, 2 tablespoons of the parsley, and a pinch of salt and pepper. Continue to boil rapidly until liquid is reduced by half. Season with the Marigold (or salt) and fresh pepper. Throw in the parsley and the clams and turn off the heat.

Drain the linguine, reserving ⅓ cup of the cooking liquid. Add the pasta to the clams and toss to coat. Add just enough of the reserved cooking liquid to keep the sauce liquid. You may add a spoonful or two of vermouth at this point to intensify the wine flavor. Taste for seasoning. Now add the butter and toss it all together. Sprinkle with another handful of parsley and the optional basil. Add a few twists of freshly ground pepper and a little lemon zest. Serve.

Note:

Some people insist upon Parmesan with their pasta. In Italy, dishes made with fish or seafood are not traditionally served with Parmesan cheese, the Parmesan being considered too intense a flavor that overpowers delicate seafood. In America, as in many things, this tradition is sometimes broken. By all means, if you like it, you won't hurt my feelings if you add it.

Fresh Clam Version

This is the most wonderful option when you find fresh clams.

Follow the preceding recipe exactly, except add 2–3 pounds (1–1½kg) fresh clams such as cherrystone or littleneck to the garlic wine mixture. Do not boil the clams, or they will become tough and rubbery. Cover and simmer until the clams have opened, about 6 minutes. Discard any clams that do not open. Add the 2 tablespoons butter to the clams and toss to thicken the sauce a bit. Cook the pasta as in the preceding recipe, adding the cooked pasta to the clam mixture. Toss gently off the heat with parsley and serve.

Pasta with Sage and Browned Butter

As you putter round the fresh markets in port sometime, you may find lovely fresh sage leaves. Gather them to serve this simple dish to delight your companions. Sage isn't used much in America except with turkey or chicken, but it's treated with more affection and respect in Italy. It takes its place as the star of this classic pasta, a miracle dish that cooks in the blink of an eye.

This sauce is nice for any wide, delicate pasta, such as tagliatelle, fettuccine, and the like. Perfect for ravioli.

GALLEY GURU

¼ pound (115g) of butter

few sprinkles hot chili pepper

18–20 fresh sage leaves (with a few extra for garnish)

salt and freshly ground pepper

¼ to ½ cup (60–125ml) freshly grated Parmesan cheese

1 pound (455g) pasta

Cook pasta according to package directions. Meanwhile, cook butter in large skillet over medium heat until just beginning to brown, about 3 minutes. Add sage leaves whole, and red pepper. Continue to cook until butter turns chestnut brown, but do not allow to burn or it will become bitter. Remove from heat.

Drain pasta, reserving about half a cup of the salty cooking water. Add pasta to butter in pan and turn on heat again, tossing to heat through. Add tablespoonfuls of the pasta water to form a nice sauce. Remove from heat. Add cheese and serve with a few torn sage leaves strewn on top.

Rice With Sage and Browned Butter

This sage and browned butter sauce also makes a lovely rice dish similar to a risotto but even easier to prepare.

3 cups (750ml) Arborio rice

Bring a large amount of salted water to the boil as if you were going to cook pasta. Add the rice and cook uncovered for 16 minutes. Drain.

Prepare the browned butter with sage as above. Add rice to butter in pan and toss. To serve, sprinkle with the cheese and garnish with the sage leaves.

Seafood Pasta au Pernod

This pasta is very light yet has a luxurious, aromatic perfume and a sharp, piquant taste. Pernod and tarragon are a match made in heaven. These seasonings are also great with salmon.

    1 pound (455g) fettuccine or tagliatelle noodles
    ½ pound (225g) raw tiger prawns, peeled
    8 sea scallops or ½ pound (225g) bay scallops
    2 cloves garlic, minced
    3½ ounces (100g) butter
    ¼ cup (60ml) Pernod or brandy
    handful fresh tarragon, chopped
    a few fresh basil leaves, torn or cut into strips
    juice of 1 lime with a little zest

Cook pasta according to package directions. Drain, reserving some of the cooking water to moisten the pasta. Season the prawns and scallops with salt and lots of fresh pepper. Melt butter in a sauté pan. Cook garlic gently until tender. Toss the prawns and the scallops in the butter, turning up the heat until scallops are just browning and prawns are pink, about 2–3 minutes. Pour the Pernod over, toss, and cook just a minute. Do not overcook. Remove from heat.

Toss seafood mixture with the pasta. Sprinkle over the lime zest, tarragon, and/or fresh basil and toss with lime juice, adding pasta water by spoonfuls just to make a glistening sauce. Season well with salt and pepper.

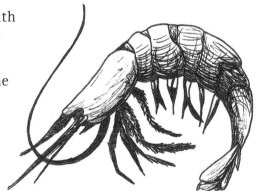

Pasta with White Bean Sauce

This is a simple vegetarian pasta that is loaded with complete protein and has the added advantage that everything comes from your trusty galley pantry. As always, if you do not have fresh herbs, substitute a judicious amount of dried, rubbed well between the fingers to release the essential oils.

¼ cup (60ml) extra virgin olive oil

1 small onion, chopped fine (or a few green onions, sliced finely)

4 cloves garlic, minced

a few sprinkles hot red pepper flakes

1 can white canellini beans

1–2 glasses white wine

1 teaspoon (5ml) Marigold bouillon powder (or to taste) (see * p. 19)

1 teaspoon (5ml) liquid aminos seasoning (Marigold, Braggs), or to taste

large handful fresh basil leaves, torn

handful chopped parsley

salt and freshly ground pepper to taste

Parmesan cheese

1 pound (455 grams) pasta cooked al dente according to package directions (any shape you like)

Heat the olive oil in a frying pan. Add the onion and cook until soft but not brown. Add the garlic and hot red pepper. Cook for 2 minutes. Stir in the beans, Marigold powder, and the white wine. Bring to a boil, reduce heat, simmer 4 minutes. Add parsley. Mash some of the beans around with a fork to thicken sauce. Taste for seasoning. Add salt if necessary and a few twists of black pepper. Drain pasta, reserving ½ cup (125ml) of cooking water. Add pasta to pan with sauce, adding cooking water by tablespoonfuls to loosen the sauce, which should cover pasta nicely. Toss over low heat for another minute. To serve, sprinkle pasta with the basil. Pass freshly grated Parmesan or Romano cheese.

Fettuccine Alfredo

This celebrated dish, rich, luxuriant with butter, giddy with cream, and extravagant with the finest Parmigiano-Reggiano, was invented in the roaring '20s by Alfredo Di Lelio, the original owner of Alfredo all'Augusteo Restaurant in Rome. Alfredo obviously had an amazing metabolism that no amount of butterfat could defeat. Not surprisingly, this fettuccini was first dubbed al triplo burro *(triple butter) for its utter lack of restraint with that ingredient.*

The closely guarded secret to the creaminess and lightness of the original is legendary and has remained shrouded in mystery, though the ingredients seem straightforward. I got hold of the simple yet elegant answer from an insider friend in Rome, and it is well within the scope of the galley chef to produce. It is the almost tasteless vodka that adds a depth and delicacy that are indescribable. No wonder its origin remains elusive.

As in all simple dishes with few ingredients, the quality of each is the key to success, especially the fettuccine and the cheese. At home, I would suggest you make this dish with fresh fettuccine only, because it is luscious and smoother than the dried version. At sea, the dried version works very nicely as long as you take care to buy the best you can find.

1 pound (455 grams) fettuccine or tagliatelle (fresh, if possible)
4 ounces (115g) unsalted butter, at room temperature
1 cup (250ml) freshly grated Parmigiano Reggiano (or Parmesan), at
    room temperature, plus extra cheese to pass at the table
1½ cups (375ml) heavy cream, very lightly whipped with
3 tablespoons (45ml) vodka
pinch of freshly grated nutmeg
salt and freshly ground pepper (use white pepper if you have it) to
    taste

Boil the pasta according to package directions. Fresh pasta barely needs cooking; about 2–3 minutes does it. Fettuccine, even dried, takes less time than spaghetti, so be careful that the pasta finishes cooking when your sauce is ready.

In a large skillet, melt the butter into the cream that has been slightly whipped with the addition of the vodka. Cook just until the butter melts.

Drain the pasta and add it to the sauce with the Parmesan, nutmeg, and salt and pepper to taste. Toss over low heat about a minute. The sauce will thicken slightly. Serve immediately.

Fettuccine Alfredo II (Vegetarian)

This one will fool you (and your friends). It has a remarkable similarity to the richness of the real thing but, get this, it has no cream and it's even healthy for you. They make quite a reasonable soy (or rice) Parmesan now, which would make your dish completely vegan. In any case, I think, if Alfredo had cared about his waistline, he might, had he known this secret, have snuck down to the kitchen at least once for this nonfattening version of his famous dish.

   1 recipe Tofu Cream*
   2 tablespoons (30ml) dry vermouth
   2 teaspoons (10ml) Marigold bouillon powder (if using substitute,
       see * p. 19)
   2 teaspoons (10ml) liquid aminos seasoning (Marigold, Braggs)
   ½ cup (125ml) grated Parmesan or soy Parmesan
   2 tablespoons (30ml) olive oil
   fresh grated nutmeg
   handful chopped parsley
   1 cup (250ml) fresh or frozen peas (optional)
   1 pound (455 grams) fettuccini

Cook fettuccini according to package directions. Meanwhile, in a large, deep skillet, heat soy cream gently with the olive oil. Add the seasonings and the optional peas. Toss in the pasta for a minute until well coated with the sauce. Serve topped with lots of fresh or a lesser amount of dried parsley and more grated Parmesan.

   * See recipe for homemade Tofu Cream, page 271.

Pasta Puttanesca

Lady of the Night Pasta

This delicious pasta is said to have originated in the bordellos of Naples.
Whatever its pedigree, its fiery spiciness has been known to release inhibitions.
By all means share a good red wine with this. Relax. You deserve it.

4 cloves garlic, finely chopped

1 handful capers, rinsed in water and drained, chopped roughly

2 large handfuls black olives, pitted

1 can anchovy filets, drained and roughly chopped

2–3 dried red chilis, crumbled

3 tablespoons (45ml) extra-virgin olive oil

1 glass dry white wine, or dry Vermouth

1 (14 oz/400gram) can tomatoes, drained and chopped fine

a couple of handfuls fresh torn basil, or chopped flat leaf parsley

salt and freshly ground black pepper

Parmesan cheese

1 pound (455 grams) pasta

Boil the pasta according to package directions until al dente. Meanwhile, sauté the garlic, anchovies, and chilis in the olive oil over medium heat for 3–4 minutes, just until the anchovies melt into the oil and the garlic begins to turn golden. Immediately add the white wine, bring to a boil, and continue to boil, reducing the liquid until wine has almost disappeared. Add the tomatoes, capers, and olives. Simmer the sauce for 15 minutes.

Drain pasta, reserving ½ cup of cooking water. Off the heat, add the pasta and toss till well coated with the sauce, adding spoonfuls of the pasta water if necessary to make a nice smooth sauce. If using basil, just tear the leaves over the dish. Sprinkle with chopped parsley. Add salt and pepper. Serve with a dish of Parmesan on the side.

Pasta With Duck Confit

This dish sounds very baroque, but it is not at all fanciful or difficult. On the contrary, it is extremely easy, and very nourishing. That is not to say that confit is not a gourmet's delight. It is also part of the artillery of a galley guru. If you are lucky (or wise) enough to have it on board, it is a great treat.

1 pound (455g) duck meat, pulled from 4 duck confit bones (reserve
    any fat from the confit)

2 tablespoons (30ml) each finely-diced carrot and onions

1–2 cloves garlic, minced

1 tablespoon (15ml) chopped thyme

½ cup (125ml) well-flavored chicken stock

2 tablespoons (30ml) dry vermouth

1 pound (455g) wide pasta (tagliatelle or papardelli)

salt and freshly ground pepper

Parmesan cheese, for garnish

fat from duck confit

In a large sauté pan heat 1 teaspoon or two of duck fat. Add vegetables and thyme, cook 5 minutes, until transparent. Add the garlic, cook another minute, then add the duck meat. Heat gently, adding chicken stock to make a nice sauce. Add vermouth. Cook gently for 10 minutes. Meanwhile, bring a large pot of salted water to a boil. Cook the pasta according to package directions, stirring to separate, until al dente. Time the pasta to be ready when the sauce is done. Flat egg noodles take a little less time than spaghetti or linguine, so be careful not to overcook them.

Drain pasta, reserving ½ cup of cooking water. Add pasta directly to sauté pan. Toss to combine with a tablespoon of fat reserved from the confit, if desired, and spoonfuls of the pasta water to achieve the perfect consistency for the sauce. Serve with freshly grated Parmesan.

Pasta Salmon

This is one of the most delicious pasta dishes that ever had a cream sauce that isn't cream. You can, if you have the time, broil or sauté the salmon specially for this dish, but it is outstanding with the salmon from last night's dinner. In fact, that is how this dish was born. It is very rich, and the smoky-sweet salmon is complimented gorgeously by the fragrant tarragon cream sauce—which isn't a cream sauce at all, but a tofu sauce! You must use a blender for the tofu cream, though the blender needn't be electric. The only thing you really need to make this is the fresh and smoked salmon. It isn't bad with canned salmon, but opt for the real thing when you can opt.

1 pound (455g) cooked salmon filet, flaked
4 ounces (115g) smoked salmon
1 recipe tofu cream
1 bunch fresh tarragon, chopped with a handful of tarragon reserved for the topping
1–2 teaspoon (5-10ml) Marigold bouillon powder (see * p. 19)
1–2 teaspoon (5-10ml) liquid aminos seasoning (Marigold, Braggs)
¼–½ cup (60-125ml) Noilly Prat or other dry white vermouth
1 pound (455g) short pasta: fussili, rotelli, or penne or the like

Galley Guru Tip:
Noilly Prat is a nice vermouth to have on hand...much herbier and more fragrant (hence more flavorful) than the more common ones.

Cook pasta according to package directions. Meanwhile, put the tarragon, Marigold, liquid aminos (Marigold, Braggs), and Noilly Prat into a blender with the tofu cream. Blend until the tarragon is almost but not quite emulsified into the sauce. Place sauce into a large saucepan or skillet and heat gently. Cook until flavors are well blended, about 3 minutes. Drain pasta, reserving ½ cup of cooking water. Add the pasta to the cream sauce in the pan and toss. Toss in the cooked salmon just to heat through, adding spoonfuls of pasta water to loosen the sauce. Taste for seasoning. Serve topped with smoked salmon and decorate with some tarragon.

Risotto

If you have never attempted risotto before, you will learn to love it on a boat. It is quick to prepare once you get the knack, and it can be dressed as many ways as you have ideas for flavors.

4 cups (1 liter) vegetable or chicken stock
1 tablespoon (15ml) olive oil
1 large or 2 medium onions, finely chopped
2 cloves garlic, minced finely
14 ounces (400g) Italian arborio or Spanish paella rice
2 glasses dry white vermouth
salt and freshly ground black pepper
4 ounces (115g) freshly grated Parmesan cheese

Heat the stock in a saucepan and keep hot. In a large skillet, heat the olive oil, then add the onion and garlic. Cook over medium low heat a few minutes until they become soft and transparent.
Add the rice, stirring. Turn up the heat. Stir rice to coat evenly with the oil and keep stirring until it begins to look translucent. Pour in one glass of the wine. Stir until absorbed. Repeat with the other glass.

When the wine is absorbed, add about a half cup of the stock. Keep stirring the rice over medium heat as the stock absorbs into it. Add more stock and allow to absorb, stirring all the while. You should keep the liquid bubbling a little around the edges. The rice should always be covered by a thin veil of broth. Regulate the heat under the pan so that all the liquid will be absorbed in about 15 minutes. Any longer and the rice will be overcooked; any less and the rice will likely retain a hard kernel inside. Remove from heat. Rice should still be al dente (chewy to the tooth).

Stir in the Parmesan and butter. Cover and allow to stand for a few minutes, during which time the rice will finish cooking. Serve.

Coconut Risotto

Here is an island risotto that is so wonderful with grilled shrimp or any fish you may have that you will want it again and again. Since it relies mainly on pantry ingredients, it is not at all difficult to make that happen. You can stir some shrimp or crab directly into this after the last addition of stock to have a lovely main course.

2 ounces (56g) butter

½ medium onion, finely chopped

2 cloves garlic, minced

¾ pound (340g) arborio or paella rice

2 (14oz/400ml) cans coconut milk

equal amount of water

1 teaspoon (5ml) cardamom

1 teaspoon (5ml) coriander

1 teaspoon (5ml) cinnamon

few twists of freshly ground pepper

½ cup (125ml) chopped cashews

juice of ½ lime

handful of chopped cilantro (fresh coriander)

Heat coconut milk to boiling with water, cardamom, coriander, cinnamon, pepper, and a teaspoon of Marigold bouillon. Sauté the onions and garlic in the butter gently for about 5 minutes until transparent. Pour the rice into the pan and stir over moderate heat for about 5 minutes until rice turns a milky color. Immediately pour in one cup of the hot liquid. Continue to stir the rice as the liquid absorbs. When it is almost completely absorbed, pour in another cup of liquid.

Continue in this manner, stirring as the liquid is absorbed into the rice and becomes dry enough that you can see the bottom of the pan when you push the rice away. The heat should be regulated under the pan so that the liquid bubbles but does not boil too rapidly. The entire process should not take longer than 18 minutes. Rice should be a tiny bit undercooked.

At this point, remove the rice from the heat. Stir in the chopped cashews and squeeze half a lime over the mixture. Cover the rice and allow to stand for 2 to 3 minutes more, during which time the rice will continue to cook and be perfectly al dente (just offering resistance to the tooth, not mushy). Fluff with a fork. Top with chopped coriander. Serve.

Jamaican Rice and Peas

A very different coconut rice, this one is fiery hot and made hearty and substantial with Gungo peas. Gungo peas (Congo peas, also known as pigeon peas) are really beans. Part of the food culture of India and Ceylon, they can also be found in Jamaica, having emigrated there from Africa. There is some notion that these peas or beans are mildly narcotic, so if you want to test that on yourself you will have to go out of your way to get the real thing. Otherwise, the Jamaicans substitute red kidney beans and you can too. Narcotics to the contrary, the scotch bonnet pepper will make you wake up and take notice. Fiery warning: use the scotch bonnet (make sure you keep it whole; don't allow it to break) only if you have a cast-iron palate and a heart for any fate. Otherwise substitute a bit of cayenne to taste. You can use any oil with this, though coconut oil, found in Caribbean markets, will give it a characteristic sweet taste.

> 1 can (16 oz/455g) gungo peas or 1 can red kidney beans
> 1 can (14 oz/400ml) coconut milk
> 2 cups (500ml) jasmine or long-grain rice
> 1 onion, chopped fine
> 2 cloves garlic, minced
> 2 teaspoons (10ml) Marigold bouillon powder (see * p. 19)

1 teaspoon (5ml) fresh thyme, chopped

½ teaspoon (2.5ml) allspice

1 tablespoon (15ml) butter

1 tablespoon (15ml) oil

1 scotch bonnet pepper (optional)

salt to taste

Sauté the onion in the oil and butter until transparent. Add the garlic. Add beans/peas and rice. Sauté until rice is well coated, about 3 minutes. Pour in the coconut milk and an equal amount of water. Bring to a boil. Add the bouillon powder, allspice, and thyme, and give rice a stir. Place whole scotch bonnet pepper (if using) in saucepan. Reduce heat to low and cover tightly. Simmer until water evaporates, about 25 minutes. Taste for seasoning. Remove whole scotch bonnet pepper before serving.

Simple Couscous

Couscous is a Moroccan and Tunisian favorite. It resembles a grain-like rice, but is actually a very small pasta made of semolina. There are all sorts of dishes that use couscous as a base. It cooks almost instantly. In fact, you can make it in a thermos, where it steams perfectly, so it is easy to make and eat in inclement weather.

Serve this couscous as a side dish with Oven Roasted Ratatouille, Tchaktchouka, or any stew of your choice.

For each cup (250ml) of couscous, bring an equal amount of broth or water to a boil. Add the boiling liquid to the couscous with a pinch of salt and stir it around. Cover.

Allow to stand, off the heat, covered for about 5 minutes. Fluff with a fork before serving.

Rosemary Roast Potatoes

Rosemary and/or thyme are perfect with potato fries done this way. You can do these potatoes in 20 minutes in a blazing hot oven, and by all means, try it that way if you haven't more time. I prefer the softer golden brown of this slightly slower method, which also makes sure that they are crispy on the outside and cooked through and soft in the center.

   2 pounds (approximately 1 kilo) potatoes, wedged lengthwise
   ¼ cup (60ml) olive oil
   1 tablespoon (15ml) chopped rosemary (or thyme)
   salt and pepper

Preheat oven to medium hot (about 425°). Spread potatoes in a single layer on a baking sheet covered with foil. Pour the olive oil over, sprinkle with the herbs and some salt and pepper, and with your fingers, toss all together to coat well. Roast potatoes about 40 minutes, turning once, until golden brown and crispy. Season with a touch more salt immediately out of the oven and serve.

Classic Roast Potatoes

If you can parboil (pre-boil) potatoes first, you will get a crunchier potato with a softer center.

Peel potatoes and cut them into chunks about 1½ inch thick. Boil potatoes 5–7 minutes in boiling salted water. Drain, shaking them around in a covered pot just to rough up the edges. Spread them on a baking sheet as in the previous directions and cook until golden brown, about 40 minutes.

Artichoke Stuffed Potato

"For me, a plain baked potato is the most delicious one . . . .
It is soothing and enough."
—M.F.K. Fisher

It can be difficult to think of what to cook for a filling meal when you have been staring at the same old cans in the hold for days. Though potatoes can be a meal indeed, and the base of any number of different meals, the fact is that sometimes ideas are slow to materialize. Here is a savory and different combination that is sure to please, as easy as it is delicious.

4 baking potatoes
1 can (10 0z/285g) artichoke hearts or bottoms
3 tablespoons (45ml) butter
4 tablespoons (60ml) cream or milk
2 tablespoons (30ml) extra virgin olive oil
2 tablespoons (30ml) grated Parmesan
salt and freshly ground black pepper

Scrub the potatoes and poke holes in them. Bake the potatoes at medium high heat until soft, about 1 hour, depending on the size of the potatoes.

Drain and chop the artichoke hearts quite finely. Cut potatoes in half and scoop the flesh into a bowl. Mash potatoes with olive oil and butter, cream, or milk. Add the artichoke hearts to the potato and mix well. Taste for seasoning. Add salt and plenty of freshly ground pepper. Sprinkle with Parmesan cheese.

Pile the mixture back into the potato shells, put them in a baking dish, and heat through for a few minutes in the oven, until hot.

Torta Tarantina

Potato Pie

Italians, especially Italian peasants, are masters at throwing a few innocent looking ingredients together and coming up with pure gold. They make delicious and healthful meals that rush headlong from the pantry straight into an art form. They can turn old bread into new salads or soups and can manipulate a few scoops of leftover risotto into delicate crunchy rice cakes elegant enough to be served in the finest restaurants. For our purposes this is good. We have appetites for the finer things. We have cans in our pantry. And we have all wistfully watched a perfectly innocent leftover or two fall overboard. This time, instead of feeding the fish, we will use our noodle—or potato—in the manner of the Italians to create a moveable feast.

This simple pie with its intense flavors is another "lucky for us" dish of a rather poor region, Puglia, the boot heel of Italy. It is great to make when you have a few potatoes lying around. Turn them into this rustic torte with only some canned tomatoes, mozzarella cheese, and anchovies to assist you. Take heart, it is easy to make. Try it next time you are hungry for pizza but seem to have left your recipe for pizza dough in your other suit.

    2 pounds (approximately 1 kilo) baking potatoes
    2 tablespoons (30ml) all purpose flour
    1 (14 oz/400g) can peeled tomatoes, chopped
    ¼ cup (60ml) extra virgin olive oil
    10 ounces (285 g) mozzarella slices
    8 anchovy filets in oil, chopped
    1 teaspoon (5ml) dried oregano
    3 ounces (85g) black olives, sliced
    salt and pepper to taste

Preheat oven to medium high (400°). Boil the potatoes in their skins in salted water until tender. Drain, peel, pass through a food mill or a ricer, and allow to cool. Sprinkle with 2 tablespoons flour and half the oil. Mix well. Season with salt and pepper.

Oil a round pizza pan (or other baking tray) and spread the potato mixture over it. Arrange the tomato over the potatoes, sprinkle with the oregano, and top with the anchovies, mozzarella, and olives. Drizzle the rest of the oil over the top. Bake in the oven for 20 minutes, or until cheese is melted and pie is golden brown around the edges. Serve hot or at room temperature.

Pouch Potatoes

Make these potatoes when you have some Onion Confit already stored away for an exquisite and almost instant side dish or base for a main course. (See page 221 for how to make the pouch. Onion confit is on page 262.)

4 medium potatoes, cut into paper-thin slices
1 cup (250ml) onion confit
2 cloves garlic, minced
4 tablespoons (60ml) white wine
chopped fresh or pinch of dried thyme or rosemary

Preheat oven to high. Place a layer of potatoes on one half of the prepared paper or foil. Season with salt and pepper. Add a layer of the onion confit. Continue layering in this manner until all used up. Sprinkle with garlic and the herbs and drizzle with white wine. Tightly seal the papillote and place it on a baking sheet. Cook in center of oven 35 minutes. To open pouch, cut a cross in the top, then pull back points, being careful as the steam is released.

Variation:
Layer potatoes and onions with a third layer consisting of a pound of sausage or ham cut into slices or diced. This will result in a good, homey, satisfying supper.

Yam Gratin

There is nothing like a lovely gratin. They are easy to cook in the oven and are the most comforting of comfort foods. Here is a decidedly decadent and delectable Caribbean island version.

2.2 pounds (1 kilo) yams (sweet potatoes or butternut squash will
    also work)
1 (14 oz/400ml) can rich coconut milk
1½ teaspoon (7.5ml) cinnamon
pinch of freshly grated nutmeg
pinch of cayenne pepper
salt
½ cup (125ml) crunchy peanut butter
¾ cup (185ml) peanuts, chopped or ground in a grinder or mill
2 tablespoons (30ml) brown sugar
2 tablespoons (30ml) butter
splash of rum, gold or dark is nicest with this

Preheat oven to 425°. Peel and slice potatoes very thinly. Use a mandoline or cut them carefully with a knife. Put potatoes in a pot of boiling salted water. Reduce heat and simmer 10 minutes. Drain. Butter an oven dish. Layer the potatoes in the dish, overlapping them slightly. Sprinkle each layer with salt, a little cayenne pepper, some cinnamon, and the nutmeg. When half of the potatoes are arranged, cover with a layer of the chunky peanut butter. Continue filling the dish with potatoes, seasoning each layer as before. Pour the coconut milk over the potatoes. Sprinkle over a bit of rum. Top with the ground peanuts and brown sugar. Dot the top with butter. Cover the gratin and cook in a medium hot oven about 40 to 45 minutes, until the potatoes are tender and the coconut milk has been absorbed. Remove top and continue to cook 10 minutes, until the butter and sugar have melted and the top is crispy.
    Serves 6.

Janssen's Temptation

"Pray for peace and grace and spiritual food,
For wisdom and guidance, for all these are good,
But don't forget the potatoes."
—J. T. Pettee

It's amazing what you can do with a few potatoes and a can or two
of anchovies. Janssen's (or Johnson's) Temptation is a Scandinavian
baked potato casserole that is astonishingly good and easy to make. My
Swedish friend Lyn serves this every Christmas Eve along with a glorious
Glögg *(hot mulled wine) to wash it down. A mandoline is the best way*
to quickly and effortlessly slice the potatoes and onions. You also get
even, uniform slices. Here is one temptation that Mr. Janssen found
utterly irresistible. You will too. By the way, you don't exactly taste the
anchovies. They stand in for salt, and add a buttery softness to the dish
that is indescribable.

2 cans of anchovies

2 large onions, sliced thin

5 large potatoes (about 1lb/400–500g), peeled and sliced thin

1¼ (310ml) cup double cream (fresh or canned)

freshly ground black pepper

2–3 tablespoons (30-45ml) breadcrumbs

2 tablespoons (30ml) butter

Open the cans of anchovies and drizzle the oil from them into a pan.
Add the onion and sauté gently until softened. Do not allow to take
on color. Stir in the potatoes and sweat over low heat until they
start to soften. Remove from the heat and stir in the cream and the
anchovies. Season with black pepper. Spread the mixture in a small
gratin dish, top with breadcrumbs, and dot with butter. Bake in a
hot oven for 35–40 minutes, until potatoes are tender and crust is
crispy and golden.

Serves 6.

Even when there is nothing so great as a storm, the sea will move you whether you wish to be moved or not. As a wave crests, you go up; it rolls and falls, and you come down with it. Taking advantage of this fact one day presented a hilarious picture when I decided to make pizza in the galley. There I was, sitting on the galley sole—wedged in for stability, of course—with my rolled dough in my hands. When the wave would crest I threw the pizza dough up, and when the wave came down so did the dough as I caught it stylishly in my outstretched hands. It could not have been better if I were a pizza cook in New York. This method made a brilliantly thin crust and everybody went crazy for that pizza. Here it is:

Pesto Pizza
...With Sausage and Tons Of Cheese

mozzarella, grated (as much as you like)

2 or 3 cooked sausages (slice thinly to put on pizza)

1 medium leek, finely chopped

1 large tomato, diced

olive oil

2 tablespoons (30ml) butter

oven-roasted sliced zucchini (courgette) and red pepper with thyme
brushed with olive oil

1 pizza base (or you can make your own from a mix)

1 teaspoon (5ml) dried oregano

Sauté leeks in a pan with butter, olive oil and garlic. Place all ingredients onto pizza base in decorative but nevertheless nonchalant manner.

Cover cheerfully with **Pesto**. Cook pizza in a hot oven for 15 minutes (or until you get back on course).

Another Pesto

½ cup (125ml) Parmigiano Reggiano or best Parmesan, grated

1 cup (250ml) pine nuts (or cashew)

1 cup (250ml) chopped fresh basil

season with liquid aminos (Marigold, Braggs)

or Marigiold vegetable bouillon powder (if using substitute,
   see * p. 19)

½ cup (125ml) olive oil

as much garlic as you can stand

Blend all ingredients in a blender.

Rice Pilaf

*This is a simple rice pilaf that you may serve alongside almost anything.
It is made by sautéing rice in a pan and then adding seasoned broth. The
main difference between a pilaf and the risotto dishes I have given you is
that this is made from long grain rice and is thus a bit lighter. It is so easy.*

1 cup long grain white rice
2 tablespoons oil
½ small onion, chopped
¼ cup dry vermouth
2 cups chicken broth or vegetable broth (low sodium)
2 teaspoons Marigold bouillon powder (if substituting, see * p. 19)
good pinch nutmeg
salt and freshly ground pepper

Heat oil in a large skillet. Add onion and sauté until just soft but not
colored. Add white rice. Continue cooking, tossing the rice in the pan
until translucent. Immediately pour in the vermouth and stir until the
rice is puffed a bit and all liquid is absorbed. Add broth in three stages.
With the first, stir in Marigold and nutmeg. After each addition bring
liquid back to a boil and stir the rice until it is almost dry before
adding more liquid. It is important to keep the broth just at the boil
while you stir and fluff the rice. This process should take about 18–20
minutes. Season with salt if needed and freshly ground pepper. Let
rice stand covered for 3–4 minutes. Fluff with a fork. Serve.

Variation: Middle Eastern Pilaf

With a few additions you have a sweet-savory, fragrant Persian pilaf.
Add a handful of golden raisins along with the rice in the pan. Add
a pinch of saffron and another of cardamom along with the nutmeg.
Toast a handful of pine nuts in a dry pan until just golden. When
rice is cooked, stir in the pine nuts. Let stand. Fluff with a fork and
top with a handful of chopped mint leaves.

Vegetable Dishes

*"Sex is good, but not as good as
fresh, sweet corn."*

—Garrison Keillor

Now we come to the crunch. *The vegetable crunch, I mean.*

How does your garden grow? Without a garden, that is, and with very little space?

When we have fresh raw vegetables, simplicity is usually the best course. One can dream of a great soft sandwich of crisp cucumber, sliced paper thin, nestled into thick or thin (each has something to be said for it) slices of whole grain bread spread with fresh creamery butter and just a twist of pepper to set it off. A bread with a soft, almost cake-like crumb, coupled with the tender crunch of a sliced cucumber, make for matchless companions.

While crunchiness is what we expect from our vegetables, there is some difficulty keeping our horn of plenty full to bursting aboard ship, especially on a long cruise. Yet we would never resort to the can, would we? Prudence dictates using the most perishable items first and trusting that our onions, carrots, and cabbages will keep longer than our lettuces, broccoli, and snow peas. We are trying to beat the demon damp here. Most of this boils down to common sense with a bit of trial and error thrown in.

Did I say boil? I didn't mean it. We love succulent vegetables with all their moisture and flavor inside. We reject them when boiled, as in grandmother's day, into hapless resignation.

As for cooking methods: steamed or sautéed lightly, what you are looking for is the lovely surprise of a perfectly tender carrot or tip of asparagus cooked "à point," that is, just enough but no more. Try throwing asparagus on the grill for just a few minutes. It will reward you with a slightly charred, smoky, and delicate taste.

Otherwise, make confit out of your onions and garlic. Tuck your veggies into the oven to develop unexpected complexity and sweetness. Tomatoes make a wonderful condiment this way, and, happily, they keep a long time.

I have here given recipes for a few of my favorite perishables, when even the most mundane of vegetables may surprise you. Carrots and cabbage, for instance, that you are actually thrilled to eat.

Remember, it's not the veggies, it's the way you cook 'em.

Grilled Corn on the Cob

This is for one of those great nights under the stars when you can grill. Perhaps you have a chicken to roast as in **Beer Can Chicken**, *or you plan to have some great steaks or fish. Corn on the cob is great anytime, but on the grill, the sweetness of the corn is intensified. Peel back the husks to reveal the silk. Remove the silk and replace the husks around the corn. If you want you can soak the corn in water for about 20 minutes before grilling. This prevents the husks from burning, but it also is an extra step that prevents the corn from getting that charred smoky grill flavor. Whichever way you choose, throw the corn directly onto the grill and keep turning over and over (if you did not soak them, turn until the husks blacken evenly). The corn is done in about 10 to 15 minutes. Serve with lots of butter or make* **Tequila Lime Butter**.

Tequila Lime Butter with Chipotle

¼ pound (115g) butter, softened to room temperature

2 cloves garlic, pressed

juice of two limes with some zest

2 tablespoons (30ml) good tequila

1 chipotle pepper minced fine (optional)

Put the butter in a food processor with the garlic and chipotle pepper. Mix well. Add the tequila and mix again. Mix in the lime juice a little at a time until incorporated.

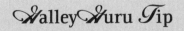

To easily zest citrus fruit, use your microplane grater. See **Batterie de Galley, page 37.**

Oven Roasted Ratatouille

If there is one place that a vegetable sheds its supporting role status and becomes a star, it is in the oven. Unlike veggies boiled atop the stove in water that leaches away their nutrients and flavors, roasted vegetables develop their sugars and concentrate their flavors deep in the privacy of the oven. From the galley point of view, it is like finding pure gold doubloons. You produce a lot of flavor from very little effort. No more prisoners below decks!

Almost any vegetable becomes rich and gorgeous this way. Vary the vegetables (and the herbs) according to what you have and what sounds good to you to eat together. The cooking time must be adjusted a bit according to how dense the vegetable and how large you cut the pieces as well as the heat of your oven, as galley ovens can vary wildly in temperature. You can do potatoes wedged or cubed this way for breakfast or any time, perhaps adding about ten minutes to the total cooking time to ensure the potatoes get that golden crust that make them irresistible. Throw in a whole head of peeled garlic (or unpeeled if you want to squeeze out the sweet flesh from its case when it's done), then toss together with the potatoes and add salt. Sinfully delicious.

You can add potatoes to the following vegetable mixture, if you cut potatoes or sweet potatoes in cubes or thin enough wedges so they will cook fairly quickly. Another way is to parboil the potatoes for about 15 minutes, or throw them in a microwave for 5 minutes, just to give them a head start against something as delicate as, say, a zucchini. Roasted carrots and roasted beets are a taste treat because both of these vegetables have a lot of natural sugars (as do parsnips), so when these get heat applied in the right way, the flavor is off-the-charts good. As always in this book, the measurements are pretty flexible. It is not about numbers here. If you roast any single vegetable with olive oil, salt, and pepper, you pretty much have the thing mastered. Add onion and garlic and you add another level of flavor and texture.

1 large onion

4 shallots, peeled

½ head of garlic, cloves separated and peeled

1 eggplant (aubergine)

2 large zucchini (courgettes)

1 pound (about ½ kilo) medium mushrooms (crimini or portobello, or whatever you have)

2 red peppers

2 tomatoes

olive oil

a handful chopped thyme (you could use rosemary or oregano or all three)

salt and freshly ground pepper

½ teaspoon (2.5ml) cinnamon

Slice onion into wedges. Cut all the vegetables into slices or wedges approximately the same size. (Roasting will cause the water from the vegetables to be released and they will get smaller and denser.) Leave mushrooms whole or slice in half if they are too big. Toss in the garlic cloves. Toss all vegetables in a large bowl with the fresh herbs and the olive oil until every vegetable is covered well with oil.

Cover a large tray with foil. Lay out all the vegetables in flat little groups. Season with salt and loads of freshly ground black pepper. Put into a medium hot oven and cook for 35–40 minutes, or until the vegetables are nicely golden at the edges, are cooked through, and have shrunk in size.

These vegetables are perfect to serve as a side dish or tucked inside an omelet, or if you prefer, cool them and serve them as a salad. Alternatively, spoon them over rice or pasta and you have a lovely vegetarian main course.

Tchaktchouka

Tchaktchouka with its exotic name is a simple Tunisian supper and nothing more than a spicy version of ratatouille served with poached eggs on top. It was taught to me by a Tunisian fisherman, though there is not a fish in sight in this dish. In this version, the vegetables are cooked in the oven, leaving just the poached eggs to watch over at the end. You can serve this exceptionally fragrant dish with or without the eggs, alone with **Couscous,** *or to accompany a lamb or chicken dish. It is good at room temperature as part of a meze with pita or any good bread alongside little dishes of* **Hummus** *and* **Baba Ganouj.**

2 red peppers, sliced

2 pounds (approx 1 kilo) tomatoes, quartered

1 eggplant (aubergine), cut into sticks

2 zucchini (courgettes), cut into sticks

2 medium onions, cut in pieces

4 cloves garlic, sliced or chopped

pinch powdered bay leaf

handful chopped fresh thyme

extra virgin olive oil

1 teaspoon (5ml) coriander

1 teaspoon (5ml) cinnamon

½ teaspoon (2.5ml) cardamom

½ teaspoon (2.5ml) allspice

10 black olives, pitted

4–8 eggs

salt, pepper, and cayenne to taste

Place all vegetables, onion, and garlic in a large ovenproof skillet. Drizzle generously with olive oil and sprinkle the spices over them. Season with salt, pepper, and a good amount of cayenne (the Tunisians like this spicy). Toss vegetables to coat well with the oil and seasonings.

Place skillet directly into a medium oven for 35–40 minutes until the vegetables have become caramelized. Remove vegetables to top of the stove over medium heat. Stir in the olives. Break eggs (one or two per person) first into a cup (to prevent breaking yolks) and then slide them gently onto the vegetables. Cover and let cook just until the white is completely done but the yolk is still soft. Serve immediately over couscous with crusty bread or garlic bread.

If you have bread that is not at its freshest, cut it into cubes for croutons. Toss in some olive oil, salt, and pepper and put it in the oven until crisp and golden, about 15 minutes. At serving time, serve the Tchaktchouka with croutons sprinkled over.

Roasted Butternut Squash

Isn't life sweet? This couldn't be simpler and is very good to serve with almost anything you can think of. You can toss the result with pasta. It makes a delightful vegetarian main dish.

1 or 2 butternut squash
4–6 tablespoons (60-90ml) butter (or olive oil)
good pinch nutmeg
salt and freshly ground pepper

Cut the squash in half lengthwise and take out the seeds. Peel the squash. Cut in cubes. Put squash into an oven dish. Toss with butter or oil and season with salt, pepper, and nutmeg. Bake in fairly hot oven, tossing in the hot fat once or twice, for 45 minutes or until cooked soft and caramelized all over.

Portobello Mushrooms Florentine

Mushrooms this way can be a side dish with a steak but they shine on their own, for they are very rich and make a fine lunch with some nice bread.

¼ cup (60ml) olive oil
¼ cup (60ml) balsamic vinegar
1 tablespoon (15ml) Tamari* soy sauce
2 cloves garlic, minced fine
8 medium or 4 large portobellos, stems removed and chopped
salt and freshly ground pepper to taste

Filling
4 tablespoons (60ml) olive oil
½ medium onion
2 spring onions, sliced
2 cloves garlic, minced
2 cups (500ml) fresh spinach leaves, shredded
handful fresh basil, shredded
½ glass white wine
1 teaspoon (5ml) Marigold bouillon powder (see * p. 19)
⅓ cup (85ml) breadcrumbs
⅓ cup (85ml) Gruyere, Emmental, or Havarti cheese, shredded
¼ cup (60ml) Parmesan, grated

Mix the oil, Tamari, vinegar, and garlic. Season with salt and pepper. Place the mushroom caps in a small baking dish and pour the marinade over them, coating well. Put the mushrooms under the broiler or in a very hot oven until lightly browned, basting with any excess marinade.

* Tamari is a special organic type of soy sauce that you can find in any health food store and some supermarkets. It is richer than conventional commercial kinds and is also less salty. It is very worth searching out, since it gives a rich, complex, meaty taste to mushrooms and onions and is very useful.

While the mushrooms are grilling, prepare the filling. Heat a skillet over medium heat. Pour in the olive oil and sauté the onions, reserved mushroom stems, spring onions, and garlic until tender. Add the spinach and basil with the white wine. Cook a minute or two, allowing the spinach to wilt. Add the Marigold, breadcrumbs, and Gruyere. Turn off the heat. Mix well and taste for seasoning.

Divide the filling among the mushroom caps, mounding it up in the center of each. Sprinkle with grated Parmesan. Return to the broiler for two to three minutes or until the top is golden and the cheese is melted.

Our Mushrooms

Mushrooms are a perfect side dish, I think, so I have given several recipes that star them. Here is a delicious way to cook them with an Oriental touch. Other than the fresh mushrooms, which are essential, this dish is made entirely from pantry ingredients. It is deceptively easy and spectacular to serve with steak or chops or chicken. I have not given measurements at all, but you can figure at least a cup of sliced raw mushrooms per person (depending on whether this is a garnish, a side dish, or the main event), since they cook down considerably.

> fresh mushrooms, sliced
> butter
> dark sesame seed oil
> oyster sauce
> Kikkoman sushi and sashimi sauce, or other light soy sauce

Melt some butter in a frying pan. Then add the mushrooms. Sauté, coating the mushrooms in the butter. As the mushrooms are cooking add a few good dashes oyster sauce, sesame seed oil, and sashimi sauce. Keep turning them around the pan over medium heat. Cook until mushrooms are browned and reduced in size by about half. The juices from the mushrooms will have turned into a beautiful sauce.

Baked Mushrooms

These are the mushrooms that go with anything. They are super billowing out of a baked potato or on top of a steak or chop. You can use wild mushrooms or those little brown crimini (which are only small portobellos), but the humble white mushroom works very well too. Even if you don't like mushrooms, try them this way. I think you may change your mind.

> 2 pounds (about 1 kilo) mushrooms
> 4 tablespoons (60ml) olive oil
> 3 garlic cloves, minced
> small handful parsley, chopped
> a good splash rich soy sauce (like Tamari)
> a splash of brandy
> salt and pepper to taste

Wipe the mushrooms. Chop stems, leaving caps whole. Arrange the caps in a shallow ovenproof dish and sprinkle with the stems. Drizzle with the olive oil, brandy, and soy sauce. Cook in a medium high oven for 20 minutes. Remove mushrooms from oven and sprinkle with garlic and parsley, season with salt and pepper.

Return dish to oven and bake another 15 minutes, basting occasionally with the liquid in the dish. Mushrooms should be bubbling and browned. They may be served hot or at room 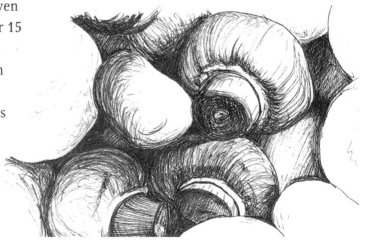 temperature. Or they may be put into a mushroom sandwich.

Spinach Sautéed in Olive Oil and Garlic

This is the classic Italian way to cook spinach. It is fast and it is delicious. For that matter, you can do broccoli—or any green vegetable in olive oil and garlic—in basically the same way. Try it with green beans. There are few Italian children who won't eat their vegetables, and this method of preparation explains it.

Spinach is a delicate vegetable. It doesn't need to be boiled to death. The drops of water left on the leaves from washing will be sufficient to allow them to steam sauté and not lose any of their integrity. If you are using another vegetable, pre-boil (parboil) just a few minutes until it is tender-crisp before tossing in the olive oil and garlic.

3–4 large bunches spinach, washed and drained

4–6 tablespoons olive oil

3–4 cloves garlic minced

good pinch nutmeg

red pepper flakes (to taste)

salt and black pepper to taste

Heat the olive oil over medium-low heat in a large skillet with a well-fitting lid. Add the red pepper flakes and the garlic and cook a minute. Do not brown the garlic, just heat it through. Add the spinach leaves and a good pinch of nutmeg, tossing the leaves in the olive oil to coat them. They will cook down very quickly. Push the leaves down in the pan. Cover. Turn heat to low and continue to cook 4–5 minutes. Take off the heat and toss again. The spinach should be wilted but not soggy. Season with salt to taste. Serve hot or cold.

Variation:

Just before serving, sprinkle with a handful of pine nuts; these are marvelous with spinach. You can toast these in a dry pan first if you like, but they are really quite nice as they are.

Asparagus

Asparagus is just about my favorite vegetable. If you have a microwave, this is one place I would use it. In 2 or 3 minutes it makes perfectly cooked asparagus that is tender but still retains its crunch. This simple seasoning doesn't mask the beauty of the vegetable but brings it out for a perfect accompaniment to any steak or piece of grilled chicken or fish. Try to get asparagus that is pencil-thin, since this is the most tender and delicate. As asparagus gets thicker it is also more rubbery and not as nice. If you find only the larger asparagus, do as the French do and peel the stalks from just under the tips, leaving only the tenderest part underneath. This also makes a pretty presentation.

If you want to boil asparagus instead, simply boil for 5–6 minutes in lots of boiling salted water into which you have dropped a bay leaf or two, and then toss with the thyme, butter, and lemon.

> large bunch very fine green asparagus
> powdered thyme
> a bay leaf
> juice of half a lemon
> butter

Wash asparagus and snap the ends off. You can tell exactly where you need to do this by holding a stalk in your hands at each end and snapping. Discard the woody stems. Put the tips into a microwave-safe dish with a bit of water and sprinkle with thyme. Place a bay leaf down into the water at the bottom of the dish. Cover. Place in the microwave and cook on high for 3 minutes (you will need to adjust this according to how much asparagus you have and how powerful your microwave). Drain. Toss with lemon juice and butter. Serve.

Asparagus Wrapped in Prosciutto

Use Italian prosciutto or Spanish jamon serrano for an elegant presentation. Cook asparagus as indicated above. Take a few stalks together and wrap them in thin slices of the ham. Drizzle with a bit of extra virgin olive oil. This is wonderful either hot or cold.

Asparagus with Morel Mushrooms

If you find fresh morels, these woodsy, flavorful mushrooms are wonderful with asparagus. However, if you keep the dried aboard, you can make this lovely aromatic dish any time you want. This is basically asparagus with a mushroom cream sauce, but try to leave the morels whole or cut through only once.

> cooked asparagus (as above)
> ½ cup (125 ml) fresh morel mushrooms, washed and patted dry
> (or 1 ounce = 28.3g dried)
> 1 bunch green onion, minced or
> 2 shallots, minced
> 2 tablespoons butter
> 1 wineglass white wine
> 1 wineglass cream
> a few sprinklings of nutmeg
> salt and pepper to taste

If using dried morels, place them in a bowl and pour a cup of boiling water over them. Allow to stand 10 to 15 minutes until rehydrated. Remove from water. Melt the butter in a large skillet. Add the onions or shallot and morels and sauté for a minute or two. Add the white wine and turn heat up. Allow the wine to bubble and reduce by about half. Add the cream and nutmeg. Continue to boil a minute or two until you have a nice thick sauce. Season with salt and pepper. Add the asparagus to the pan and very gently toss to coat. Serve.

Spiced Carrots in Cider

Carrots are pretty easy to keep, as vegetables go. But they can be dead boring if you don't do something with them. Here is something rather exotic to do with them and it definitely isn't going to put you to sleep. The sweetness of the carrots is brought out by this method. Sweet, rich, and delectable!

    1 pound (1/2 kilo) young carrots, peeled
    1 cup (250ml) cider or apple juice
    1 teaspoon Marigold bouillon powder (see * p. 19 if using a
        substitute)
    2 tablespoons brandy or cream sherry
    pinch nutmeg
    pinch cardamom
    2 teaspoons butter
    salt and freshly ground pepper to taste

Cut the carrots on a diagonal. In a heavy skillet or sauté pan bring them to a boil in the cider or apple juice with a pinch of salt. Reduce the heat, cover, and simmer about 20 minutes, until the carrots are tender but still firm. Uncover the carrots, add the Marigold, and continue to cook, allowing all the liquid to evaporate. Add the butter and the brandy and nutmeg and cardamom. Continue to cook the carrots, tossing them over medium high heat until they are shiny and lightly glazed. Add salt and lots of freshly ground pepper to taste.

Sautéed Red Cabbage with Country Ham and Port Wine

Cabbage is one of those things with leaves that is kind to us at sea. It keeps for ages. I prefer the red cabbage to the white if I must make a choice, because the red is so much more versatile, lending itself not only to coleslaws and the like but to heavenly dishes such as these. If you have a piece of country or other cured ham, it will make this dish, of German origin, perfect. But . . . as always, feel free to improvise.

8 ounces (225g) country ham or fresh ham or lean bacon
   cut into small pieces or cubes
2 tablespoons olive oil
1 small head red cabbage, halved then sliced into thin strips
1 small wineglass port wine
¼ teaspoon allspice
1 tablespoon whole grain French mustard
salt and freshly ground black pepper to taste

Heat the olive oil in a large skillet. Add the country ham or bacon pieces and cook until crisp over medium heat. Remove the ham to drain on some paper towels and pour out all but 2 to 3 tablespoons of the fat in the pan.

Add the cabbage to the pan and toss and cook over medium low heat until it is tender, adding half the port wine as needed for moisture. When cabbage is done (about 12 minutes) add the rest of the port wine, the mustard, and the ham. Season with allspice, salt, and lots of freshly ground pepper. Toss to coat and heat through for about two minutes. Serve.

Mashed Breadfruit

You will find breadfruit wherever you go in the tropics. It is indeed a fruit yet seems almost like a potato in texture. In general breadfruit can be substituted for potatoes in any recipe. Here is a way to make them velvety with coconut in the island style.

2 cups (500g) breadfruit, peeled and seeded
1 can rich coconut milk, heated
½ cup toasted coconut flakes, unsweetened
sprinkle of nutmeg
salt and freshly ground white pepper to taste
few chives, minced

Cook chunks of breadfruit in boiling water until soft but not mushy. Drain and put through a ricer or a food mill or simply mash with potato masher. Place mashed breadfruit into a saucepan on medium heat and slowly add heated coconut milk, whipping with a balloon whip or fork to make a thick purée. Adjust thickness with coconut milk and continue to mix until smooth. Season to taste with nutmeg, salt, and lots of freshly ground pepper; add chives. Mix well and serve hot.

170

Oven-Dried Tomatoes

These tomatoes are oodles better than the sun-dried tomatoes you get in the stores. So if you have an abundance of fresh tomatoes that you don't know what to do with, definitely make these. You can use them for a great side dish along with chicken or meat, but also as a garnish or relish with a sandwich, with cream cheese on a bagel and, of course, over some freshly made pasta, maybe with another handful of basil leaves.

16 ripe plum or 8 large ripe tomatoes
3–4 cloves fresh garlic, chopped
½ wineglass olive oil
a bunch fresh basil leaves or
a handful of freeze-dried basil
sea salt

Preheat the oven to medium (325F). Slice the tomatoes in half lengthwise. If using large tomatoes, cut in half crosswise. Place the tomatoes on a baking sheet, cut side up. Pour the oil over them. Sprinkle with salt, garlic, and the basil leaves. Bake for about 2 hours until tomatoes are shrunken and wrinkled just as sun-dried tomatoes are. You can let them go longer depending on how juicy you want them. As they cook, the flavor just intensifies. Just don't let them dry out completely. You may serve them immediately or cool them and store in olive oil in a covered container in the refrigerator and use as needed. They will keep at least a couple of months this way.

Cipolle di Parma
Baked Onions with Prosciutto

Onions. Glorious, simple, elegant and ... quite overlooked. Herewith the onion, returned to former glory. When it has come down to nothing more than a few onions rolling around at the bottom of the bin, do not lose heart. Think not of the simplicity of your ingredients. Make this dish. It is fantastic. Consider it an ode to an onion.

4 large white onions, peeled
3 ounces (90g) prosciutto, finely chopped
2 cloves garlic, minced
¾ cup (75g) freshly grated best Parmesan
1 egg, beaten
½ cup (50g) dry breadcrumbs
small handful finely chopped fresh parsley (or freeze dried)
pinch of nutmeg
olive oil
salt and freshly ground pepper
½ wineglass Marsala wine or cream (Oloroso) sherry

Preheat the oven to medium hot, 350°F (180°C). Cook the onions in boiling salted water for 15 minutes. Drain and allow to cool. Cut a slice from the top of each onion and scoop out the centers with a spoon, leaving about ¼ inch of the onion intact to make little bowls.

Finely chop the scooped-out onion. Heat a frying pan and add a little olive oil, the chopped onions, and the garlic. Sauté until softened, then remove to a bowl. Toss in the bread crumbs with the prosciutto, cheese, and parsley. Moisten all with the beaten egg. Season with salt and pepper and a good pinch of nutmeg. Fill the onions with the stuffing, mounding it up on the top like a little exploding Vesuvius. Stand the onions in a small enough baking dish that they touch each other. Pour a little olive oil around to moisten the outside of the onions. Then pour the Marsala over. Bake 45 minutes, until soft and tender, basting the onions occasionally with the pan juices. Serve.

Eggs Your Way

"It's very provoking,"
Humpty Dumpty said after a long silence,
looking away from Alice as he spoke,
"to be called an egg—very!"

"I said you looked like an egg, Sir," Alice gently explained.
"And some eggs are very pretty, you know," she added,
hoping to turn her remark into a sort of compliment.

—Lewis Carroll, *Alice Through the Looking Glass*

Perfect Hard-Boiled Eggs

The secret to boiled eggs is not to boil them at all. These eggs are perfect every time and peel easily.

Place eggs in the bottom of pot. Cover with warm water. Bring to a boil on high. Once water has boiled, immediately remove from heat. Cover the pot and allow eggs to sit for about 15 minutes. Remove eggs from pot and allow to fully cool. Do not run under water or place in refrigerator. They must cool at room temperature.

The French Omelet

A well prepared omelet, fragrant with just a few herbs, served accompanied by a simple green salad, can be an achievement of such perfection that I often choose it on terra firma over much grander fare. It bears no resemblance to the doorstep affairs served in those insults to the palate: chain coffee shops. You too can pull off a little French miracle in the galley on a regular basis if you follow a few simple guidelines.

The most successful egg pan has curved, sloping sides for easy stirring and removal. This is the one pan in my arsenal that I insist should be nonstick because it makes the cooking process foolproof and clean up painless.

Making each omelet separately gives you more control over the tenderness of the finished product.

Crack 3 eggs in a bowl. Add two tablespoons or so of water, cream, or soymilk but not regular milk, which will tend to make the omelet tough. With a fork, break the yolks and scramble gently. Do not over whip.

Heat the pan over medium heat. Drizzle in some extra virgin olive oil. Butter is not essential for eggs; indeed, I find the taste and health value of olive oil preferable. Pour in the egg. Let the egg settle for barely a minute, then lift it at the sides with a spatula, tilt the pan, and let the runny egg on the surface run underneath the cooked part. As the egg mixture cooks, lift the sides and allow the egg to slide under to form a firm surface underneath. Do not overcook—three to four minutes should do it. When the center is still tender, you are ready to turn the omelet out onto a plate. The egg will continue to cook for a bit even off the heat.

To serve the omelet, grab the pan's handle with your left hand (if you're right handed). Hold the pan over your plate. Loosen the omelet by running a spatula under it so it will slide out of the pan. Now tilt the pan and slide half the omelet out onto the plate. Then tilt the remaining half of the omelet over it so the remaining half of the omelet will fold over the omelet on the plate.

For vegetable filled omelets, sauté your vegetables—such as chopped onion, chopped red pepper, chopped mushrooms (anything that you have around)—before you start the eggs. You can also add chopped meats such as ham or bacon. If you want to add cheese, grate some cheddar and have it ready. Take out half the vegetables from the pan and pour your omelet mixture, as described above, over the remaining half. When the omelet is cooked underneath but the center is still tender, pour the rest of the vegetables and cheddar into the center of the omelet. Slide half the omelet onto a plate and tilt the pan so that the other half folds over the center.

There are endless variations to produce a meaningful omelet. Instead of cheese, try a generous spreading of hummus, olive tapenade, or pesto. You can do a masterpiece with ratatouille and basil, crab or portobello mushroom and hollandaise or Béarnaise sauce, Gruyere and some fresh sorrel or, failing that, spinach.

Valley Guru Tip
You don't need very much filling, so an omelet is a good way to stretch a little bit of food into a satisfying meal.

Basic Crepes

Sweet or savory, crepes are not beyond the grasp of the **Galley Guru**. *They are really quite foolproof with the blender method. As a matter of fact, crepes are a wonderful way to make a great deal out of a little bit of something—jam or cooked leftovers. Crepes are fun. Crepes are lovely with only a little practice. The great bonus is that they can be made ahead, stacked between sheets of wax or parchment paper, and refrigerated, even frozen. So if you haven't made them before, don't allow the evil demon crepe gods to plant fearful thoughts in your head. Toss them the first crepe or two (which never turn out perfect anyway) to shut them up.*

First, you get out your nice nonstick 8- to 10-inch pan (the one you make omelets in). You whiz the ingredients briefly in a blender and then you set the batter aside for a while in a plastic jug with a lid and a pourable spout. At the moment of making the individual pancakes, all you have to manage is to stow the jug comfortably within reach as you cook each one. You should only need to coat the pan with butter once to start the crepes. After that the following pancakes should release from the pan just fine with no extra help.

4 eggs
¼ tsp (1.25ml) salt
2 cups (500ml) flour
2 cups (500ml) milk
⅓ cup (85ml) melted butter

Put all ingredients in a blender. Whiz for 60 seconds. Scrape down sides, pulse batter once more to incorporate. Refrigerate batter for at least 1 hour.

To cook crepes, heat a small nonstick pan. Add butter to coat. Swirl ¼ cup of the batter around to cover the pan evenly. Cook for 30 to 60 seconds over medium-high heat until bubbles form in the crepe and the edges turn golden brown. Flip crepe over and continue to cook about 10 seconds or just to dry the bottom of the crepe. Slide crepe out to cool. Stack crepes as they are done. After they are cooled you can store them in plastic freezer bags in the refrigerator several days or freeze them. Unfreeze thoroughly before gently peeling apart.

Makes 20-30 crepes.

Some ideas for easy sweet fillings:

Plain with sugar
Jam (any kind)
Chocolate Sauce
Bananas with **chocolate sauce**
Maple syrup
Grand Marnier (Crepes Suzette)

Some ideas for easy savory fillings:

Smoked salmon and sour cream
Ham or any leftover chicken with **cheese sauce**
Any baked or sautéed mushrooms
Sliced beef with mushroom sauce (or leftover Stroganoff, or any
    leftover stew)
Onion Confit
Prawns (with lemon butter, with avocado, with mayonnaise, with
    Mornay Sauce)
Oven Roasted Ratatouille
Brandade de Morue

Tortilla Española

This wonderful Spanish omelet has nothing whatever to do with the Mexican bread wrapper thing that makes burritos. Equally, it is more like an egg and potato cake than a French omelet. It is cooked, cut in wedges, and placed on the bar to serve as a tapa in Spain with a glass of sherry. Perfect for cruising, because it actually improves when it stands around at room temperature. It won't take long to master the technique for flipping it over to cook on both sides and will give you a sense of ascendancy as you toss your head at the elements. I have Mercedes, a savvy Andalusian local in my village of San Pedro de Alcantara and thoroughgoing expert in the art of tortilla turning, to thank for teaching me.

Be careful to leave the eggs a bit runny in the very center of the tortilla. Like a custard, it will continue to set up as it cools. There is nothing worse than an overcooked tortilla whose tender succulence has turned to something very akin to cooked cardboard shoeboxes.

> 4 good-sized potatoes, peeled and sliced thin
> 6 eggs
> ½ cup (125ml) olive oil for frying
> 1 large sweet onion, finely sliced
> 4 cloves garlic, chopped
> 2 tablespoons (30ml) chopped parsley
> salt, to taste

In a large bowl, beat eggs and salt. Set aside. Heat the oil in a large, heavy, nonstick frying pan and add the onion and garlic. Soften for a few minutes. Add the potatoes. Fry until tender, turning them to cook on all sides. When potatoes are cooked, remove them with a slotted spoon to drain as much oil as possible before placing into egg mixture. Pour out oil and clean pan. Coat the pan with olive oil, place over medium high heat. Pour combined potato/egg mixture into pan. As tortilla cooks, shape with spatula, flattening, pushing away from sides. Continuously shake the pan so that the tortilla does not stick on bottom.

Slide a spatula under the tortilla to see how it is cooking. When golden brown on the base, turn tortilla by inverting the frying pan onto a flat lid so that the tortilla falls onto the plate cooked side uppermost. Then you simply slide it back into the pan to heat the other side. Continue to shake pan to prevent sticking and shape the round sides with the spatula. When browned but not completely hard, remove the tortilla to a plate. Sprinkle with parsley.
This marvelous creation is equally good hot or cold.

Variation:
Add some sliced red bell pepper to the egg mixture before cooking. You could add Spanish ham, chorizo, or cooked bacon if you have them.

Easy Microwave Poached Eggs

There is a use for a microwave besides reheating your coffee. The first time I tried to cook an egg in the microwave I didn't put in the water, and that was a disaster. Eggs come out really well in the microwave as long as you set them to cook in a little water and remember to prick the yolk gently. Otherwise you will find your eggs will explode rather than cook.

Put 3–4 tablespoons water into a custard cup or small bowl. Break and slip in one or two eggs. Gently prick yolks with tip of knife or wooden pick. Cover with a dish or plastic wrap. Nuke the eggs on full power. One egg will take 30 to 45 seconds. Two eggs will take 1 to 1½ minutes. Eggs will continue to cook when taken out of the microwave.

Let the eggs stand, covered, for another minute or two, until whites are completely set, during which time the yolks will begin to thicken. Pour off water. Serve in custard cup or remove to plate with slotted spoon.

Eggs Benedict

*With your **Blender Hollandaise**, these classic eggs are a snap to make.*

1 toasted English muffin, split
2 slices Canadian bacon
2 poached eggs
hollandaise sauce to cover

For each person, place a slice of Canadian bacon on each half of a toasted English muffin. Place a poached egg on each ham slice and top with some freshly made hollandaise sauce.

Smoked Salmon Benedict

Substitute two nice slices of smoked salmon for the Canadian bacon in the preceding recipe.

Artichoke Benedict

Instead of the toasted English muffin, place two artichoke bottoms (from a can or jar) on the plate and set a poached egg inside of each. Top with hollandaise and serve with crisp bacon or thin slices of prosciutto.

Fried Eggs For Lunch

Egg and bacon revisited makes a simple, sumptuous hot lunch or supper. Save this for when you find that perfect, beautiful, thin asparagus that is so delicate in texture and flavor.

4 slices pancetta (or other bacon), diced
24 stalks asparagus
8 eggs
8 ounces (225g) butter
Parmesan cheese, grated
salt and pepper to taste

Render the pancetta over medium heat until crisp and golden. Drain on a paper towel. Snap or trim off the ends of the asparagus. (If all you have is thicker asparagus, peel the skin, then slice through the stalks lengthwise to give them a flat side and make them cook quicker.) Lay flat in a pan with salted water. Bring to a boil and cook until just tender, about 5 minutes.

Meanwhile, fry the eggs to desired doneness in the butter. Drain water from asparagus. Drizzle some butter from the eggs over them and give them a toss to coat. Place the asparagus on serving plates. Top with two eggs and sprinkle Parmesan and crisp pancetta over top. Pour over any extra butter.

Serve with buttered toast.

You can also cook asparagus beautifully in the microwave. Sprinkle on a little thyme, add a bay leaf and a little water. Cover and cook two minutes on high. Drain water, remove bay leaf, add a little butter and lemon juice.

 Galley Guru Tip

If adding lemon juice to asparagus, add after it is cooked to prevent the lemon from discoloring it.

Scrambled Eggs Vaudois

For perfect scrambled eggs, you must be a little patient. The fire must be low and you must stir and stir with a gentle hand. Then again, these unique eggs, said to have been favored by the famed composer/actor Noel Coward, are more than just perfect. They have a certain panache. They are elevated to this resplendence by the stunningly simple substitution of vermouth for the usual milk or water. Then add crab or shrimp and serve on toast with a sprinkling of almonds. Not difficult. And not really time consuming. But what a dish.

> 6 eggs
> 2 tablespoons (30ml) butter
> 3 tablespoons (45ml) dry vermouth (Noilly Prat or Martini)
> 6 ounces (170g) crab, fresh or canned,
> or
> 16–20 cooked shrimps
> 2 tablespoons (30ml) sliced almonds

Whisk the eggs with 3 tablespoons of vermouth. Melt butter in nonstick pan over low heat. Tip in the eggs and begin to stir with rubber spatula.

Allow eggs to cook very slowly, eventually building up into the center. As the eggs solidify, push them gently to the center of the pan. Do not overcook. Eggs should still be very runny and glossy. Add the crab meat or shrimps. Stir for just a minute. Eggs should still be fluffy.

Turn out onto plates on top of buttered toast. Top with almonds.

> ### Galley Guru Tip
> You don't need a lot of ingredients or a lot of time to put something delicious on the table.

Quiche Lorraine's Distant Cousin

It is an unqualified triumph of ingenuity that we can have quiches without having to worry about making crust. If you have digestive biscuits (or any good crumbly crackers) in your larder you are ready. Thus you bypass pastry crust, which seems a bit ambitious in a boat, making this mixture of cheese and cream with bacon, crab, or other delights pretty simple to make. It isn't a classic quiche Lorraine, since it has cheese in it, but that having been said, it is very, very good and works hot or cold.

Crust
2 cups (500ml) crumbled digestive biscuits or other suitable crumbly
   crackers
4 tablespoons (60ml) butter, melted
salt and pepper

Filling
2 cups (500ml) grated Gruyere cheese (or substitute any cheese of
   your choice: fontina, cheddar, smoked gouda, et cetera)
1 wineglass cream
3 egg yolks
generous pinch nutmeg
pinch cayenne
½ pound (255g) bacon, cooked crisp
salt and pepper to taste

Preheat oven to medium high. Mix the crust ingredients together in
a 10-inch tart pan and then press them down to form a crust.
Beat the eggs with the cream and nutmeg. Put the grated cheese
into the pie crust and pour over the cream mixture. Season with
salt and pepper. Lay the crispy bacon on top of the pie, pressing
down into the cream. Bake for 25 to 30 minutes. Allow to cool
slightly. Cut in wedges to serve. Serves 4 to 6.

You can use the same recipe but add crab with the bacon or instead of the bacon. Try shrimp and bacon. Or asparagus or corn. Again, you have here a basic recipe for endless variation.

Migas

Migas is a Spanish word that literally means "crumbs." If these are crumbs, let us grab every last one. Actually, the method has a lot in common with croutons. This is a peasant recipe, served all over Spain, which appears reincarnated in Mexico and South America. As with all such dishes, there are probably as many ways to prepare this as there are cooks, and in Mexico the bread is replaced by corn tortillas. The following dish (and its alternative) is the way I learned it in the south of Spain. It is a wonderful way to use up some leftover ingredients.

    1 loaf day-old peasant bread
    2 or 3 cloves of garlic, sliced
    1 chorizo (Spanish sausage), sliced
    1 tablespoon (15ml) paprika (preferably Spanish smoked)
    olive oil
    salt

Break or cut the stale bread in squares and wrap in a damp towel, allowing bread to sit for at least 30 minutes. Sauté the garlic with the chorizo in some olive oil. Add the pimento and the bread cubes, stirring the mixture over medium heat until the bread is golden brown. Add salt to taste. Serve with eggs.

Migas II

1 loaf day-old peasant bread (French bread type)

2 or 3 cloves of garlic, sliced

1 chorizo, cut into thin slices

1 tablespoon (15ml) paprika (preferably Spanish smoked)

3 eggs

1 cup (250ml) milk

large handful leftover grated cheese

olive oil

salt

Preheat oven to medium. Follow previous recipe. Instead of serving Migas alongside the eggs, at this point put the breadcrumbs and sausage mixture into an ovenproof dish. Scramble eggs with the milk, pour over the bread cubes, and sprinkle cheese over the top. Bake in a medium oven for 25 minutes, or until the top is brown and bubbly.

Oeufs en Meurette
Poached Eggs with a Bacon and Red Wine Reduction

From the Burgundy region of France—where some of the world's finest grapes grow in abundance and can be heard, if you listen on the wind, begging to be made into wine—comes that most excellent of beef stews, Boeuf Bourguignonne; the unpretentious masterpiece that is Coq au Vin; and, last but not least, this simple dish of poached eggs with red wine sauce. Simple, yes, but do not think for a moment that it is not also simply divine. The rich perfume of the bacon and the concentrated wine is exquisite. Though little known in America, this is one of the splendid classic dishes of French country cooking. I have used Marigold bouillon here to stand in for the mirepoix of slow-cooked carrots, onion, and celery that would otherwise form the basis of the sauce. It adds subtle flavor, and, as is our wont, cuts a corner or two. Though Marigold bouillon is not very salty, bacon usually is, and you shouldn't need any more salt in the sauce, but please taste to see.

8 eggs
2 shallots or 1 half small onion, minced fine
4 ounces (125g) bacon minced
2 wineglass burgundy or other full bodied red wine
1 wineglass chicken or beef stock (low sodium, please)
1–2 teaspoons Marigold bouillon powder (see * p. 19)
4 ounces (115g) butter
4 thick slices peasant bread
2 cloves garlic, sliced in half lengthwise
1 tablespoon wine vinegar
small handful chopped parsley (fresh or freeze dried)
freshly ground black pepper
salt (if needed)
a few slices extra bacon

For the Sauce Meurette:
Melt about one ounce of the butter in a frying pan over low heat. Add shallots and the bacon. Cook gently without allowing to color, about 10 minutes. Add the stock, the Marigold and the red wine. Continue to cook over low heat until liquid is reduced by half. Just before serving stir in the rest of the butter and add the parsley. Add freshly ground pepper and taste for salt. Add if need be.

For the poached eggs:
Fill a large saucepan about half full with water and bring to a boil with the vinegar. Break each egg separately into a small bowl. Stir the boiling water around clockwise to form a vortex. Add one egg delicately to the center of this boiling water. Let poach 3 to 4

minutes to achieve a soft yolk and tender but firm white. To bring the egg whites together, stir the water around the egg in a circular motion. This will bring the white in around the yolk and make the finished egg more compact. Remove egg with slotted spoon and allow to drain on a plate covered with absorbent paper. Repeat with remaining eggs.

Toast the bread to desired doneness in a toaster or in the oven. Rub the cut garlic over each slice. Place 2 eggs on each slice of the bread and pour over the sauce. Serve immediately with additional slices of cooked bacon on the side.

So You've Caught a Fish

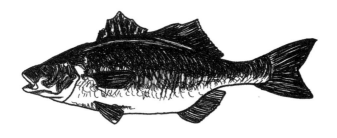

*"In the hands of an able cook, fish can become
an inexhaustible source of perpetual delight."*
—Brillat-Savarin

*Well, the first and unquestionably most succulent way to cook fish is to
roast it whole. This makes pretty light work.*

*Once the fish has been cleaned, there's practically nothing more to
it. The skin and bones add flavor during cooking; they also seal in all the
juices. The flavor and texture of a whole fish cooked like this is perfection.
With little more than some salt and pepper and perhaps a drizzle of olive
oil you have the beginnings of a maritime banquet. The only difficulty
with this recipe will be if you have caught a fish that will not fit into your
pan or small oven.*

*On the other hand, there might be a more compelling reason to resist.
Once, drifting in the translucent sapphire waters of the Bahamas, a friend
and I snagged a barracuda while trolling the line. Oh, it was a handsome
specimen, sleek, long, and exceptionally toothy. This fellow swam
uncomfortably close to our little boat and stared at me, fixing me with his
fishy eye. Perhaps he suspected I was wondering how to prepare him.*

*My reverie was abruptly cut short by my companion. "Poisonous,"
he pointed out. "They feed on the fishes that swim here, who get ciguatera
poisoning from the coral reefs—at least, some of them do. You don't want
to get fish poisoning," he added after a few beats.*

I didn't. Further study has informed me that there is no way to know if your particular prize barracuda is poisonous, unfortunately. Other than asking him. Which probably explains why there are so few barracuda recipes to be found in the cookery section of the Sunday papers.

 # Baked Fish

Cover a baking sheet with foil. Place your fish on the foil. Season the cleaned fish generously with salt and pepper on both sides, rubbing well into the skin. Sprinkle with extra virgin olive oil and a squeeze of lemon juice. Put the pan into a hot (220°C–425°F) oven for about 7 to 8 minutes per inch of thickness.

To serve, sprinkle with a little more olive oil and lemon and some fresh chopped parsley. Present the fish whole and carve it in front of the assembled company, or carve it in the galley and place the filets on a platter. Either way you will have a meal to be proud of.

To De-bone Fish:

Using a fish knife and a fork, slice through the skin down the back of the fish. While holding the fish with the fork, slide the knife against the tiny bones that run along the ridge of the back. Push the bones out into the plate. To loosen the filet, cut through the fish just behind the head until you reach the bone. Now, make an incision through the skin along the center of the top filet with the knife until you run into bone. Continue along the whole length of the fish from the head to the tail. Turn your knife flat and slide it along the bone, separating the flesh from the bone along the length, dividing the top filet in half. Lift the back half up off the bones and lay back on the plate. Lift the front half towards you on the platter, exposing the entire bone. Pull bone from one end and remove. You can then replace the fish pieces to keep the fish whole, or cut off serving size pieces from the filet.

Broiled Whole Fish
with Preserved Lemons

This is a nice way to do a whole fish using the lovely **Moroccan Preserved Lemons** *you have made for just such an occasion. You don't need much of the preserved lemon to flavor a dish. You can, of course, get some nice fish filets and do them the same way. A one-inch-thick fish or filet will take 4–5 minutes on each side in the broiler.*

> 2 small or 1 large fish such as red snapper, yellowtail, grouper, sea
>   bream
> ¼ preserved lemon, sliced into paper-thin slices
> 2–3 tablespoons (30–45ml) Persillade
> 2 tablespoons (30ml) olive oil
> butter for melting
> handful of toasted pine nuts

Cover a broiler pan with aluminum foil. Place your cleaned, dried fish on the foil. Mix the preserved lemon with the **Persillade** and the olive oil. Reserve a little Persillade for the garnish. Spread the lemon mixture on both sides of the fish. Broil 5 minutes on each side.

Melt the butter in a small pan or in the microwave. Pour over the fish and top with a few toasted pine nuts and a little more of the Persillade. Serve immediately.

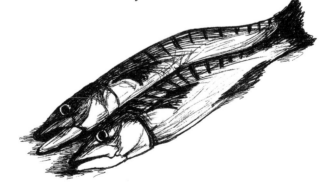

Fennel Crusted Tuna
with Avocado Mango Salsa

Oh, the good life! The balmy days and nights when you can cook and dine on deck. This crunchy, succulent fish is great on the barbecue, but you can do it very well below decks in a pan with a little butter or oil if the mood strikes you.

    4 thick tuna steaks
    4 teaspoons (20ml) fennel seeds
    2 teaspoons (10ml) cumin seeds
    2 teaspoons (10ml) coriander seeds
    1 teaspoon (5ml) ground ginger
    ½ teaspoon (2.5ml) ground nutmeg
    1 teaspoon (5ml) salt
    1 teaspoon (5ml) black pepper

Preheat the grill or barbecue. Roughly grind the whole spices in a mortar and pestle or small grinder or crush with a heavy pan. Mix all spices on a plate or on a flexible cutting board and spread them out. Dip each tuna steak into the spice mixture to coat thoroughly on each side. Cook on hot grill about 3 minutes on each side for medium-rare tuna. Serve with **Avocado Mango Salsa** (see next page).

    Substitute any firm-fleshed fish for this, such as swordfish or mahi mahi.

Avocado Mango Salsa

This pretty salsa is fruity and smooth and very refreshing.

　　1 ripe avocado, peeled and diced
　　1 ripe mango, diced
　　3 spring onions, chopped
　　handful fresh coriander, chopped
　　juice of 1 lime with zest

Combine all ingredients. Spoon a large dollop alongside grilled fish.

Cod in Salsa Verde

This is a simple dish that is prepared in the blink of an eye. Nevertheless, it is a classic way to prepare fish that is often made in Spain with hake (merluza), which is similar to cod. Sea bass also works very well. It is very good with fresh peas, but you can do it with frozen if you haven't got them. (If you haven't got either, leave them out. I would only use canned if my life depended on it.)

4 large pieces cod (or 8 pieces of hake)
2 cloves garlic, minced
large bunch fresh parsley, chopped
12 ounces (340g) clams
4 ounces (115g) fresh peas (or frozen)
1 tablespoon (15ml) flour
1 teaspoon (5ml) Marigold bouillon powder (if substituting,
    see * p. 19)
1 wineglass white wine
olive oil
salt and freshly ground black pepper
lemon wedges

Cook fresh peas 10 minutes in boiling water until tender. (If you have frozen peas, leave out this step.) Cover the bottom of a skillet with olive oil. Add the garlic and 1 tablespoon of the parsley. Sauté a few minutes until the garlic is golden. Add the clams to the pan. Stir in the peas, the flour, 1 glass white wine, Marigold bouillon powder, and mix.

Put the fish in the sauce, cover the pan, and allow to cook on low heat 3 minutes. Turn the fish over, pour spoonfuls of the sauce over the top of the fish. Add another spoonful of parsley, cover and cook 3 minutes more. Taste for salt, add if necessary, and pepper to taste. Serve immediately with lemon wedges and a generous amount more fresh parsley tossed over the top.

Steamed Clams

A bucket of steamers never goes amiss. Here are two ways to do it.

4 dozen cherrystone or other steamer clams
handful fresh parsley, chopped
1 onion, chopped fine
3 cloves garlic, chopped
1 bottle dry white wine
4 ounces (115g) butter
pinch of Marigold bouillon powder
    (see * p. 19 if substituting)
red or black pepper

Wash the clams thoroughly.   Heat
butter in a large saucepan over medium heat and cook garlic and
onion gently until translucent.   Add the wine and the parsley and
cook for 3 minutes. Add the clams and cover the pan for 5 to 10
minutes until the clams open. Discard any clams that do not open,
and remove clams to serving bowls. Boil sauce for a minute. Taste
for seasoning. Add a pinch of Marigold in place of salt and red or
black pepper. Pour sauce over clams. Sprinkle with fresh parsley
and serve hot with French bread.

Beer Steamed Clams

Substitute beer or any nice ale for the wine.

Moules Mariniere ... Mariners Mussels

This is the most classic French or Belgian mussel dish. The Belgians, who are famous for their "french fries," always serve them to accompany their mussels, which dish they call Moules Frites. You can make up a big batch of rosemary roast potatoes to have with these. You can use green onion or leeks instead of or in addition to the shallot.

4½ pounds (2kg) fresh washed (and de-bearded) black mussels

2 cups light, dry white wine or 1 cup dry white vermouth

2 tablespoons (30ml) olive oil

3 minced shallots or 1 small onion, chopped

2 cloves of garlic, finely sliced

1 bay leaf

1 tablespoon (30ml) fresh thyme or pinch dried thyme

1 teaspoon (15ml) Marigold bouillon powder
   (see * p. 19 if substituting)

freshly ground pepper, to taste

6 tablespoons butter

handful fresh parsley, chopped

Rinse the mussels under cold running water. Discard any mussels with broken shells or mussels that will not close. Heat olive oil and 4 tablespoons butter in a large pot over medium heat. Add the shallots, garlic, fresh or powdered thyme, and bay leaf. Cook about 5 minutes. Add the mussels to the pot and give them a good toss. Pour in the white wine. Bring to a boil. Cover and steam over medium-high heat for 5–6 minutes, stirring occasionally, until all the mussels open. Discard any mussels that do not open. Season with Marigold and pepper. Toss in the remaining 2 tablespoons of butter. Sprinkle with the parsley and serve immediately in big bowls with the wine sauce. Serve with plenty of crusty bread.

Sea Urchins

Chef Umberto Vezzoli, * *who runs the very wonderful* **Ristorante Fiore** *in London, is also a keen sailor. He was delighted to hear I was writing* The Galley Guru *and very graciously agreed to contribute a recipe to this book.*

When we were sailing in Greece, we discovered the Island of Kalamos, Porto Leone. Kalamos, Greece is a village that stretches along two bays, the first a long ribbon of pebbled beach, the second more of a natural harbor. The water is marvelously clear and inviting and one cannot help but spend endless hours in those cooling waters. In this small bay there were only three sailing boats.

The Chef, Umberto, was not going to the market this time. He went underwater to scrape the fresh sea urchins from the rocks. Remember that the female urchins (violet color) are the better ones.

Sea Urchins as a Starter

Open the sea urchins with scissors/knife (see below). Place the opened sea urchins on a tray. Serve fresh and eat with a teaspoon. Serve a nice bottle of champagne with it: you are in paradise!

To open the sea urchins :

Hold the sea urchin with the small hole upwards. To protect your hands it is best to use a kitchen towel or even gloves. Put the scissors or knife in the hole, scrape some of the "needles" away with the blade of the knife, and cut the shell of the sea urchin, making sure no pieces of the shell fall inside. Enlarge the cut of the shell enough and finish the opening with your finger till the hole is wide enough to insert a teaspoon and take the coral/pulp out of this delicious sea urchin.

* Chef Umberto Vezzoli, Ristorante Fiore, 33 St. James's Street, London SW1A 1HD, Telephone: +44 20 7930 7100, Fax: +44 20 7930 4070, info@fiore-restaurant.co.uk, www.fiore-restaurant.co.uk

As a "Pasta" Dish

12 ounces (340g) linguine pasta
2.2 pounds (1kg) sea urchins
10 basil leaves
small bunch of parsley
4 tablespoons (60ml) extra virgin olive oil
salt

Wash the parsley and the basil leaves; dry them gently. Chop parsley and basil. Open the sea urchins and take out the pulp with a teaspoon. Place the pulp in a separate bowl. Place a pot with boiling water on the fire and bring the water to the boiling point. Add salt to the water and boil the linguine pasta. In the meantime, take a frying pan and heat the olive oil very gently (just to lukewarm). Add a bit of basil and parsley and the pulp of the sea urchins. (Cook 2 minutes)

Once the pasta is cooked al dente, remove the water, keeping 3 spoons of the boiling pasta water. Place the cooked pasta in the frying pan with the olive oil and the sea urchin pulp. Add 3 spoons of the boiled pasta water, stir gently for 1 minute, take the pan off the fire, and add the rest of the chopped basil & parsley. Mix gently. Serve hot.

Smoked Salmon Cakes
with Wasabi Dill Mayonnaise

In Maryland and all over the Chesapeake they will serve you their famous crab cakes. They are outstanding and we could never get enough of them. Smoked salmon cakes are an unexpected twist and equally delectable. You can use leftover mashed potatoes. Smoked salmon does not improve with cooking, so have the pan nice and hot to brown the potato cakes quickly. The spicy wasabi mayonnaise is the kicker.

    4 cooked potatoes, mashed roughly
    freshly ground white pepper
    2 tablespoons (30ml) mayonnaise
    1 large egg, separated
    3 or 4 spring onions, chopped fine
    1 teaspoon (5ml) Marigold bouillon powder (for subs., see * p. 19)
    1 tablespoon (15ml) butter
    4 ounces (115g) smoked salmon, chopped
    4 thin slices smoked salmon
    small handful fresh dill, chopped
    ¼ cup (60ml) dried breadcrumbs
    2 tablespoons (30ml) vegetable oil, or oil and butter

To mashed potatoes, add mayonnaise, egg yolk, chopped spring onion, and dill. Season with freshly ground pepper and Marigold to taste. Stir chopped smoked salmon lightly into potato mixture. Shape into cakes by placing a layer of potato, a slice of salmon, then covering with another layer of potato.
Beat the egg white in a bowl. Place the breadcrumbs on a plate. Dip the salmon cakes into the egg white and then in the breadcrumbs to make a crust.

    Heat the oil and butter in a pan over medium heat. Fry the salmon cakes until golden. Do not overcook or salmon will be tough. Serve with the **Wasabi Mayonnaise** drizzled over the top.

Wasabi Dill Mayonnaise

4 tablespoons (60ml) mayonnaise

juice of a lime, with a little zest

2 tablespoons (30ml) fresh dill, chopped

1–2 teaspoon (5–10ml) dried wasabi or wasabi paste

Place the mayonnaise in a bowl. Beat together with the powdered wasabi, lime and lime zest, and fresh dill.

Fisherman's Pie

This fish pie takes on extra richness because of its golden sweet potato topping. You can use a mixture of fish if you want to. It requires three cooking pots (sorry) but it will delight your crew and after you put it in the oven you can pretty much forget it until it's ready.

1 pound (about 1/2 kilo) baking potatoes

1 pound (about 1/2 kilo) sweet potatoes

1½ pound (680g) salmon, cod, or other flaky fish

1 medium onion, chopped

4 strips bacon, chopped

1 medium-sized onion

2½ cups (625ml) milk

3 tablespoons (45ml) sherry

4 tablespoons (60ml) flour

6 tablespoons (90ml) butter

2 teaspoons (10ml) Marigold bouillon powder (for subs., see * p. 19)

few gratings fresh nutmeg

liquid aminos seasoning (Marigold, Braggs) to taste

salt and pepper to season

fresh parsley
fresh tarragon

Heat the oven to medium to medium-high heat. Boil the potatoes and the sweet potatoes until soft in salted water. Drain and put through a ricer to mash. Stir in 3 tablespoons of butter. Season with salt, pepper, and Marigold. Stir in a handful of chopped parsley.

Cook the bacon in a skillet until crisp, about 5 minutes. Drain the bacon fat. Add 2 tablespoons of butter. Stir in the onion. Cook until wilted, about 5 minutes. Add the flour and cook a minute or two. Whisk in the milk. Cook over a low heat, stirring all the time, until the sauce has thickened. Add 1 teaspoon Marigold and a few dashes liquid aminos (Marigold, Braggs).

Add the pieces of fish to the sauce. Add the sherry, 1 tablespoon each of tarragon and parsley. Simmer gently about 3 minutes. When fish is opaque, flake with two forks. Taste for seasoning. Pour into the baking dish. Pile the mashed potatoes over the fish and sauce. Use a fork to spread the potatoes out to the edges. Dot with the extra butter. Place in oven for 20–25 minutes, until the top is just starting to brown. Remove from oven and allow to cool 15 minutes before serving.

Use a ricer to mash potatoes. They will come out creamy and wonderful.

Tuna Tonnato

This is a twist on a divine Italian dish. In its new incarnation, it is basically tuna with tuna sauce. It sounds simple and is, but tonnato sauce is a luscious concoction, more than the sum of its parts. Traditionally served at room temperature over tender veal that has been poached gently in the oven and allowed to cool, it is melt-in-your-mouth delicious. Perhaps not surprisingly, the sauce works just as well when served with tuna. We did this tuna on deck one night to rave reviews. It can be served hot or not, your choice.

> 4 tuna steaks
> crushed fennel
> dried basil
> salt and pepper

Season tuna steaks with salt, pepper, and dried basil and crust generously with the fennel spice. Grill them on the barbecue just until rare to medium rare. Do not overcook or tuna will be dry. If you do not have a grill, you can sauté them in a pan or even poach them gently in some vegetable broth.

Serve with: **Tonnato Sauce**

Tonnato Sauce

> 1 (6oz/170g) can Italian style tuna fish in olive oil, drained
> 4 anchovy filets, drained and patted dry
> 1 tablespoon (15ml) capers, drained and rinsed
> 4 cornichons, or one small sweet and sour pickle
> juice of half a lemon
> 1 cup (250ml) mayonnaise
> 1 cup (250 ml) heavy cream
> 3 tablespoons (45ml) chopped flat leaf parsley

In a manual or electric food processor with a metal blade, puree the first 4 ingredients. Add the lemon and mayonnaise and gradually pour in the cream. Stir in parsley.

You might serve with this some string beans tossed in olive oil and garlic and an Italian salad.

Moqueca
Brazilian Fish Stew

"Moqueca is for anytime . . . Its delicate taste and fine aroma
are permanent and eternal pleasures . . . But I prefer them preceded by a
chalice of the best cachaça, away from air-conditioning systems,
cold floors and, if possible, a few meters from a bed
willing to share with me the dreams of an unforgettable afternoon . . . .

—Marcos Alencar

Moqueca is a beautiful mixture, delicate, subtle yet rich, whose flavors are very typical of the influences of many cultures on Brazil. The catch of the day, or any fresh white fish, will be excellent in this recipe. You can do it with only fish or only shrimp or try scallops another time. You will make it again and again. If you can find the red dende oil it is worth carrying some for this, as it adds something, but I have tried it with just olive oil and paprika and it is quite passable that way. As to the cachaça of the quote: It is the Brazilian national drink. More of a sugarcane brandy than a rum, it is the main ingredient in the Caipirinha, a traditional cocktail made with cachaça, limes, and sugar. Try one to sharpen your appetite for the Moqueca.

1 pound (455g) fresh fish in thick slices
8 ounces (225g) fresh shrimp
2 garlic cloves, smashed
1 lemon
1 lime
1 whole onion, chopped
2 firm tomatoes, chopped
pinch cayenne pepper
handful of cilantro (fresh coriander), lightly chopped
1 or 2 green chilis, seeded, and minced finely

1½ (14oz/400ml) cans coconut milk

2 tablespoons (30ml) dende oil

(or 2 tablespoons [30ml] olive oil and 1 teaspoon paprika)

½ cup (125ml) chopped cashew nuts

¼ cup (60ml) chopped peanuts

2 tablespoons (30ml) chopped chive or green onion

cilantro for garnish

1 teaspoon (5ml) Marigold bouillon powder (or to taste)

(if using substitute, see * p. 19)

freshly ground pepper

Make a marinade with lemon, lime, coconut milk, and salt. Marinate the fish and shrimp for 30 minutes. Heat oil on medium heat. Add the onions and paprika if using. Sauté gently until onions are transparent. Add cilantro, chilis, garlic, cashews, and peanuts. Sauté for a minute or two. Add the marinade from the fish and bring the mixture to a simmer. Cook, stirring, until reduced slightly, about 6 minutes. Add Marigold and pepper to taste. Add the fish to the sauce, cover, and cook about 5 minutes until fish is opaque and shrimp are pink. Do not overcook.

Serve sprinkled with fresh chives and cilantro with cooked white rice or use couscous, which is so easy and traditional in Brazil with this dish.

* Dende oil is a red palm oil, originally from Africa, used in Brazilian cooking. You can get it in Brazilian shops. For the African version, see "Where in the World?" page 294.

Saint Pierre Veronique

"Fish, to taste right, must swim three times...
in water,
in butter,
and in wine."

—Polish proverb

I must warn you: this is kind of rich. Veronique refers to a velvety sauce of wine, cream, butter, and grapes and while it is a time-honored (some might say retro) French recipe with chicken, the grape and fish combination (with a very rich sauce indeed) I remember from my Russian roots. The Saint Peter fish, so named because it is said to bear the thumbprint of the fisherman Peter, is also highly prized as one of the most delicate and delicious white fishes in existence. If you do not have it, substitute any other delicate white fish of your choosing. The dish is simple and elegant, the tarragon superb. It really is better if you slice the grapes, but if even that seems too much, I suppose you could just throw them in whole.

> 1 pound (455g) San Pedro (also called John Dory or San Pierre) or any delicate white fish
> 2 wineglasses white burgundy or other dry white wine
> 1 wineglass Noilly Prat or dry vermouth
> 1–2 shallots, chopped
> 1 wineglass double cream, or heavy cream
> (or you can use a can of cream)
> 1 teaspoon (5ml) Marigold bouillon powder
> 1 ounce (28g) chilled butter, cut into small cubes
> salt and freshly ground black and white pepper
> 1 small bunch white grapes, sliced in half
> 2 handfuls fresh tarragon, chopped (or 2 teaspoons dried)
> salt and freshly ground black pepper to taste

Turn oven on to medium hot. Place the white wine and vermouth in a saucepan with the shallots, Marigold bouillon, and half of the tarragon. Reduce to half. Pour in the cream and bring to a boil. Season with salt and pepper. Remove from heat. Season the fish with salt and pepper. Place the fish in a baking dish. Sprinkle over the halved grapes. Pour the sauce over to coat, dot with pieces of butter, and sprinkle with the remaining tarragon. Taste for seasoning. Cover baking dish with foil.

Bake in a medium hot oven for 15 minutes. Remove foil and allow to bake 5–10 minutes more. Fish should just flake when tested with a fork.

Perfect Pan Fried Grouper
. . . or any other fish, for that matter

The fish is caught, cleaned, and fileted and you are ready to enjoy the catch of the day. What better way than a simple pan fry, whisked from galley to table in the time it takes to find your shaker of salt and gulp down that first ice-cold Margarita.

   4 grouper filets
   2 tablespoons (30ml) olive oil
   4 tablespoons (60ml) butter
   flour for dusting (optional)
   1–2 lemons or limes
   handful chopped parsley
   salt and freshly ground pepper

Season the fish generously on both sides with salt and pepper. If you wish, you can dust both sides lightly with flour, shaking off the excess. This will give a slightly firmer result to the outside of the fish and is nice but not at all necessary. Melt the butter in the olive oil in a hot skillet until the butter is just foaming. Immediately add the seasoned fish. Cook for about 3 minutes on each side (depending on the thickness of the fish) until the fish just turns white and loses its transparency, but do not overcook. Squeeze some lemon/lime over. Toss a handful of chopped parsley into the pan. Spoon over the juices once to coat the fish and serve immediately with more lemon or lime wedges.

Tequila Shrimp

These shrimp are a favorite any time. They couldn't be more simple. The tequila makes them delectable.

24 jumbo shrimp, peeled
½ cup (125ml) tequila
juice of 1 lime
a few sprinkles of cayenne pepper
pinch of salt
butter for sautéeing

Season the shrimp with salt and cayenne pepper to taste. Marinate in the tequila and juice of a lime for a half hour. Melt some butter in a large frying pan. Add the shrimp and cook for a minute or two on each side, until the shrimp turn a nice bright pink color. These shrimp do not take long to cook. Be careful not to overdo them or they will become rubbery. Serve with plain rice or any rice pilaf.

Shrimp and Grits

Grits vs. Polenta

Grits and polenta are pretty similar, coming from corn, though polenta, which comes from Italy, is yellow and fine, while grits, which come from the American south, are white and bigger. Other than the method of processing, they are interchangeable and a great alternative to other starches. Both are quick cooking; both are glorified with the addition of milk, cream, or cheese. They can substitute for pasta or mashed potatoes or rice.

You could serve these cheesy grits on their own, with eggs, and the shrimp mixture with pasta or over couscous on another day. The beauty is that these recipes are flexible. Use whatever herbs you might like on the day. You can use soymilk to add extra protein to the grits instead of regular milk. They come out equally creamy and just a little bit more nutritious than if you had used dairy milk.

For the Grits

2 cups (500ml) grits (or polenta)

4 cups (1 liter) water, milk, or soymilk (or half soymilk and half water)

2 tablespoons (30ml) butter

2 teaspoons (10ml) Marigold bouillon powder (see * p. 19)

1 cup (250ml) shredded cheddar cheese or soy cheddar (you can vary this with any melting cheese: try Fontina or Havarti)

salt and pepper to taste

In a large saucepan, bring the water to a boil with the Marigold bouillon. Slowly whisk in the grits and cook over moderate heat, stirring frequently with a wooden spoon or whisk until grits are soft, smooth, and very thick, about 15 minutes. Add 2 tablespoons butter. Remove from heat and stir in the cheese. Taste for seasoning. Cover and keep warm.

For the Shrimp

1 pound (455g) shelled and deveined large shrimp

2 tablespoons (30ml) olive oil

2 tablespoons (30ml)butter

1–2 jalapeños, chopped (or ½–1 teaspoon (2.5–5ml) red pepper
flakes)

½ teaspoon (2.5ml) smoked paprika

1 bay leaf

6 garlic cloves

1 wineglass white wine

1 tablespoon (15ml) chopped parsley or basil

Season the shrimp with salt and pepper. In a large skillet, melt
the 2 tablespoons butter in 2 tablespoons olive oil over medium-
high heat. Sauté the garlic, bay leaf, and chopped jalapeño (or red
pepper flakes) until garlic just begins to turn golden. Immediately
add the shrimp and paprika, and cook until cooked through, about
2 to 3 minutes. Do not overcook. Remove the shrimp from the pan.
Add wine and boil until wine has reduced by half. Discard bay leaf,
return the shrimp to the pan. Heat shrimp through. Pour shrimp
over grits and serve sprinkled with parsley.

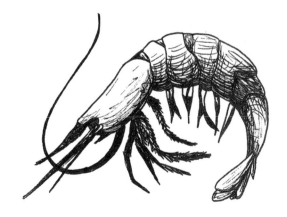

Crab Mornay

In the days before refrigeration, meat, poultry, fish, and seafood didn't last long. More than a few diners didn't last too long either, given that sauces and gravies were actually used to mask the flavor of tainted foods. Though such an idea would be abhorrent today, you can't beat some of those sauces. Put this one under the heading of comfort food and enjoy with the freshest of seafood.

1 bunch green onions, chopped

3 tablespoons (45ml) butter

2 tablespoons (30ml) all-purpose flour

1 teaspoon (5ml) dry mustard

1 cup (250ml) heavy cream

2 cups (500ml) shredded Swiss cheese

1 wineglass dry sherry or dry white wine

pinch of nutmeg

2 teaspoon (10ml) Worcestershire sauce

salt, pepper, cayenne pepper to taste

1 pound (455g) crab meat

2 tablespoons (30ml) Parmesan cheese, grated

In medium saucepan, sauté green onions in butter until tender. Stir in flour and dry mustard, allowing to cook about 3 minutes to get the raw taste out of the flour. Add wine, stirring until sauce is smooth. Add cream, Worcestershire, and seasonings. Add cheese, stir until cheese is melted. Be careful not to scorch. Gently stir in crab meat. Heat thoroughly, sprinkle with Parmesan, and serve on toast or over cooked pasta or rice.

Crab Imperial

You can make a great gratin out of this Chesapeake specialty by putting it in the oven topped with breadcrumbs and dotted with butter.

- 1 cup (250ml) breadcrumbs or cracker crumbs
- 2 tablespoons (30ml) butter
- 2 tablespoons (30ml) finely chopped mixed fresh herbs (or 1 teaspoon [5ml] dried)
- 2 tablespoons (30ml) Parmesan, grated

Pour **Crab Mornay** into an ovenproof dish, reserving the Parmesan. Sprinkle with the breadcrumbs mixed with the herbs. Dot with butter and top with Parmesan. Put in a medium hot oven for 5–7 minutes, or until bubbly and golden.

Salmon Hash à la Russe

Smoked salmon and sour cream turn this "hash" into a dish so elegant and so Russian you could imagine yourself floating down Mother Volga making your way out to sea. It is easy to keep little unopened packets of smoked salmon in the refrigerator. Or if your fridge has very recently gone on strike, what a fine time to throw this together to use up all these toothsome ingredients.

4 medium potatoes, boiled in their skins 15 minutes

1 large onion, minced fine

4 tablespoons (60ml) olive oil

¾ pound (340g) cooked fresh or canned salmon

¾ pound (340g) smoked salmon

1 cup (250ml) sour cream

1–2 tablespoons (15–30ml) good Dijon mustard

1–2 teaspoons (5-10ml) fresh dill, chopped, or freeze-dried dill

1 teaspoon (5ml) Marigold bouillon powder
    (if using a substitute, see * p. 19)

freshly ground pepper

2 or 3 scallions, chopped fine

finely chopped dill pickle

Chop or slice the smoked salmon into thin strips. Stir it into the sour cream along with a teaspoon of the dill. Season to taste with a little Marigold and pepper. Set aside. In a large bowl, flake the fresh salmon. Set aside. Peel still-warm potatoes and shred them. In a skillet, sauté onion in oil over medium high heat until translucent, 3 to 5 minutes. Season with a little Marigold and pepper. Add potatoes. Season again. Fry until potatoes are very brown and crusty on the bottom. Add flaked fresh salmon, the mustard, and the rest of the dill. Cook for 3 minutes or until salmon is just opaque. Check for seasoning.

To serve, tip the potato mixture out onto the plate with the crusty side up. Spread with the smoked salmon sour cream as if you were frosting a cake, or set a generous dollop of it on the side. Sprinkle the top with chopped pickle, scallions, and some more dill and freshly ground black pepper.

Of course, a Russki might top this with a spoonful of caviar. Great caviar comes from America now and it is very affordable. If you happen to have some of any variety in your stores, don't let it go to waste. Now is the time to use it.

Serve with buttered toast or dark rye bread (and a shot of vodka, if you are so inclined).

Langostinos San Pedro

I made this in the lovely Puerto José Banus in the south of Spain and was asked for it evermore. Even St. Peter might have a hard time thinking of any low cholesterol way to prepare this dish. Frankly, we are so self-disciplined on a regular basis that we deserve to allow ourselves the occasional slide down the slippery slope. (Apart from cooking, I am known for my faultless logic.)

Pernod (or Pastis), a strongly anise flavored liquor the French are very fond of, is also an ingredient in traditional bouillabaisse. It complements fish sautéed, grilled, or battered, so is nice to have around. If you are unfamiliar with it, it is vaguely related to absinthe and is drunk as an aperitif—never on its own—always with a bit of water and (optional) ice. The water turns the clear liquid a rather pretty milky yellow. Exercise a modicum of care, though, for this unassuming little drink can turn you bowsprit to stern before long.

There are a few ingredients to assemble, but it is not at all difficult. The unusual combination of the curry powder and the anise of the Pernod works. Try it and see.

4 tablespoons (60ml) butter

2 tablespoons (30ml) flour

24 large prawns, shelled and deveined

2 cloves garlic, minced

2 shallots or 1 small onion, finely minced

1 cup (250ml) chicken or vegetable stock

1 glass dry white wine

¼ wineglass Pernod

1 teaspoon Marigold bouillon powder (if substituting, see * p. 19)

1 teaspoon (5ml) dried tarragon (rubbed between fingers)

½ teaspoon (2.5ml) dried thyme

1 teaspoon (5ml) curry powder

1 bay leaf

pinch nutmeg

½ cup (125ml) heavy cream (or 1 small can Nestlé cream)

1/2 wineglass good quality cognac

salt and freshly ground pepper

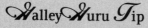

Assemble all your ingredients on flexible plastic cutting boards that you can stack on top of each other. If you need to, you can put these in the sink with the one you need first on top.

Season prawns with salt and pepper. Put in a bowl to marinate with the Pernod for 10–15 minutes. In a large skillet, melt 2 tablespoons of the butter. Cook shallots or onions over high heat for 3 minutes. Add garlic and prawns, reserving Pernod. Continue cooking over high heat just to color prawns, about 1 minute on each side. Pour the reserved Pernod over the prawns. Remove from pan and set aside.

Add the rest of the butter and the flour to the pan. Stir a minute or two over medium heat. Add the chicken stock and the wine. Raise the heat slightly and cook, stirring, until the resultant sauce is thick and smooth. Season to taste with salt and pepper. Add the curry powder, all the spices, and the Marigold, stirring all the while. Continue to cook over medium heat 5 minutes.

Return the prawns to the skillet, cover, and simmer slowly for 3–5 minutes or until prawns are cooked through. Stir in the cream. The sauce will thicken immediately. A minute before serving, remove the bay leaf and stir in the cognac. Taste for seasoning. Add salt if necessary and lots of freshly ground pepper.

Serve with **Pilaf** and perhaps **Baked Mushrooms**. Method works equally well with lobster or scallops or any combination of the three.

Stuffed Lobster

This is a splendid lobster dish. So good and so very pretty. A green salad and baked potato makes it a feast! I have apportioned half a lobster per person, but those with heartier appetites may want more.

If you have live lobsters, cook them according to approved method. Then split and clean them. Julia Child said that cooking lobsters was not for the squeamish or faint hearted. Julia, of course, was neither—as many chefs are not. (I refer you to the Alice B. Toklas Cookbook *chapter* "Murder in the Kitchen".*)*

On the other hand, if you have the option to buy lobsters already cooked, cleaned, and split, this would solve the problem.

2 large lobsters, split in half
4 ounces (50g) finely chopped fresh parsley
4 ounces (50g) seasoned bread crumbs
2 tablespoons (25g) melted butter
2 tablespoons good quality cognac
juice of half a lemon

Let the lobsters cool. Cut the flesh away from the shell and cut these halves in half again to make them easier to eat. Replace the flesh in the shells. Lay the split lobsters on a baking tray.

Mix the melted butter, lemon juice and cognac into the bread crumb and parsley, making a bright green, crumbly stuffing. Firmly press into the lobsters' cavities, and slightly overlap the edge of the meat. Dot the remaining meat with extra butter.

Squeeze on some more lemon and pop under the broiler for 5 to 7 minutes. The lobsters are beautiful in their bright red shells with green stuffing.

Serve with a lemon wedge and lobster picks, if available.

Mainly Chicken

"A chicken—its shining skin crisp, its flesh soft and buttery—is a splendid thing to bring to the table."

—Nigel Slater, *Real Cooking*

Pouched in Mystery

Appealing as the thought might be, you can't leave all the pots and pans at home. There is a way, however, that you can reduce the unnecessary cargo and leave more room for the things you love. Cooking in a pouch wins hands down as the perfect way to prepare food in a galley.

The term en papillote refers to the French word for butterfly because the parchment packet (the papillote) used for wrapping up the food looks like a butterfly or a heart, depending on your point of view. By any name, cooking in a sealed packet is elegant yet simple, as fast as ever a fast food could be, yet healthful. Each element locked inside the packet retains its integrity yet becomes extra succulent because this method forces the food's own juices back into itself as it steams. Dinner is served locked inside its puffed-up little parcel, the mystery of whose contents is revealed with a satisfying little puff of steam that escapes when it is unsealed at the table.

You can get foil bags that make this whole thing very easy. But if you don't have them or can't find them, here are the simple directions to make a traditional parchment paper packet:

To make a parchment paper papillote, begin with one rectangle of parchment paper (measure about 18 inches long for each portion). Fold the paper in half. Starting at one end of the fold, cut a point, then cut around into as wide a semicircle as possible, ending at the opposite end of the fold with a rounded point. When opened out, the paper will resemble a heart. Lay the paper flat and place the food to be cooked on one side of the heart, season and cover with vegetables, wine or sauces. Fold the paper over the food, making a packet by sealing with a series of overlapping folds. If this seems daunting to you, you can also make a quick packet using a straight piece of foil instead of parchment paper.

Place your sealed food parcel onto a baking tray. Put it in the oven for the required number of minutes and serve the packet directly from the oven onto the dish. The heat will make the pouch puff up and then you or your dinner companions cut into it, allowing the steam to escape and discovering a beautifully cooked meal inside. Every time. After a delicious dinner, you have but to throw away the cooking utensil and the serving dish (your pouch). Beats working for a living.

This method works equally well with fish or chicken breasts, which are delicate and cook quickly, but sometimes it is used for longer cooking of meats.

Basic Papillote Method

Coat your fish or chicken breast with oil, then season with salt and pepper. Slice whatever vegetables you are using into batons or julienne. The trick here is to make the pieces as uniform as possible so that they will cook at the same time. You can also use artichoke hearts, olives, sun-dried tomatoes, or mushrooms, all from a bottle or can. The pouch is very forgiving. It will all work.

Place the fish (or chicken) on the paper, cover with a nice mound of vegetables, and add a generous amount of fresh herbs and or spices. Sprinkle wine or pre-prepared sauce over the top and seal the packet. Place on a baking sheet in a moderately hot oven. Fish will take 10–12 minutes, chicken 20–25 minutes.

Chicken Marco Polo

I adapted this from one of my mother's recipes. She does a great deal of entertaining and has a busy life, so she comes up with many lovely and effortless meals. You will enjoy an aromatic Asian fusion sort of poached chicken with no clean-up.

4 skinless chicken breasts

4 slices of prosciutto (cured ham)

4 tablespoons (60ml) soy sauce

24 stalks tender, thin asparagus

2 large red bell peppers, sliced into thin strips

glass of dry vermouth

poultry seasoning, to taste

1 teaspoon (5ml) shredded ginger or pinch of dried ginger

4 cloves garlic, minced

¼ cup (60ml) olive oil

1 teaspoon (5ml) Marigold bouillon powder (if substituting,
   see * p. 19)

freshly ground pepper

Preheat the oven to medium hot. In a small pan, sauté the garlic with the ginger in the oil for a few minutes. Season the chicken breasts well with poultry seasoning, Marigold, and pepper. Rub with soy sauce. Snap off or cut off the asparagus stems. Place a bed of asparagus on the middle of an individually prepared parchment paper or aluminum foil. Layer the prosciutto next, then the chicken breasts over. Pour over the olive oil, along with the sautéed garlic and ginger. Cover with thin strips of red pepper. Dust again with Marigold (be careful, prosciutto is salty) and freshly ground pepper. Sprinkle over a nice amount of vermouth for each packet. Tightly seal each papillote and place it on a baking sheet.

Bake in a hot oven for 25–30 minutes or until pouch is puffed and brown.

Orange Blossom Chicken

This Pan-Asian chicken owes its Oriental touch to wonderful, fragrant, five-spice powder. The potatoes will, if they are cut thinly, cook at the same time as everything else, thanks to the high heat inside the pouch.

4 chicken breasts

handful of green beans

1 large carrot, sliced into fine strips

1 baking potato, peeled and sliced into fine strips

1 orange, peeled and cut into segments

1 teaspoon (5ml) Chinese 5-spice powder

3 tablespoons (45ml) soy sauce

hot red pepper flakes, to taste

2 tablespoons (30g) butter

2 cloves garlic, chopped

2 tablespoons (30ml) honey

1 glass medium (or sweet) sherry

Preheat the oven to medium hot. Season the chicken by rubbing with soy sauce and 5-spice powder. Cook the garlic in a little pan with butter for a couple of minutes. Place a bed of potato, carrot, and green beans in pre-prepared paper or foil. Lay the chicken over vegetables and top with the orange segments. Pour the butter and garlic over the top. Drizzle with honey, a little hot red pepper, and a nice amount of sherry. Tightly seal the papillote and place it on a baking sheet. Bake in a hot oven for 25–30 minutes or until pouch is puffed and brown.

Kleftiko

Lamb in a Pouch, Thieves Style

Kleftiko was the first Greek dish I tried soon after we docked in Piraeus, the port of Athens. That Kleftiko was delicious. I enjoyed it in tavernas in Corfu (Kerkira) and all over the Greek islands. It is very popular and I have heard the locals of more than one place lay claim to its origins. Kleftiko is lamb, traditionally baked in paper, redolent of garlic and cinnamon, fragrant herbs and wine, cooked long and slow until it is so tender it is melting softly into its juices.

The method of cooking is thought to have been invented by a band of anti-heroes, the Klefts, whose name translates literally as thieves, although they are reputed to have been heroes for fighting the Turks during the Ottoman occupation. Whatever side of the law they were on, these fellows could evidently cook a mean stew. Their idea, to carefully seal their food inside paper to prevent any smells from escaping and thereby giving away their whereabouts, indicated method in their madness. Thus the intrepid outlaws made enterprising chefs. Though the history surrounding the Klefts is a bit murky, their exploits are renowned, for they gave their name to this dish as well as any kleptomaniacs amongst us.

Today, the parchment paper is often dispensed with and Kleftiko's ingredients go to the oven in a casserole dish covered tightly with foil, but the original method still works beautifully. The long, slow cooking is all done in the oven, it doesn't require tending or turning, and you can make a choice as to which method you will use to prepare this. Either method is ideal for producing big flavors from a little galley.

2.2 pounds (1kg) boneless lamb, cut into 4 serving pieces
¼ cup (60ml) olive oil
2 large onions, chopped
4–6 spring onions, sliced
1 carrot, chopped

4 garlic cloves, minced

4 bay leaves

2 sprigs fresh rosemary, cut into 4 pieces

2 teaspoons (10ml) cinnamon

1 glass white wine

1 teaspoon (5ml) Marigold bouillon powder (if substituting, see * p. 19)

1 medium can tomatoes, chopped

2 teaspoon (10ml) oregano

salt and pepper

Preheat the oven to medium high. Season the lamb with salt and pepper. Heat the olive oil in a large pan and brown the meat on all sides over high heat. Add the onions and cook until soft. Add the garlic and cook 2–3 minutes.

Cut 4 large sheets of foil or parchment paper. Distribute the lamb pieces, then distribute the tomatoes, carrot, and herbs evenly among them. Pour the wine over. Season with Marigold, salt, and pepper. Seal each pouch completely. If there is any doubt that your pouch will survive the time in the oven without bursting at the seams, cut a second piece of foil and rewrap the entire parcel.

Place the pouches in a shallow pan and bake for 2½ hours. Meat should be meltingly soft.

Sometimes you find Kleftiko with a slice of feta cheese or Greek kefalotiri on top of the lamb to cook with it. This is also very delicious and if you have the cheese, by all means, cut a thick slice and lay it on top before you seal your packet.

Chicken Sautéed in Marsala Wine

One of the pleasant surprises you may meet when shopping in foreign markets, is chicken. Often the chicken you find in foreign ports will be the best you have ever tasted. That is because our "civilized" chickens are raised in an uncivilized manner. They are pumped full of hormones, force-fed, and expected to live their entire lives literally on top of each other in batteries until the moment they are slaughtered, wrapped in plastic, and sent to the supermarket. Often, the simpler life we hope to encounter when we are cruising means that foods are raised the old-fashioned way, the way that some farmers are turning back to, now that we are realizing that our food tastes better and is better for us when it is treated with care and respect. A chicken allowed to roam around in freedom has great taste and bears little resemblance to his impoverished cousins.

Chicken lends itself to so many different ways of cooking, most of which are easy to accomplish. A chicken sauté, done in only one pan, makes wonderful eating. If you get a whole chicken, nothing could be easier than smearing it full of butter and garlic, perhaps putting some herbs under the skin, and roasting it in the oven. Boneless, skinless chicken breasts can do just about anything veal can do for much less cost and are even more tender than veal if cooked quickly as a schnitzel or sliced for a quick stir-fry.

This beautiful chicken sauté is accomplished in one pan and is rich and savory. It has all of the character of coq au vin yet is much simpler to prepare. The basil and tarragon both have licorice and anise overtones and complement each other. Thighs are a much more succulent part of the chicken than breasts and stand up to this kind of cooking very well. The Marsala wine is the pièce de résistance in the sauce, its complexity giving the sense of having cooked all day.

1 large onion, chopped
3 garlic cloves, minced
olive oil (to coat pan)

3 tablespoons (45ml) butter

4–6 chicken thighs (depending on the size)

1 pound (about ½ kilo) mushrooms, sliced (crimini or sliced
  portobello are nice)

1 wineglass Marsala

1 wineglass chicken broth

½ cup (125ml) heavy cream

few fresh basil leaves, torn

few leaves from fresh tarragon, chopped (about 1 tablespoon)

salt and freshly ground black pepper

Season the chicken pieces with salt and pepper. In a large skillet heat the butter in the oil. Fry the chicken, over medium heat, skin side down. Allow to cook until the skin is nice and golden, about 10–12 minutes. Do not disturb chicken during this process. The skin will get lovely and crusty.

Turn the chicken pieces and cook, covered, until the chicken is done and the other side is golden, about 10 minutes. Remove chicken from the pan. Pour out any excess fat from the pan, leaving about 3 tablespoons.

Add the onions. Turn heat to medium low and cook until onions are soft and turning apple color. This process, which will take about 15 minutes, will give a sweet caramelization to the onions. Do not allow onions to burn. Add the mushrooms and garlic together, and season with salt and pepper.

Raise heat to high and sauté 4–5 minutes until mushrooms begin to color. Pour the Marsala into the pan. Cook over high heat, scraping up all the bits from the bottom of the pan, about 3 minutes. Stir in the chicken broth and let the sauce reduce and thicken a bit. Lower heat again. Pour in the cream, add the fresh basil and tarragon, and stir.

Put the chicken pieces back into the pan to heat through in the sauce. Taste for seasoning.

Parmesan Chicken Two Ways

This is a wonderful crispy pan-fried chicken breast, kind of a schnitzel. You only need the two chicken breasts to serve four. You need a bit of calm weather to manage the breading technique, but it is otherwise simple. As with most of these recipes, the measures needn't be precise at all. You can make your own breadcrumbs by putting stale bread into your food processor and giving it a good whiz. Serve sprinkled with **Persillade**, *or top with* **Salsa Verde**.

2 whole chicken breasts
flour to dust
1 cup (250ml) panko or other large crumb breadcrumbs
⅓ cup (85ml) Parmesan cheese, grated
1 egg
salt and pepper to taste
4 tablespoons (60ml) butter
½ cup (125ml) pine nuts, lightly toasted in a pan

Beat the egg in a soup plate or other flat bowl. Season with salt and pepper. Set out another bowl with the breadcrumbs and the Parmesan cheese mixed together. Place the chicken breasts on a large cutting board (flexible is best). Butterfly the chicken by holding your hand on the top of the breast and slicing evenly through the entire breast. Then cut in two, so that you have four cutlets. Salt and pepper the cutlets. Dust with flour to coat lightly but evenly on both sides. Dip the cutlets first into the beaten egg. Let the excess run off and then dip them in the crumbs to coat well.

Melt the butter over medium heat in a large frying pan. When it is foaming, add the chicken pieces. Cook until golden brown on one side, about 3–4 minutes. Flip the cutlets over. Turn down heat slightly and continue to cook them until they are just cooked, 2–3 minutes. Do not overcook the chicken. It will continue to cook in the pan even after the fire is turned off. Sprinkle with **Persillade** or serve with a generous drizzle of **Salsa Verde** over the chicken. Top with a few toasted nuts.

Persillade

Persillade (Pear-see-yade) takes its name from persil, which is French for parsley. It is a simple mixture of parsley chopped finely with a lot of chopped garlic. It packs a punch, enhances many dishes—meats, fish, chicken—and can be thrown on a plain chop or piece of fish at the end of cooking to lift it out of the ordinary.

You can vary it by adding to or substituting other herbs such as basil or tarragon for the parsley. Mixed with an equal amount of dried or fresh breadcrumbs, persillade makes a superb crust for roasted lamb or chops. If you add lemon and/or orange zest to your persillade you get gremolata, a traditional Italian garnish for osso bucco (braised beef or lamb shanks) that is stirred into the sauce during the last few minutes of cooking.

I have also included a recipe for salsa verde that includes anchovy and is done in melted butter and poured over grilled or breaded fish or chicken as a sauce. Salsa verde works as a sort of deconstructed pesto sauce: you simply toss a few pine or other nuts over the sauce to serve.

½ **bunch of parsley, about ½ cup**
2 **garlic cloves**
salt and pepper

Chop parsley by hand or put in a food processor and whiz it. Press garlic and add to parsley. Season with salt and pepper.

Salsa Verde

2–3 anchovies
4 ounces (115g) butter
1 bunch cilantro (fresh coriander) or flat leaf parsley
2 handfuls fresh basil
1 bunch chives
4 garlic cloves, minced
juice and zest of a lemon

Chop the fresh herbs finely with the garlic. Melt the butter in a small saucepan. Add the anchovies. Cook, stirring, over medium low heat to melt anchovies into the butter. Add the herbs and garlic mixture. Cook 3–4 minutes until the garlic is transparent. Add the lemon juice and zest. Cook, stirring another minute or two.

Chicken Mole Poblano (the Fast Version)

"Everything I eat should contain either garlic or chocolate, but rarely both." —**Anonymous**

Mole (pronounced mo-lay) poblano is one of those dishes that does indeed contain both, and what a good idea it is too! Normally this dish is a huge production number in Mexico, requiring endless hours of toasting and stirring and pounding of ingredients in a molcajete (a Mexican mortar and pestle made of lava rock), after which the resulting sauce of many different roasted peppers and spices is thickened with flour tortillas and made rich with the addition of chocolate. It is still prepared in the old way in the Puebla region of Mexico and is traditionally found adorning a turkey for holiday celebrations. Don't be daunted by all the ingredients here (they aren't even half of the original); this is a fairly quick dish to make, mostly a matter of assembly, and the result is exceptional.

4 boneless chicken breasts or thighs, butterflied (sliced into two
    thinner pieces) and pounded thin

2 tablespoons (30ml) butter

4 tablespoons (60ml) olive or peanut oil

1 onion, chopped

4 cloves garlic, minced

4 tablespoons (60ml) chopped almonds or cashews

1 teaspoon (5ml) cinnamon

½ teaspoon (2.5ml) allspice

½ teaspoon (2.5ml) anise seeds, crushed

pinch oregano

1 teaspoon (5ml) cumin

1 teaspoon (5ml) coriander

2 teaspoon (10ml) Mexican chili powder

pinch hot red pepper flakes

1 bottle beer

1¼ cup (310ml) chicken broth

2 tablespoons (30ml) peanut butter

2 tablespoons (30ml) sesame tahini (or 4 tablespoons sesame seeds)

3 tablespoons (45ml) raisins

1 ounce (28g) unsweetened chocolate

salt and pepper

Salt and pepper the chicken breasts. Sauté them in butter and oil
in a large skillet until golden. Remove from pan. Add onion to pan,
sauté over medium heat until onion begins to caramelize. (Do not
let onion burn; it should soften and turn apple color.) Add garlic and
spices with the almonds, allowing to cook gently a few minutes. Add
the beer and chicken broth, turn up heat, and reduce to half, scraping
up all the bits from the bottom of the pan. Pour this mixture into a
blender. Add peanut butter, tahini, and raisins. Blend until smooth.
Return sauce to pan over low heat. Add chocolate and stir, allowing
to melt into the sauce. Taste for seasoning. Return the chicken to the
pan and gently reheat in the sauce.

Poulet Sauce Moutarde au Pernod

*Enter the great Pernod doing one of the two things it does best. As
an aperitif, Pernod is a seductive drink, possibly even hypnotic, for it
bears a similarity, in taste anyway, to its scandalous relative, absinthe.
In cooking, Pernod snuggles a fish in its soft anise warmth, adds an
indefinable but imperative note to a classic bouillabaisse, and completely
redefines the quotidian chicken. With few ingredients a masterpiece
can be wrought. If you haven't the shallots, you can use a bit of very
finely chopped onion, a clove of pressed garlic, or leave it out altogether.
Tarragon is a natural companion to Pernod, so try to use fresh tarragon in
this dish.*

> 4 boneless skinless chicken breasts
> 3 tablespoons (45ml) butter
> 2 shallots, finely chopped
> 1 cup (250ml) cream
> 1–2 teaspoons (5–10ml) Marigold bouillon powder to taste
>   (if substituting, see * p. 19)
> Dijon mustard
> ¼ wineglass Pernod (or to taste)
> handful fresh tarragon, chopped (or 1 teaspoon dried tarragon)
> salt and freshly ground pepper

Pound the chicken breasts to flatten a little with a heavy pan or
mallet. Salt and pepper them on both sides. Brown chicken pieces
in 2 tablespoons butter. Lower heat and cook for 5 minutes on each
side until done. When cooked, keep warm, put into foil in a low
oven or a hot covered dish. Add shallots with 1 tablespoon butter to
the pan. Cook for a minute or two. Add cream to the pan, stirring
to scrape up the bits at the bottom. Into this put a large dollop of
Dijon mustard, stir in the Marigold, about two teaspoons of the
chopped tarragon (if using dried tarragon, rub it between your
fingers to release the oils), and finally, finish with a good splash of

232   GALLEY GURU

Pernod. Cook gently until this sauce has mixed thoroughly. Taste for seasoning, adding a bit of salt if necessary and loads of freshly ground pepper. Return chicken to the pan just to coat with the hot sauce.

Serve sprinkled with fresh chopped tarragon.

Roasted Chicken with Garlic Confit

*This is beyond fantastic and simple if you have **Garlic Confit** on hand, which, of course, you do.*

a dozen or so garlic cloves from Garlic Confit with a little of
    the garlic oil
1 large chicken, quartered
1 tablespoon (15ml) butter, softened
salt and freshly ground pepper

Preheat oven to high. Rub chicken pieces all over with butter and a tablespoon of garlic oil. Sprinkle all over with salt and pepper. Arrange chicken, skin side up, in a shallow baking pan and roast 20 minutes. Put garlic into a small bowl along with 1 tablespoon garlic oil, and mash well with a fork. Spread mashed garlic over the skin of roasted chicken, then return chicken to oven and roast until skin is crisp, about 5 minutes.

Serve with potato purée (boiled potatoes put through a ricer) or rice pilaf or pasta that you have tossed with a little garlic confit.

Beer Can Chicken

He looks quite handsome there, impaled (sorry) upon the beer can, but not half as handsome as he tastes as the malty liquid slowly and steadily infuses this fellow with flavor. For the most tender, succulent roast chicken, try it this way on the barbecue. It is awfully easy, and quite good fun. Beer has a special affinity with chicken (as it does with people), so it doesn't take much imagination to see why this has become a near classic recipe amongst barbecue aficionados.

You open a can of beer (making sure to drink some), enhance the remains with a sprinkling of well chosen seasonings, and slide the open cavity of a chicken—or his rear end, to be quite graphic—over the can of beer. (This recipe is not for the squeamish). You then set the thus vertical bird onto a metal pie plate, splaying out his legs and sort of wedging them against the plate's sides like a tripod, so that he can stand upright without tipping over. You put the whole thing right onto the grill. The beer can acts as a self-basting tool as well as a stand for your plump little bird. The flesh turns out unusually moist and the skin becomes excellently browned and exceptionally crispy this way. The pie plate catches all the juices, thereby saving them to pour over the cooked chicken instead of letting them run off and be lost in the coals. Barbecue is a fine way to cook on board with everybody up on deck lolling about under the shade of the bimini, appetites sharp, sipping sundowners while the balmy breezes blow. Pretty hard to beat this, you might think, as you watch another perfect sun settle into the silent embrace of the sea.

    1 large whole roasting chicken, about 5 pounds
    olive oil
    3 tablespoons (45ml) dry spice rub
    1 12-oz can of beer at room temperature

Remove the neck and giblets from chicken. Rinse inside and out and pat dry. Rub oil all over the chicken skin. Next, smear 2 tablespoons of the dry rub all over the chicken.

Open the beer. Pour out (heaven forefend; drink it!) about ¼ cup and make a couple of extra holes in the top of the can with a can opener. Put the remaining dry rub right into the can. Settle the chicken down on top of the can and then stand it on a metal pie plate. Put this in the center of the grill over indirect medium heat. Cover the grill and cook the chicken for 1¼ hours or until the temperature in the breast area comes to 165°. No need to baste, the basting is done for you by the beer. When cooked, remove chicken from grill and let rest for 10 minutes before carving. Do not skip this step, because letting meat rest after cooking causes it to reabsorb its juices.

Serve chicken with **Grilled Corn on the Cob, Rosemary Roast Potatoes, Pan con Tomate**.

Dry Spice Rub for Chicken or Pork

3 tablespoons (45ml) smoked paprika

1 tablespoon (15ml) fleur de sel (or other good coarse salt)

⅓ cup (85ml) brown sugar

2 teaspoons (10ml) chili powder

1 tablespoon (15ml) ground cumin

3 tablespoons (45ml) garlic powder

3 tablespoons (45ml) onion powder

2 tablespoons (30ml) oregano

Combine all ingredients. For a smoother rub, whiz this in a spice grinder (coffee grinder) till fine. Can be stored in an airtight container for up to 6 months.

Spanish Chicken in a Pot

This very simple Spanish chicken dish is accomplished quickly in a pressure cooker. The wine makes a lovely juice for the chicken and the potatoes. Use this method for any chicken braise that you want to do. Timings with pressure cookers vary. It is best to follow the instructions provided with your pressure cooker. Delicate vegetables such as mushrooms must be sautéed and added to the pot at the end of the cooking time.

4–6 whole chicken breasts

1 pound (455g) small potatoes

1 medium onion, chopped

3 cloves garlic, minced

3 tablespoons (45ml) olive oil

2 teaspoons (10ml) smoked paprika

2 teaspoons (10ml) Marigold bouillon powder (if using a substitute, see * p. 19)

1½ wineglasses white wine or sherry

salt and freshly ground pepper to taste

Season the chicken well with salt and pepper. In a pressure cooker, cook the onion over medium low heat in the olive oil until it is transparent. Add the chicken pieces and brown them gently about 15 minutes, turning them occasionally. Add the chopped garlic and the potatoes. Cook three or four minutes. Add the paprika, Marigold, salt and pepper, wine, and a half glass of water. Close the pressure cooker and cook 8 minutes at 15 pounds pressure (or follow the instructions for cooking chicken in your pressure cooker's manual).

If you make this dish without pressure cooking, cook the chicken gently for 25 minutes, adding a bit of water if needed.

Pork Tenderloin Asturiana

This delicious dish, often finished with cream, is traditional in Asturias in the north of Spain but can also be found in Normandy in France, for in both locales, cool, grassy lands mean that apples and cream are in abundance. If you have cream and want to use it, stir in about a half to three quarters of a wineglass at the last 3 minutes of cooking. This will make a smooth, velvety sauce and the cream will serve to thicken it a bit. In Asturias, you will find sidra, an alcoholic cider similar to the one produced in England. Calvados, the exquisite apple brandy, comes from Normandy. You will love using this if you have it, for it brings out the essence of the apple, or you may use any good French or Spanish brandy or cognac.

2 pork tenderloins
3–4 apples peeled, cored, and sliced
2 medium onions, quartered then sliced thin
1 wineglass Calvados, cognac, or brandy
1 wineglass cider, sidra, or apple juice
3 tablespoons (45ml) olive oil, or mix olive oil and butter
½ teaspoon (2.5ml) powdered thyme
pinch powdered rosemary
good pinch nutmeg
salt and pepper to taste

Season the tenderloins with salt and pepper and a sprinkling of thyme. In a nonstick pan, sauté in the olive oil until golden brown. When browned on all sides, remove and set aside while you cook the onions. Add onions to the pan and cook gently over medium heat for 5 minutes. Add sliced apples and the remaining seasonings. Cook gently together with the onions until the apples are becoming soft, about 8 minutes. Return the pork to the pan and add the Calvados or cognac. Let the pork tenderloins cook over low heat about twenty minutes or until done, turning a few times to keep them covered with the apples and onions. Taste for seasoning.

This is perfect served with rice. Slice the pork into medallions and fan the medallions out with some of the garnish on top and the rest alongside.

Once, *while port hopping in the Mediterranean, I found myself wandering down a dark road in Tunisia with my assistant cook, when we noticed we were being followed by a group of Arab youths. As we hurried down the tiny street, the young men sped up behind us. When we slowed, our followers slowed too. A chill ran up my spine and down again.*

Finally, being able to stand it no longer, I turned and asked them in French where they were going. We soon discovered that the fellows only wanted to be friendly. They seemed to think we weren't safe to wander these streets at night and that we needed someone trustworthy to guide us, for which task they volunteered cheerfully. My sailmate and I didn't take long to agree.

Our newfound friends took us to a small square on the quay surrounding an ancient harbor with palm trees overshadowed by the walls of ancient Roman ruins. There we stopped at a street vendor, where we were treated to typical Tunisian street food—a bowl of soft, grainy pudding, full of spices, dipped from a wood-fired copper vat.

The young Arabs, who were fishermen, then decided that we should visit them on their steel fishing boat and enjoy some couscous. So, surrounded by a large group of Arab men, we laughed and talked, drank thick black coffee, and ate couscous.

Later, aboard our boat, they taught us how to make their couscous.
It was different than the method I learned in Morocco and different again from the one on the next page, which is also delightful but has an American twist.

* See Tchaktchouka

Jambalaya with Couscous

Whether you are of the American persuasion where the word prawn is replaced by the word shrimp, or of the Louisiana persuasion where the entire shrimp is often replaced by his buddy, the crawfish, jambalaya by any other name would mean a Creole take on Spanish paella. This illustrates that no matter where you travel, there is nothing new under the sun . . . except, perhaps, making this with couscous. Couscous will puff up in hot water and requires no further cooking, so after a little sautéing and a little throwing together of this and that, this dish literally prepares itself.

2 stalks celery, finely chopped

1 green pepper, chopped

1 onion, chopped

4 cloves garlic

¼ cup (60ml) extra virgin olive oil

3 ounces (85g) chorizo or Andouille sausage, sliced or chopped

1 chicken breast, sliced into bite-size strips, seasoned with salt and
    pepper

½ pound (225g) prawns, peeled and deveined, seasoned with salt and
pepper

1 tablespoon (15ml) tomato paste

pinch of allspice

2 bay leaves

1 teaspoon (5ml) dried oregano

½ teaspoon (2.5ml) dried thyme

1 teaspoon (5ml) Tabasco sauce

pinch cayenne pepper

10 ounces (285g) couscous

1¼ cup (310ml) well-seasoned chicken stock, heated to boiling

2 tablespoons (30ml) dry vermouth

salt and freshly ground black pepper

Heat the oil in a large skillet with a lid. Put the chopped celery, green pepper, and onion into the oil and sauté over medium heat until wilted, about 5 minutes.

Add the garlic and sausage. Cook 2–3 minutes. Add the chicken pieces. Sauté 3 minutes more. Add the prawns. Cook until they turn pink, about 3 minutes. Do not overcook the prawns or they will become tough.

Add the tomato paste to the pan and toss around with the meats and prawns. Add the couscous with the stock, vermouth, bay leaves, allspice, oregano, thyme, Tabasco, and cayenne.

Give the mixture a stir, cover, and turn off the heat. Allow to stand for 15 minutes. Remove cover and toss with a fork. Remove bay leaves, taste for seasoning, and serve.

Baked Sausages in Cider Cream

*Simplicity is often best in a galley. Sausages and cider are old mates. If you have **Onion Confit** already made, this dish is a snap to assemble. It's a fine comfort-food kind of meal.*

    1 cup (250ml) onion confit
    2 apples, peeled and sliced
    12 sausages
    pinch allspice
    1 tablespoon (15ml) fresh thyme, chopped
    1 bottle dry cider
    1 teaspoon (5ml) Dijon mustard
    ½ cup (125ml) cream

Put sausages in a roasting pan. Pour over the cider and throw in the onions and apples, pinch of allspice, and a tablespoon of chopped thyme. Cook in a medium hot oven until sausages are done, about 30 minutes. Remove pan from oven, stir in cream and mustard. Return to oven and cook until nice and bubbly, about 10 minutes. Serve with mashed potatoes, spooning some of the sauce over the mash.

Lamb Romanesque

The pairing of anchovies with meat is very Roman and dates back to the Caesars. The rest of this sauce may be an afterthought, but it is a very good one.

    4 lamb steaks or chops
    3 cloves garlic, finely chopped
    2 tablespoons (30ml) capers, rinsed in water and drained, chopped
        roughly

1 handful black olives, pitted

4–6 anchovy filets, drained and roughly chopped

1 dried red chili, crumbled

2 tablespoons (30ml) extra-virgin olive oil

1 tablespoon (15ml) butter

½ pound (225g) fresh porcini or portobello mushrooms, sliced (you may use dried and reconstituted)

1 glass dry white wine, or dry vermouth

1 (14 oz/400g) can cannellini beans, drained

1 teaspoon (5ml) Marigold bouillon powder (if using a substitute, see * p. 19)

pinch allspice

salt and freshly ground pepper

Heat a large skillet. Add the olive oil to the pan and heat. Season the lamb chops with salt and pepper and add to pan. Cook for 6–7 minutes on one side. Turn the lamb over. While it is still cooking, add the garlic, anchovies, and hot pepper to the pan. Stir the anchovies into the oil and allow to melt. Cook the lamb about 5 minutes more for medium rare. Remove lamb from pan and keep warm.

Add the butter and the mushrooms to pan and cook over medium high heat until golden. Add the capers and olives to the mushrooms, along with the white wine. Bring to a boil. Simmer the sauce for 5 minutes. Taste for seasoning. Pour sauce over lamb.

Meanwhile, purée the cannellini beans in a food processor or with an immersion blender. Heat through in a pan with the allspice, Marigold powder, salt, and pepper.

Serve alongside lamb with some of the sauce poured over.

Pre-Socialist Beef Stroganoff

This is one of those romantic old Russian émigrés that I always come back to. It is rich, but who cares, it is great. It is a one-pan meal and, if you can read, is hardly more difficult to make than that hamburger assistant in a cardboard box that purports to be so time-saving and delicious but is only dreadful. Stroganoff, being of noble heritage, should always be made with the best meat you can find, which means tenderloin. This is not a stew. It is a luxurious dish of steak napped with a sour cream mustard sauce highly flavored with sherry. No tomato. No Worcestershire. And for pity's sake, no ketchup! We are not trying to hide any flavors here, but let the ingredients speak for themselves. This is one of those cases where if you've got it, flaunt it.

> 1½ pounds (680g) tenderloin, cut into even strips ½-inch thick
> 1 teaspoon (5ml) allspice
> 4 tablespoons (60ml) butter
> 1 onion, sliced paper-thin
> 2 cloves garlic, minced
> ¾ pound (340g) mushrooms, sliced
> 2 tablespoons (30ml) flour
> 1 teaspoon (5ml) dry mustard
> 1 cup (250ml) rich beef stock (from a box)
> ½ cup (125ml) sour cream
> ½ glass medium sherry
> salt and freshly ground pepper

Season the steak with salt and pepper and ½ teaspoon allspice. Sauté quickly in 2 tablespoons butter until browned but still rare inside. Remove to a plate but keep warm in the oven. Add 2 tablespoons butter to pan. Over medium high heat, sauté the mushrooms, shaking the pan to allow them to brown nicely. Add 2 tablespoons of the sherry to the mushrooms. Shake the pan well to allow the sherry to burn off. Season with the rest of the allspice, salt, and pepper and remove from pan. Add remaining butter to pan. Sauté the onion gently, until soft and just beginning to turn gold. Add garlic to pan. Cook for 2 minutes. Add flour and dry mustard to the pan, turning the onions in the flour and butter to coat. Cook 2 minutes to get rid of the floury taste. Add the sherry and the beef stock as well as any juices that have been released from the meat and the mushrooms. Bring to a boil, stirring constantly as the sauce thickens to prevent lumps. Add the sour cream. Stir over medium heat for 2 minutes until flavors meld together. Taste the sauce for seasoning. Just before serving, add the meat and mushrooms back into the pan, tossing and allowing to come to temperature in the sauce. Remove from heat.

Serve with boiled egg noodles or boiled new potatoes tossed in butter.

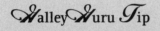

To keep the plate warm while you are working, turn the oven on and then, when it is warm, turn it off. This should be just enough heat to keep the meat warm without cooking it further. Also, you will not have to worry about keeping the plate from sliding around.

Chili Aboard

When you are pleasantly in port somewhere and want to invite some friends from neighboring boats, this chili will wow 'em. It will serve 8–10 people comfortably. It has received rave reviews from everybody who has tasted it.

Cubed beef chuck (a fattier cut of meat, chosen for its tenderness in long cooking) is the best, but you can make it with ground beef if that is what you have. However, the cooking time must be reduced to half an hour if you do, for ground beef will not improve with long cooking.

This chili, or a version of it, bubbled atop a pot-bellied stove in one corner of my restaurant in Spain, warming many a winter evening. Guests at the bar could help themselves to a steaming bowl and return to their endless discussions and their backgammon. This recipe is as authentic as it gets and it does not have beans. I got it from a Mexican chef. I imported it to the south of Spain from the south of Texas via Mexico. Contrary to the accepted wisdom of the day, chili con carne, while not a Mexican dish, does have Mexican origins. How else do you find these particular spices in it? It uses ingredients introduced to Spain in the days of the conquistadores and currently in use in the characteristic cooking of Catalonia. I thought the cross-culturization fitting.

The whole process, though it requires quite a few ingredients, is worth the effort and is a snap in a pressure cooker. Otherwise, give it the long, slow cooking it deserves. It is satisfying and rich and very delicious. To make the whole process much simpler for a boat, you can make up little zip-lock baggies beforehand with all the 8 dried ingredients so you will have your own homemade chili spice powder ready whenever you want it.

4 pounds (1.8kg) boneless beef chuck cubed (or use ground beef and
    adjust cooking time)
1 pound (455g) chorizo (or other Spanish-type sausage)
2 large yellow onions, chopped
8–12 cloves of garlic, chopped (one garlic bulb)
2 tablespoons (30ml) olive oil
4 tablespoons (60ml) ground ancho (pasilla) chiles
3 tablespoons (45ml) ground cumin
4 teaspoons (20ml) dried oregano
4 teaspoons (20ml) paprika (smoky Spanish paprika is wonderful for this)

1 teaspoon (5ml) ground coriander

1 teaspoon (5ml) ground cinnamon

good pinch of ground allspice (about 1/4 tsp/1.25ml)

¼–½ teaspoon (1.25ml) cayenne

2 tablespoons (30ml) brown sugar

2 teaspoons (10ml) Marigold bouillon powder (see * p. 19)

large can diced tomatoes

2 bottles beer (you get a good result with either dark or light, but the nut brown ale tends to be sweeter so I use it if I have it)

½ cup (125ml) strong coffee

dash of vinegar

2 squares dark unsweetened chocolate

salt and pepper

2 tablespoons (30ml) masa harina*

In a large pot, sauté the onions in the oil until soft. Add garlic and stir for 2 to 3 minutes. Pour into a bowl and set aside. Season beef with salt and pepper. Put beef cubes in pan. Brown on all sides over high heat. Add sausage meat to pan. Turn heat to medium and continue to cook a minute or two, stirring to break up sausage. Return onions and garlic to pan. Pour beer over meat and onions. Bring to a boil. Continue boiling gently, adding tomatoes, coffee, sugar, and all the spices, reserving the chocolate and vinegar for later. Liquid should completely cover meat. If you do not have enough liquid, add a little beef broth or water to make up the difference. Boil gently a minute or two. Reduce heat to a simmer. Cook, covered, for 2 hours, stirring occasionally. Put masa harina in a cup and add ⅓ cup warm water. Stir until smooth. Pour into chili and stir to combine. Cook uncovered over low heat, stirring frequently, ½ hour, until meat is very tender and sauce is thick. Now add the dash of vinegar and stir in the chocolate, allowing it to melt well into the mixture. Serve.

It is nice to serve this with grated cheddar cheese and a dollop of real sour cream. You can further garnish chili with sliced avocados. Pass a bowl of chopped onion and a little chopped cilantro (fresh coriander) if available.

* Masa harina is a flour made from dried corn. Used to make tortillas, it is available at most supermarkets.

Daube Provençale

*"Talk of joy: there may be things better than beef stew
and baked potatoes and homemade bread...there may be."*
—David Gayson

*Here is an excellent and traditional French stew, flavored with herbs,
orange peel, and red wine, that is as easy as throwing a few ingredients
into a pressure cooker and waiting for it to cook. Use this classic method
for whatever stew you may want to prepare under pressure, where you get
quick and savory results.*

    2 pounds (900g) of beef chuck
    3½ oz (100g) bacon, cut into ½-inch pieces
    2 cloves garlic, crushed
    4 carrots, sliced
    2 medium onions, sliced
    2 canned tomatoes, sliced
    ½ cup (125ml) black olives (Niçoise or other French olives)
    1 tablespoon (15ml) extra virgin olive oil
    2 pinches Herbes de Provençe
    or a Bouquet Garni
    2 or 3 cloves
    2 glasses good light red wine
    zest of half an orange
    salt and freshly ground pepper

Cut the meat into bite-size cubes. Brown the bacon in the bottom of
a pressure cooker. Add the meat, and brown on all sides. Pour out
all but 1 tablespoon of the fat. Add the onion slices, carrot, garlic,
and tomato slices. Season with salt and pepper.

> * Herbes de Provence is a mixture of savory, rosemary, fennel,
> thyme, basil, tarragon, lavender and marjoram. You can buy
> mixtures of these herbs in the spice section of any market.

Add the oil, the orange zest, the Herbes de Provençe, the cloves, the olives, the wine, and then add enough water to cover the meat completely. Seal pressure cooker and cook for 20 minutes from the moment of the rotation of the valve. Turn off heat and do not open pressure cooker. Let stand until all pressure is released. Remove top of pressure cooker. Turn heat on under pan and cook until meat is very tender, about 15 minutes.

Galley Guru Tip

The pressure cooker is a godsend in a galley. Buy the best one you can. It performs all the cooking in a sealed pot, thus keeping your meal from being tipped over in unruly seas, which goes a long way to preserving your sanity. Uncovered, it can also double as a pot to boil anything like pasta or potatoes in.

Beef in Port

The port in this dish is port wine, so the preparation of this stew does not require that you be docked. You can cook this as a normal stew, in which case you would bring it to a simmer and then turn down the heat to low. Cook for 2–2½ hours. Pressure cooking will make the meat tender in far less time. The secret to this dish is the deep mushroom flavor you get by using just a teaspoon or two of mushroom powder.

2 pounds (900g) of beef chuck cut into 1-inch cubes
2 tablespoons (30ml) extra virgin olive oil
4 cloves garlic, crushed
2 medium onions, cut in half and sliced thin
1 pound (455g) mushrooms, sliced (use any you have)
1 tablespoon (15ml) butter
1 tablespoon (15ml) tomato paste
1 teaspoon (5ml) wild mushroom powder*
1 glass dry red wine
1 glass ruby port
salt and freshly ground pepper

Brown all sides of the beef in the olive oil in a large stew pot or pressure cooker. Add the onion, garlic, salt, and pepper. Cook gently for about 10 minutes, stirring frequently. Add mushrooms. Stir in the tomato paste and cook for a minute or two. Add the mushroom powder and the red wine and port. If cooking in a stew pot, cook over low heat, stirring occasionally, for approximately 2½ hours, or until the meat is tender.

If using a pressure cooker, close it and when it comes to full pressure, cook for 20 minutes (for exact timing, follow the directions that come with the cooker).

* Dried porcini or other wild mushroom, ground to a powder in a spice grinder.

Swedish Meatballs

These meatballs are nudged around in a pan and before you know it you have a lovely and unusual supper. This is a fast and authentic recipe and if you haven't got the lingonberry jam in the larder, you can substitute something else for the tart sweet taste: red currant, perhaps, or even plum sauce.

1 pound (about ½ kilo) minced beef (or veal and pork)

1 onion, finely chopped

½ cup (125ml) half and half (light cream)

1 egg

½ teaspoon (2.5ml) allspice

good pinch of nutmeg

¼ teaspoon (1.25ml) ground pepper

1 teaspoon (5ml) Marigold bouillon powder (or to taste) (see * p. 19)

salt and pepper

3 tablespoons (45ml) clarified butter (ghee)*

½ cup (125 ml) sour cream

Mix together all the ingredients but the salt. You can fry a small piece of the mixture in the ghee to taste for salt. Make small meatballs, about 3cm (1¼ inches). Fry in the clarified butter. When the meatballs are nicely browned, stir in the sour cream to the pan juices. Season with salt and pepper. Serve with boiled potatoes or noodles tossed in butter. The traditional accompaniment is lingonberry sauce or jam, or red currant jam will work in a pinch.

* Clarified butter can be bought in jars as ghee (the Indian name for it). It is butter from which the milk solids have been removed, leaving a clear golden liquid that keeps without refrigeration and has a high smoking point, which makes it suitable for frying since it does not burn the way whole butter does. It is sold in health food stores and many supermarkets.

Picadillo
Spicy Beef Hash

Picadillo, a Cuban institution, is an ambrosial chopped meat dish. My dear friend Paz introduced me to this divine thing in Spain. She had been married to a Basque who was at one time ambassador to Cuba, so she regaled me with tales of international intrigue during many dinners. She proved to be a terrific international cook who could, with utter nonchalance, throw a paucity of ingredients together in a pan and come up with the meals dreams are made of. Which is what we aim to do whenever we are in the galley. Picadillo is nothing more nor less than an elegant sort of hash. On land, Paz presented it to me piled high in the center of a plate surrounded by fried plantains sliced lengthwise and arranged in rays fanning out from the meat so that the entire dish resembled a sunflower. It needn't be so ornate to be utterly enjoyable, unless you have the plantains and a safe harbor, where a little ostentation never goes amiss.

3 tablespoons (45ml) olive oil

1 large onion, chopped

4 cloves garlic, minced

3 tomatoes, seeded and chopped

1 pound (455g) ground beef (or coarsely chopped leftover beef)

2 red bell peppers, seeded and chopped

2 small green hot chili peppers, chopped

1 teaspoon (5ml) dried oregano, rubbed between fingers

1 teaspoon (5ml) cumin

pinch ground allspice

½ cup (125ml) pine nuts

½ cup (125ml) raisins

2 tablespoons (30ml) capers

12 green olives, pitted and quartered

1 wineglass sherry, dry vermouth, or white wine

1 teaspoon (5ml) Marigold bouillon powder (see * p. 19 for subs.)

salt and pepper to taste

Heat the oil in a large skillet. Add the onion, sauté gently until the color of golden apples. Do not rush this. It will take about 15 to 20 minutes. Add the garlic. Cook 3 minutes. Add the beef, bell peppers, and chopped tomatoes, hot pepper, oregano, and allspice. Sauté, stirring, over medium heat until beef is beginning to brown and caramelize. Add the rest of the ingredients. Simmer until sherry has almost evaporated.

This dish can be made with soy minced beef (TVP) and is quite wonderful, so if you are vegetarian or haven't got beef aboard, no worries. Toss the TVP with some liquid aminos seasoning (Marigold, Braggs) to give it some extra meat-like flavor when adding it to the pan.

Serve this with potatoes, couscous, plain white rice, or "Moros y Cristianos," a traditional Cuban black bean and rice dish. Make a ring around the outside of the dish with the rice and pile up the meat mixture inside. For another day, this makes the greatest taco filling ever.

Day after day of calm. The sparkling crystalline sea smoothing out under azure skies as far as the eye can see. You would think that you were in heaven. But with the motor out there comes the problem of what to do with all that time while you are waiting for a tiny breath of wind. Books. Backgammon games on deck. Cooking. With no meat in sight and not a fish on the lines, I pulled out the trusty TVP (textured vegetable protein)* and made this dish. After all, we had to keep up our strength for the relentless, cutthroat backgammon.

Shepherdless Pie

1 pound (1/2 kilo) potatoes

½ pound (1/4 kilo) sweet potatoes

2 tablespoons (30ml) chopped parsley

2 tablespoons (30ml) butter

olive oil for sautéing

4 cloves garlic, chopped

1 teaspoon (5ml) thyme

1 teaspoon (5ml) dried oregano

3 bay leaves

2–3 onions, chopped (or a cup of prepared Onion Confit)

3 stalks celery, diced

1 medium zucchini (courgette), diced

1 red pepper, diced

2 carrots, chopped

2 cans plum tomatoes

1 cup (250ml) TVP, rehydrated with ¾ cup (185ml) boiling water

½ cup (125ml) grated cheddar

liquid amino seasoning (Marigold, Braggs)

1–2 teaspoons (5–10ml) Marigold bouillon powder (if using
	substitute, see * p. 19)

Preheat oven to medium high. Peel, dice, and boil potatoes. Put through a ricer to mash them and stir in the parsley and butter. Sauté onions gently in the olive oil until caramelized, about 20 minutes, or add onion confit to the pan over low heat. Add garlic, thyme, and bay leaves. Add celery, zucchini, pepper, carrots, and mashed plum tomatoes. Add reconstituted TVP and dried oregano. Season to taste with liquid aminos (Marigold, Braggs) and bouillon powder. Simmer 15 minutes. Put mixture in baking dish and top with potato mixture. Sprinkle with grated Cheddar.

Bake for 20 minutes (until cheese is golden brown).

Know your onions. To replace tears with laughter, get out your swimming goggles and plant them securely on your face before chopping that onion. You'll be laughing, all right, especially at all those simple folk who gird themselves to attack their onion by running water (wasteful) and sticking a piece of bread in their mouths (for the tears to fall onto, I suppose). This goggle trick is particularly amusing when you get back to land and are preparing a chummy dinner in the kitchen with some friends.

* To rehydrate TVP add ¾ to 1 cup (180-240ml) boiling stock or water to 1 cup (240ml) TVP. Let it sit for a few minutes. This can now be used in spaghetti sauces or for taco meat or chili, et

Peking Duck (Deconstructed)

This is my sophisticated version of that wonderful crispy duck served with Chinese pancakes in restaurants. The duck here is tender duck breast and it is cooked medium rare like a steak. The elements remain the same but this is pure and elegant and, oh yeah, easy.

4 plump duck breasts
2 cups Hoisin sauce
1 tablespoon toasted sesame oil
1 teaspoon Tamari or other good soy sauce
4 cloves chopped garlic
2 teaspoons plus a pinch 5-spice powder
pinch cayenne pepper
1 glass white wine or sherry
salt and freshly ground pepper
1 large cucumber, peeled, seeded and sliced into matchstick strips
1 bunch scallions (green onion)

Cut scallions into pieces about 2 inches long. Using a sharp knife, cut about a ½-inch cross in each end of the onion piece. (Slice through once, then give it a quarter turn and slice again. This will make decorative little onion flowers or brushes.) Place into a bowl of ice water while you prepare the rest of the dish.

Place duck breasts fat side up. To allow fat to melt faster, score the fat right down to the flesh but no further. Season all over with the five spice powder and salt and pepper. Place duck breasts in a large, cold skillet skin side down. Turn heat to medium and cook without moving them in the pan until skin is seared, brown, and crispy and fat is in the pan, not the duck (about 7 minutes, depending on how much fat you need to render). Turn the duck breasts over and cook to medium rare, another 4–5 minutes on the flesh side. Remove from heat. Keep duck warm.

To make sauce, place sesame oil and garlic in a saucepan and heat, low, for about a minute. Add wine, Hoisin, and Tamari. Season with a pinch of five spice powder and the cayenne. Continue to cook about 10 minutes over low heat, until reduced to 2 cups. When ready to serve, place each duck breast on a plate with the Hoisin reduction all around. Garnish with cucumber and green onions. Serve with a simple rice pilaf.

Sauces, Confits,

Relishes & Spreads

"Cheese is milk's leap toward immortality."
—Clifton Fadiman

"So I thought to myself, a little fermented curd will do the trick."
—Monty Python

Cheese: smooth, velvety, delicate, runny, crumbly, creamy, or sharp. Consider the cheese tray beckoning sensuously after dinner. Give me good ripe Camembert, or **le vrai** Roquefort. When it comes to the Brie, run, don't walk, straight to Coulommiers or Brillat Savarin with the extra cream—and, yes, calories . . . and lusciousness. A little wedge accompanied by a couple of sweet succulent dates and a drink of cold champagne is the dessert of the century. They know something, these French.

Leave France, if you can tear yourself away, and head south for Italy to pick a blossoming Taleggio, and while you're there, get thee a sublime Dolce Latte which is nearly impossible to get in good condition in the States, or (who can live without it?) Pecorino or Parmigiano Reggiano. On the north side of the Channel there is a whole other class of cheese, like the English, a breed apart: Cheddar, Cheshire, Lancashire, Wensleydale, Red Leicester, Sage Derby. Take a noble Stilton with a bit of crumbly biscuit and a small glass of port wine and heavenward rise. Then again there is the apt simplicity in a plain cheddar cheese sandwich, which is specially good melted. Oh yes, let us not forget the reassuring comforts of Grilled Cheese, a perfectly browned rustic Croque Monsieur, or that other mustard-spiked cheese on toast, **Welsh Rarebit**. The profligate joys of melted cheese bring us to such temptations as Raclette. Raclette, **says**

Switzerland, has its own special grill and ritual of service. Then there is fondue, that ultimate homage to cheese, with its chummy ceremonial lore and observances, sacraments celebrated with skewers and conversation and endless variations on a theme that prod us lightly but inexorably down the path of unctuous indulgence. Cheese and bread. Cheese and wine. Cheese and cheese. What did I leave out? Just about everything. I haven't even scratched the surface.

But we are here to talk about cheese sauce and its usefulness on board a ship. So, to begin the construction of this sauce, we need the base, the foundation, that which holds and emulsifies the cheese to a pourable consistency.

A properly made cheese sauce is an extrapolation of a simple but singularly important white sauce, a Béchamel. Achieve a Béchamel and voilà, the list of embellishments and complements begin to come a-knocking like a burgeoning cast of thousands. You have only to introduce a spoonful or two of a favorite flavor into this "mother sauce" and you quickly rise to master a whole category of French sauces. Stir in a suspicion of grainy Dijon mustard and you have a fine Sauce Moutarde. Sauce Aurore? It's nothing more than a Béchamel with the addition of tiny spoonfuls of tomato purée that render the sauce delicately sweeter and pleasingly pink (how nice, presumably like some dawns we have seen and have yet to see under way). Well, now, this isn't rocket science. More like playing with our food. Just so you know, a Béchamel is also the basis, with a few whipped-up eggs, for that mystery of mysteries, the soufflé. A soufflé on a sailboat? Maybe not. But stranger things have happened.

The proper and classic way to make a Béchamel involves scalded milk, some rich veal or chicken stock, an onion stuck with cloves, and a bay leaf. The liquid so perfumed is then stirred into a roux of butter and white flour and boiled until thick. While there is no question that this produces the finest taste, substituting Marigold bouillon powder for the stock and seasonings comes in a close second. Our sauce will be spectacular but will also offer the added advantage of being just about effortless, keeping counters clean and tempers as smooth as the calmest sea.

Cheddar Cheese Sauce

This and the Mornay sauce that follows are classic cheese sauces for pasta, macaroni, or vegetables, or for fish or seafood as in a gratin. Pour either into a baked potato or, instead of hollandaise, over poached eggs on English muffins or any nice slicing bread, even brioche, perhaps with ham or tomato for breakfast. In either of these, substitute a cup of dry white vermouth (or any dry white wine) for some or all of the cup of milk, then add the ½ cup cream for a richer yet mysteriously lighter sauce.

1½ cup (375ml) scalded milk (or mixture of milk and cream)

2 tablespoons (30ml) butter

2 tablespoons (30ml) flour

1 cup (250ml) grated Cheddar cheese

1 teaspoon (5ml) Marigold bouillon powder (see * p. 19 if using substitute)

big pinch grated nutmeg

pinch salt

¼ teaspoon (1.25ml) white pepper

Melt the butter in a saucepan. Whisk in the flour and cook for a minute, stirring gently. Add the milk, whisking until the mixture comes to a gentle boil. Stir in the Marigold. Cook until sauce is smooth, shiny, and thick, about 3 minutes. Add cheese. Immediately lower heat and stir until melted. Remove sauce from heat. Season with salt and pepper and nutmeg.

You can keep the sauce by putting it in a covered container if you press plastic wrap to the surface. Heat before serving.

Mornay Sauce

A couple of crepes filled with leftover chicken, a few mushrooms, perhaps some spinach, and just this sauce poured over. Now pour yourself a glass of wine. You will fantasize you are in one of those wonderful little Paris bistros. Mornay Sauce is the French kissing cousin to our Cheddar cheese sauce. It is, arguably, more elegant. Any Swiss cheese will do here but the Gruyère has the delicacy, to my mind. You can do all Swiss (nuttier, smoother) instead of the Parmesan/Swiss mix (more of a bite, more piquant, saltier).

1½ cup (375ml) scalded milk (or mixture of milk and cream)
2 tablespoons (30ml) butter
2 tablespoons (30ml) flour
½ cup (125ml) grated Gruyère or Emmentaler cheese
½ cup (125ml) grated Parmesan cheese
big pinch grated nutmeg
½ teaspoon (2.5ml) salt
pinch cayenne pepper

Melt the butter in a saucepan. Whisk in the flour and cook for a minute, stirring gently. Add the milk, whisking until the mixture comes to a gentle boil. Stir in the Marigold. Cook until sauce is smooth and thick, about 3 minutes. Add cheese. Stir over low heat until melted. Remove sauce from heat. Season with salt and pepper and nutmeg.

Onion Confit

This is not just a recipe: it is an institution. Rich, with an indescribable depth of flavor, onion confit is a versatile condiment, a base for sauces. Or try a spoonful or two on a little pasta. It completely transforms a sandwich . . . the list goes on. Best of all, it will keep in a jar for months. This confit is lovely with meat, any kind of chicken or fish. It is a huge time-saver for any recipe that starts out with slow-cooked onions. This is one of the rare things that I suggest you can do at home and bring aboard with you. You may even want to double the recipe. For the onions, a sweet variety is preferable but normal brown or yellow will do fine, because slow cooking develops the sweetness of any onion. They cook about an hour but sometimes need a bit more. The end result should be sweet and tender. The addition of the sweet wine as well as the brown sugar adds depth of flavor.

⅓ cup (85ml) olive oil

2 tablespoons (30ml) butter (optional)

10 onions peeled, thinly sliced

2 bay leaves

1 teaspoon (5ml) coriander seed

¼ teaspoon (1.25ml) allspice

¼ teaspoon (1.25ml) nutmeg

1 teaspoon (5ml) sea salt

2 tablespoons (15ml) brown sugar (or to taste)

⅓ cup (85ml) Port wine, Marsala, sweet sherry, apple concentrate, pomegranate molasses

⅓ cup (85ml) white or red wine

¼ cup (60ml) crème de cassis or other liqueur

Combine the olive oil and optional butter in a large, heavy-bottomed saucepan. Place over medium heat. Add onions and stir to coat with oil. Add spices and salt. Stir for 3 minutes but do not let onions color. Reduce heat to very low, and cook gently from this point for 30 to 40 minutes to bring out the sweetness of the onions, stirring frequently.

Stir in the sugar, port, and white wine and turn up heat slightly. Stir from the bottom to deglaze pan. Boil mixture gently 15 to 20 minutes longer to let the wine evaporate. Pour in the crème de cassis and cook for about 5 minutes. The onions must be very soft and the sauce should be thick and cling to them. Allow them to cool in their juices.

These utterly delicious onions may be served immediately or canned into mason jars and kept at room temperature for a few weeks, or in the refrigerator for months.

Garlic Confit

Invaluable. Simple. Store for every time you need garlic. Fish the garlic cloves out of the oil, or use the oil for seasoning dishes. Garlic goes bad easily on land. On sea it is impossible to keep a long time—unless you do it like this.

    8 whole heads garlic, peeled and separated into cloves
    3 fresh thyme sprigs (optional)
    2 cups (500ml) olive oil

Place garlic and thyme sprigs in olive oil in a saucepan. Cook gently over low heat until soft and golden in color, 45 to 50 minutes. Store in jars.

"All this mad dashing and splashing of the waters of the big ocean, which the mischievous wind caused without any good reason whatever, resulted in a terrible storm, and a storm on the ocean is liable to cut many queer pranks and do a lot of damage."
—L. Frank Baum, *Ozma of Oz*

For five days the billows rose and fell. The vast ocean could on a whim have swallowed us and never been made different by the event. We had set sail from Miami to Greece. All was well till the day we found our spacious, well-appointed, fifty-foot trimaran bravely hurling and pitching upon a savage sea. Forget four-course meals. Good thing we had a lot of chocolate on board. I will say we made excellent use of the plentiful canned tuna and hearts of palm during that storm—so much use that I couldn't look tuna or hearts of palm in the face for a long time afterwards.

A trimaran is different from a monohull in many ways. We found one of the ways in practice when a massive wave hit us broadside and lifted one of the pontoons out of the water at as near a right angle as made no difference. Normally surfing the seas as much as sailing them, a shallow drafted, broad tri-hull is nearly impossible to flip sideways, but this was clearly going to be the exception proving the rule. Fate had scooped us up and held us. Time stood still. The world teetered and so did we. Tossed rudely across the cabin, we contemplated our imminent destiny as fish food.

But fate suddenly lost interest in us. Varvara righted herself, and we slammed back down hard upon the ocean. It was not over. We had a few more lessons to learn about a wild sea before the night was through with us.

By morning we awakened to a pristine dawn of such exquisite calm we could hardly remember the extraordinary hours we had come through together. We were quite far south of our course and needed to correct if we were to enter the Med at the Straits of Gibraltar as planned, but the gods had somehow been appeased and we sailed northward over glimmering water into crystalline skies.

In the light of the new day, we looked around to see what needed repairing or restoring. Amazingly, nothing was broken, but the galley was a hell of a mess and there was a lot of sea water where it shouldn't have been: in our food. In the confusion, I spied a large bottle wedged in the back of the pantry. Its bright yellow contents fairly sang to me. One of my favorite French jars was still hermetically sealed around the most delectable lemons, preserved before we embarked as the Moroccans do, in salt and lemon juice. This stuff is as indestructible as it is incredible; it only took a little bit of it to make a terrific scampi for dinner. I added some garlic confit and a bag of shrimp that happily remained frozen in the still-functional freezer, then I threw this delicious concoction over some angel hair pasta. Saved again.

Preserved Lemons

Make these lemons in port or at home and bring them aboard. You will be delighted with them. They are not only beautiful, but they also last longer than any sea voyage on record. Chop and use these salt lemons over pasta with olive oil and some olives, or slice some over fish before putting into the oven or sealing to cook in a pouch. Put slivers inside and under the skin of a chicken and roast it with some garlic. Use to season rice and couscous. You only need a part of one lemon to scent and lend magic to a whole dish. Traditionally, preserved lemons are used in Morocco with cracked green olives in heavenly chicken and lamb dishes that take their name from the clay pots they are cooked in, which have conical shaped lids called Tagines. The Tagine's special shape creates rich, aromatic stews as the food inside slowly steams and gently simmers for hours. Meat cooked in a Tagine becomes fragrant and meltingly tender. You can achieve a similar result with a sealed casserole in the oven as long as you keep the heat low and the liquid content high.

a handful of beautiful lemons
about ⅓ cup (85ml) sea salt
fresh lemon juice (to cover)

Cut a cross into the lemons—almost to the base, so that they open like a flower. Push sea salt into the lemon segments. Put a layer of salt into the bottom of a sealable jar and pack the lemons into the jar, pushing them well down as tightly as they will go.

Cover the lemons with the lemon juice, secure the lid, and leave the jar at room temperature for a week, shaking it occasionally. Allow to sit at room temperature for at least three weeks, turning them every day. When they are ready, they will go tender and slightly translucent. The juice becomes thick and intensely lemon flavored from the lemon oils in the peel—which, along with the lemon flesh, is edible. It is important to keep the lemons covered with juice at all times, adding fresh lemon juice if necessary. You can also save leftover lemon pieces from cooking or drinks by adding to the jar with the pickling liquid.

Charmoula

Charmoula is a colorful Moroccan relish, akin to pesto, that is often served to accompany fish but is just as good on chicken or used to dress up a sandwich. This version is spectacular with the addition of olives and tomatoes. Spread it on bread before covering with cheese and toasting in the oven or under the grill. Toss a couple of spoonfuls with some shrimp sautéed in butter or olive oil; use this to top pasta or to eat with some crusty French bread.

2 teaspoons (10ml) ground cumin

1 teaspoon (5ml) ground coriander

4–6 cloves of garlic, minced fine

1 tablespoon (15ml) sweet paprika

1 tablespoon (15ml) hot paprika or ½ teaspoon (2.5ml) cayenne

½ cup (125ml) lemon juice

¼ cup (60ml) pine nuts

½ cup (125ml) chopped parsley

½ cup (125ml) chopped cilantro (coriander)

1 wineglass extra virgin olive oil

1 or 2 bottled roasted red peppers, chopped

10 Kalamata or Greek olives, chopped

12 cherry tomatoes, quartered

salt and black pepper to taste

Place the first 9 ingredients in a food processor and mix well. Add the olive oil a little at a time until a nice paste is formed. Place in a bowl. Stir in the red pepper, olives, and tomatoes.

Taratour Sauce

This earthy sauce of sesame butter goes over fish, rice, or pasta. As part of Greek meze, serve hot and dip in some pieces of pita bread. Taratour is not as well known but is the basis, with the addition of mashed chick peas and some olive oil, for **hummus**.

½ cup (125ml) tahini (sesame paste)
¼ cup (60ml) water
⅓ cup (85ml) lemon juice
½ teaspoon (2.5ml) ground coriander
pinch hot red pepper
2 cloves garlic, crushed with ½ teaspoon (2.5ml) salt
handful finely chopped fresh parsley

Place sesame paste in mixing bowl. Add water and lemon juice gradually, beating with a fork. The mixture will become thick and then thin as the liquid is added. It should resemble cream. Add garlic and beat well. Add lemon juice and salt to taste. It should be quite lemony and sharp. Stir in the parsley.

Blender Hollandaise

Hollandaise is one of those sauces most cooks find mysterious. It traditionally requires the expert use of a double boiler and the undivided attention—along with the intense effort—of the chef, who must stir deftly, even frenetically, to keep the rich egg and butter mixture from "cutting" or breaking—in other words, refusing to be a "good little sauce" and homogenize when it is told to. The use of a blender makes all this anxiety unnecessary. Using this method you can make a lovely hollandaise that is great on vegetables and fish. Hollandaise is, of course, the classic sauce for Eggs Benedict.

3 egg yolks

2 tablespoons (30ml) lemon juice

¼ tsp (1.25ml) salt

dash of cayenne pepper

½ cup (115g) butter

Melt butter in microwave or in a small pan just until bubbly. Put egg yolks, lemon juice, salt, and cayenne in blender jar. Cover blender and blend at high speed for 2 or 3 seconds. Remove center section of cover or entire cover. Set to blend at lowest speed while slowly drizzling melted butter into the mixture. When butter is incorporated, continue to blend a few seconds. Voilà! Almost instant and definitely perfect hollandaise. You may refrigerate this, but try to use it up when you have made it. Do not let it stand at room temperature too long.

Blender Bearnaise

½ cup (125ml) white wine or dry sherry

2 tablespoons white wine or tarragon vinegar

¼ cup (60ml) diced onion

cayenne pepper to taste

1½ teaspoon (7.5ml) dried tarragon (or 2 sprigs fresh chopped)

3 egg yolks

½ cup (115ml) melted butter

1 tablespoon (15ml) fresh tarragon, chopped (optional)

Boil the wine, onion, tarragon, cayenne, and vinegar together until almost all the liquid is absorbed. Add it to the blender with the egg yolks. Cover blender and blend at high speed for 2 or 3 seconds. Remove center section of cover or entire cover. Set to blend at lowest speed while slowly drizzling melted butter into the mixture. When butter is incorporated, continue to blend a few seconds. Stir in fresh tarragon and serve with steak or eggs or vegetables.

Madagascar Green Peppercorn Sauce

This sauce is a divine accompaniment to a fantastic steak.

1 can beef broth or consommé

1 whole shallot, or ¼ small onion minced finely

2 tablespoons (30ml) butter

1 cup (250ml) heavy cream or crème fraîche

3 tablespoons (45ml) brandy/cognac

sprinkling of nutmeg

2 tablespoons (30ml) drained Madagascar green peppercorns in brine

Melt butter in a medium skillet, add chopped shallots or onion, and sauté 2 minutes. Add beef broth. Boil broth until reduced by half, about 4–5 minutes. Add cream, brandy, and green peppercorns to the pan. Continue to boil, stirring until mixture thickens to sauce consistency (coats a spoon), about 5 minutes. Add nutmeg. Taste for seasoning.

Serve over steaks or chops.

 Galley Guru Tip

Cans, cans, cans! The Galley Guru is not above a shortcut. If you must use a soup or sauce directly out of a can, remember that about a half glass of white wine, vermouth, or dry sherry will greatly add to the flavor as you are heating it up. For beef stews and soups, add red wine or brandy. This will go a long way to obliterating that canned taste in the soup. Wine tends to marry the flavors and cut the saltiness of most pre-prepared foods. Turkey gravy can be made quite serviceable indeed by the addition of a couple of slugs of bourbon and a dollop of fresh (or even canned) cream.

Tofu Cream

This is the little miracle that will allow you to have many more options in your cruising cuisine than might be expected. It does not contain additives to make it thick nor does it contain any sugars of any kind, as many store-bought soy creams do.

1 package (349g) Mori-nu silken firm tofu (or other firm tofu)
equal amount favorite unsweetened soy milk
pinch of salt

Blend the tofu until perfectly smooth in a food processor. Fill the empty tofu carton with the soy milk. Add the pinch of salt. Pour it into the tofu with the machine running. In about 30 seconds you will have smooth and thick soy cream that can be used immediately or stored in a tightly sealed jar in the refrigerator for up to a week. Use in any recipe where thick liquid cream is required. This cream can be made sweet for desserts, or on its own it can go into many savory dishes.

For cinnamon tofu cream, add 1 teaspoon of cinnamon and 2 tablespoons honey or brown sugar to this to make a dessert cream. Try it over sliced apples.

Tofu Sour Cream

1 package (349g) Mori-nu silken firm tofu
¼ cup (60ml) lemon juice
juice of a whole lime
¼ cup (60ml) olive oil (can substitute any good oil, nut oil is nice)
pinch of salt

Blend ingredients until smooth. This sour cream can be made savory with the addition of more salt. Use it to fill a baked potato or anywhere you might need sour cream: to top off a bowl of chili, sauce some noodles Romanoff, or make vegetarian Stroganoff. Add fresh chopped chives if you have them, or any fresh herbs. By adding honey or brown sugar you can serve with fruit or desserts.

Soy Mayo

This soy mayonnaise is so good that you will not realize it is very low in fat and high in protein. Slather it on sandwiches, use it as a basis for salad dressings; soy mayo can go anywhere you would use real mayo. All of the seasonings are to taste here. It very much depends on you.

1 package (349g) Mori-nu silken firm tofu
¼ cup (60ml) lemon juice
½ - ¾ (120-180ml) cup grape seed oil (or any mixture of good oil:
    canola, olive, grape seed oil)
½ teaspoon (2.5ml) dried mustard
1 teaspoon (5ml) liquid aminos (Marigold, Braggs)
1 teaspoon (5ml) Marigold bouillon powder (see * p. 19 for subs.)
salt to taste

In the blender or food processor, mix the tofu into a cream with the lemon juice. Add the seasonings and the oil and continue to blend into a smooth mayonnaise.

Desserts to Live For

Sweets are not always bad for you.
On board, you will be expending a lot more energy
than at a leisurely picnic dockside.
Here are a few simple and ultra simple ways to finish a meal.

Tropical Baked Apples

Baked apples are easy to assemble. Use these dried fruits or any you have on hand. Dates are always nice with apples. Raisins, of course, are good and traditional.

4 apples
½ cup (125ml) chopped dried pineapple
½ cup (125ml) chopped dried papaya
½ cup (125ml) chopped dried cherries
juice of 1 lemon or lime
½ cup (125 ml) apple juice
½ teaspoon (2.5ml) cardamom
½ teaspoon (2.5ml) cinnamon
2 tablespoons (30ml) brandy
2 tablespoons (30ml) brown sugar

Heat the oven to medium high. Cut the tops off the apples and core them. Place them into a baking dish. Toss the dried fruit in a bowl with the lemon juice, sugar, and brandy. Stuff the apples with the fruit, pour the apple juice over, and sprinkle with the cardamom and cinnamon. Bake the apples for 25 minutes covered with foil. Remove foil and bake for 10 minutes more. Serve hot or at room temperature.

Strawberries Nimmo

A bowlful of fresh, ripe, sweet strawberries. What else could you possibly need? What more wonderful, elegant way could there be to finish a delightful repast? Well, this one. Don't be put off by the idea of eating pepper on your strawberries. Italians do it all the time, with good reason. It is the Sambucca here that is the kicker! I inherited this recipe from a good friend and fellow traveler of impeccable taste who taught me that very often the loveliest things are the simplest. In this case that is emphatically so. Perfection!

    1 pound (455g) fresh strawberries
    Sambucca
    black pepper

Cut the strawberries into halves or quarters, depending on the size. Toss strawberries with two or three good slugs of the Sambucca. Finish with a few twists of freshly ground black pepper. Serve. Note: If you want to be thoroughly decadent, make up some whipped cream in a bowl to dip the strawberries into like a fondue.

Chocolate Covered Strawberries

This is a classic after-dinner indulgence, nice for a get-together, that requires only a little work. Adjust the quantities to the number of people you need to serve.

Melt good dark chocolate in a bowl set in a saucepan filled with water over a low flame. Stir until creamy. Wash strawberries, leaving on the stems. Dip them into the chocolate, just covering half of the berry. Set the berries aside to cool. The chocolate hardens quite quickly. You can serve them right away or store them in the refrigerator.

Bananas au Rum

For the banana lover, the rum lover, or anyone in need of a quick and easy dessert. You will be in heaven.

8 bananas
4–6 tablespoons (60–90ml) brown sugar
4 tablespoons (60ml) butter
1 teaspoon (5ml) cinnamon
½ wineglass good golden rum

Peel the bananas and slice them in half lengthwise. Place them in a shallow baking dish. Sprinkle with sugar and cinnamon, and dot with the butter. Make a second layer of bananas, covering this too with sugar, cinnamon, and butter. Cover with foil and bake in a medium hot oven for 15 minutes. Remove from oven. Pour the rum over the bananas. Return to oven for 5 minutes, uncovered. Serve hot.

Note: This is also awfully good with Cachaça, the Brazilian liqueur.

Russian Grapes

Smetana, or sour cream, is used in abundance in Russia. This dessert is delicious and has a lovely texture with the smooth cream enrobing the crisp grapes.

12 ounces (340g) (large bunch) seedless white grapes
1 cup (250ml) sour cream
⅓ cup (85ml) brown sugar
1–2 tablespoons (15–30ml) sweet sherry
4 coconut or almond macaroons, crumbled

Stir brown sugar and a good swirl of sherry into the soured cream until well mixed. Stir in grapes to cover well. To make the individual portions, layer the grapes with the crumbled macaroons into cups or glasses, finishing with a few grapes on top. Serve very cold.

Poached Pears in Red Wine

A simply lovely dessert made from fresh pears. This is so easy to make.

1 bottle red wine
1 cup (250ml) sugar
2 cinnamon sticks
1 vanilla pod, slit down middle and scraped
or 1 teaspoon (5ml) vanilla
½ teaspoon (2.5ml) cardamom
4 ripe pears (Bosc are nice), peeled, with stems left on

Core the pears from the bottom and cut a flat piece at the bottom so the pears can stand upright. In a medium saucepan, bring the water, wine, and sugar to a boil. Add the cinnamon stick, vanilla, and cardamom, along with the pears. Simmer 30 minutes or until the pears are tender but not falling apart.

Remove pears to a serving dish. Increase heat to medium high. Boil sauce until it is reduced by half. Remove cinnamon stick. Allow sauce to cool. Spoon it over the pears. Cover the dish with plastic wrap and set in the refrigerator to chill. When chilled, baste again with the wine sauce and serve.

Pain Perdue au Chocolat
French Toast With Chocolate Sauce

I am never very sure whether this should be breakfast or dessert. The thing is that it is so good, it doesn't much matter. Have it twice.

8 ounces (225g) very good (70% or higher) dark chocolate

¼ cup (60ml) strong coffee or Kahlua

1 cup (250ml) cream

¼ cup (60ml) sugar

1 teaspoon (5ml) ground cinnamon (optional)

8 slices country style bread, crusts removed

1 cup (250ml) milk (can be soy milk)

1 teaspoon (5ml) vanilla

4 eggs

4 tablespoons (60ml) butter

For the Chocolate Sauce

Break up chocolate into small pieces. Place in a non-reactive bowl. Heat cream to almost boiling but do not boil. Pour hot cream over chocolate and whisk until smooth. Stir in the vanilla and coffee or coffee liquor. This is a ganache. You are now in the realms of haute cuisine. Don't fall overboard; keep this sauce warm until the French toast is done.

For the Pain Perdue

Place the bread in one layer in a baking dish or other shallow dish. Mix the cinnamon with the sugar. Sprinkle half the cinnamon and sugar evenly over the bread. Beat the eggs together with the milk and a bit of sugar in the bowl. Pour over the bread. Turn bread to soak all sides. Place a skillet over moderate heat and melt some butter in it. Remove bread from soaking liquid and allow to drain a bit. Place in the frying pan and cook until golden on both sides.

To serve, slice the bread into triangle shapes. Lay on serving plates. Sprinkle with the cinnamon and sugar. Drizzle with chocolate sauce.

"Not Guilty" Chocolate Tofu Pie

A little refrigerator time is all this sinless chocolate pie has to serve. Just until it is very cold.

> 1 pound (455g) good dark Belgian chocolate, chopped finely, or chocolate chips
> 1 package silken firm tofu
> 1 teaspoons (5ml) vanilla extract
> 4 tablespoons (60ml) coffee liqueur or strong coffee
> 2 tablespoons (30ml) honey
> prepared chocolate cookie crust or graham cracker crust

Melt the chocolate with the honey in the coffee in a small bowl over a saucepan with simmering water over very low heat. Stir in vanilla. Blend tofu in a food processor or in a bowl with an immersion blender. Add melted chocolate. Liquefy until smooth. Pour the filling into the crust and refrigerate several hours.

If you haven't got those prepared crusts that come in pie shells already, not to worry. All you need is a box or two of your favorite cookies or crackers and some melted butter. See recipe for **Crumb Crust**, below.

Crumb Crust

> 1½ cups (375ml) graham crackers, chocolate cookies or ginger snaps
> 6 tablespoons (90ml) melted butter

Crumble graham crackers, chocolate cookies, or ginger snaps until fine. Stir in melted butter. Pat the crumbs into a pie pan. Bake in a medium oven for about 15 minutes. Allow to cool before filling.

Mexican Chocolate Pie

Add 1 teaspoon (5ml) cinnamon with the vanilla.

Orange Chocolate Pie

Instead of coffee, use an orange liqueur such as Cointreau or Grand Marnier and zest from an orange.

Chocolate Ginger Pie

Add ¼ cup (60ml) diced candied ginger after mixture is blended smooth. This is a favorite of mine. Pour into ginger snap crust.

You can substitute maple syrup for the liqueur if you haven't any or wish to avoid the alcohol.

Uncle Neil's Cookies

This recipe makes the most amazing, delectable oatmeal coconut cookies in the universe! I wasn't going to put these delights in this book because I thought there might be some difficulty at sea. What was I thinking? Everybody has their SilPat ready, don't they? So that won't be a problem, now, will it? I learned early on in my cookie career to double this recipe. After your first batch you will likely do the same. Kind of hard to keep these in the tin.

    1 cup flour

    1 cup oatmeal

    1 cup coconut (from a packet, unsweetened is best)

    1 cup butter, at room temperature

    2 teaspoons vanilla extract

    1 cup brown sugar

    ½ teaspoon baking powder

    1 egg

Preheat oven to medium (350º). With a hand mixer, cream the butter and brown sugar together until light and fluffy. Add the egg and vanilla extract. Continue to beat until incorporated.

Mix the baking powder with the flour. Stir into the liquid mixture. Add the cup of oatmeal. Stir in the coconut.

Grease a cookie sheet or place a SilPat on it. (SilPat is recommended). Use an ice cream scoop to drop balls of dough on the mat about an inch apart. With a moistened hand flatten the top of each cookie slightly. Bake 15 minutes.

Makes 20–24 cookies.

Boat Drinks

"I hate storms, but calms undermine my spirits."
—Bernard Moitessier

OK. In order not to undermine anybody's spirits, I include this section because, as we all know, it's five o'clock somewhere.

Adventure in Paradise

This is a sweet/tart long drink.

2 parts white rum or vodka
2 parts pomegranate juice
1 part orange juice
freshly squeezed juice of a lime
ice cubes

Put all ingredients into a large jug and mix. Serve over ice with extra lime wedges.

Gløgg

Scandinavian Hot Mulled Wine

Gløgg (Danish) or glögg (Swedish) is served in colder climes as a Christmas holiday tradition. This will perform an attitude adjustment no matter what the temperature. In rain-lashed weather, it warms the cockles of your heart and turns old grievances to new joys. There are some starlit nights when it is just the thing.

3 sticks cinnamon
peel of ½ orange
2–3 knobs whole ginger (not ground)
10 cardamom seeds (whole)
10 cloves (whole)
½ cup (125ml) brown (or white) sugar
½ cup (125ml) water
1 bottle dry red wine
1 glass ruby port, or Madeira or Marsala

1 glass brandy (plus a shot)
handful raisins
handful blanched almonds
orange peel

Put sugar and water in a pan over medium heat, stirring to melt the sugar. This will make a simple syrup. Add the rest of the ingredients, stir and cover. Keep pan over a low heat for an hour. To serve, strain into mugs with an extra shot of brandy if desired. Garnish by twisting a fresh piece of orange peel over the mug and rubbing around rim to release the oils.

Topheavy Piña Colada

1 part coconut milk
I part pineapple juice
2 parts white rum
½ part Malibu or other coconut liqueur[*]
½ tsp (2.5ml) vanilla
1 tablespoon (15ml) sugar
float dark rum

Combine all ingredients and shake. Serve over ice. Pour a float of dark rum on top before serving. For blended drink, put ice with everything but the dark rum in blender. Serve with float of dark rum on top.

[*] In the Philippines look for the very popular drink called Lambanog, a strong liquor made from the sap of the coconut flower. They make it straight or there are many flavors (there is even a bubble gum flavor). In any case, it is powerful and great on its own over ice or it makes an exciting Piña Colada.

Falling Overboard

Pernod originally made a drink called absinthe that had a whopping 65–75% alcohol content. As if that weren't enough to boggle the mind, Peernod's one-two punch was packed by the notorious hallucinogen, wormwood. After it came to the notice of the French government that too many of its citizens were either going blind or having too much fun, the French blamed wormwood and banned it. The Pernod company, never daunted, modified their formula and came up with something a little less mind-bending but still as delicious. Never mind. Pernod is deceptive. It may taste like a charming little anise-flavored aperitif (the lovely cafés of Paris are filled with Pernod aficionados, sipping) but it is as strong as any Scotch, being 40% alcohol (80 proof). Here's what to do when you have used Pernod in every recipe you could think of. It is simple yet agreeably addictive. This is the recipe for one, but then, who wants to drink alone?

    2 shots vodka
    1 shot Pernod
    orange juice, fresh is nice
    orange slice split on rim

Fill a tall glass with ice cubes or crushed ice. Pour vodka and Pernod over the ice. Top with orange juice. Stir. Add a slice of fresh orange. Enjoy.

Mast Climbers

(Known as Porch Climbers to Landlubbers)

Now, I know what you are all thinking after perusing this recipe: "This sounds awful!" But I'm still here (barely) to tell you that this is a wonderfully refreshing drink, especially on a hot day. Even those who do not like beer will love this. But I warn you, be careful, be very careful.

This stuff tastes like lemonade and is as refreshing as lemonade, but is mostly all alcohol and it will sneak up on you. My first mate is still up in the crow's nest, naked, howling at the moon (it is broad daylight in the middle of the afternoon).

    lots of ice
    4 beers
    1 can frozen lemonade, not that pink stuff
    vodka

Fill a large pitcher or jug with ice. Pour in the frozen lemonade. Now, the part where the lemonade can says to add 4 parts water? Skip that part. Add one part vodka instead.

    Open the 4 beers and add to the jug. Stir gently and drink immediately.

Picasso

"Remember, it's not the drinking that causes the hangover, it's the stopping."
—Anonymous

Try this blue and delicious drink.

    2 parts white rum
    1 part Blue Curaçao
    1 part pineapple juice
    freshly squeezed juice of half a lime
    ice cubes

Shake ingredients together in a cocktail shaker and pour into chilled martini glasses.

Perfect Margarita

Make this drink when you have plenty of ice. Then again, it works really well without ice, so don't let that stop you.

The first thing to distinguish a really fine drink is presentation. A properly presented cocktail has an exquisite simplicity, is more appealing and, well, just tastes better. Start with your best martini glasses or Margarita glasses. Fill them full of ice and set aside to properly chill. You needn't put them in the freezer at all—in fact, better not. Now take your cocktail shaker and fill it full of ice.

The secrets to making a good Margarita:

✳ Use good tequila. You may choose Patron or Tres Generaciones or any other top shelf tequila you like.

✳ Having retrieved a fine tequila from your stores, remember that whatever you do to it next, you want to complement the flavor of the tequila, not mask it. This Margarita is not drowned in Margarita mix. See below.

✳ Use Cointreau, not Triple Sec, because it has a better, more natural orange flavor than Triple Sec.

✳ There is no salt in this Margarita. Good tequila doesn't require salt.

2 parts very good tequila
1 part Cointreau
half part freshly squeezed lime or
very nice margarita mix
a few drops of citrus sugar syrup
½ part Grand Marnier

Shake everything together (except for the Grand Marnier) till nice and chilled. Next, dump the ice from your glasses back in the freezer (to save ice) and strain the mixture into the cold glasses.

Now get the Grand Marnier and pour a float (about ½ part) on top. You can use key limes, they are nice. If you haven't made **Citrus Sugar Syrup,** you might substitute a splash of orange juice.

Now drink. Enjoy. But beware: This drink is almost all alcohol. It is not frozen because this much alcohol won't freeze. If it freezes it isn't potent enough.

There are those who drank one and survived. There are those who drank two and survived. Those who drank three, however, are still missing at sea. Just a warning.

Citrus Sugar Syrup

This is an aromatic simple syrup. You can make it at home or when you are in a calm sea. It should be stored in the refrigerator, where it will last for months or forever, whichever comes first, but it will last at least a couple of weeks or so without refrigeration.

> **2 cups (500ml) granulated sugar**
> **1 cup (250ml) water**
> **peel of 2 lemons, 1 orange, 1 lime and ½ grapefruit, cut in long, thin slivers**

In a heavy saucepan, dissolve sugar in water over medium heat. Add citrus peel and bring to a boil, reduce heat. Simmer gently for 3 to 4 minutes. Allow to cool. Pour into a glass bottle, such as an empty tequila bottle or jar. Store.

Caesar

Make Caesars only when you have enough ice. Caesars must be very cold to be very right.

✳ Ring highball glass with fresh lemon or lime and dip into celery salt or Clamato Rimmer. Fill highball glass with ice.

For each serving add:

1–2 good shots of vodka
juice of half a lime
two or three good slugs Worcestershire sauce
two or three good dashes Tabasco
extra spicy Clamato juice to fill glass

Stir with knife (for some reason or other this seems to mix the drink best, although I have no idea why). Serve. I suppose you could substitute tomato juice for Clamato juice, but then it wouldn't be a real Canadian Caeser, eh?

Ginger Sunset

Chill Martini glasses and rub rims with a bit of lime peel. Fill cocktail shaker with ice. For each serving add:

2 parts ginger infused vodka
3 parts apple juice
juice of a lime
3 teaspoons (15ml) Citrus Sugar Syrup (or 3 tsp [15ml] sugar)

You may stir or shake this one, then strain into chilled glasses.

Chocoholic

Chill martini glasses with ice. For each drink you need:

> **1 part white rum**
> **1 part dark rum**
> **1 part white crème de cacao**
> **1 part cream**
> **½ part dark crème de cacao to float**
> **cocoa powder and sugar**

Dump the ice in the glasses. Dip the rim of each glass in water, then in mixture of sugar and cocoa powder. Shake the first four ingredients with ice in cocktail shaker until really cold. Strain into prepared glass. Float the dark crème de cacao on top.

And of course, there is the tried and true . . .

Cuba Libre

> **2 ounces golden rum**
> **juice of ½ lime**
> **ice**
> **cola**
> **wedge of lime**

Place rum, lime, and ice in a tall glass and fill with cola. Garnish with wedge of lime.

Champagne Sangria

"I only drink champagne when I'm happy, and when I'm sad. Sometimes I drink it when I'm alone. When I have company, I consider it obligatory. I trifle with it if I am not hungry and drink it when I am. Otherwise I never touch it—unless I'm thirsty." —Lily Bollinger

You need not use the likes of Bollinger in the following recipe. But do use a nice bubbly that is the driest variety. "Dry" is not, for example as dry as "brut" champagne. Some of the Spanish "Cavas," which refer to sparkling wine made in the méthode Champenoise—or Champagne method—are excellent. Freixenet or Segura Viudas are two that I like very well, they are eminently drinkable and they don't cost the earth.

The green chartreuse is the nicest part about this drink. It is full of secret herbs that have gone undiscovered these long years, but that make this sangria outstanding. You may, of course, make substitutions. Any fruity or herby liqueur will make a dandy Sangria. You may branch out with almond or hazelnut liqueur. For the fruit in this, you may substitute whatever fresh fruit you have on hand. Tropical fruits such as mangos and papayas are lovely too.

1 bottle white wine (or champagne)
½ bottle green chartreuse
1 apple, sliced
1 orange, sliced
1 peach, sliced
fresh strawberries, cut in half
1 lime, sliced
1 can lemon lime soda
1 can club soda
float of brandy

Fill a large jug with ice cubes. Pour all ingredients over the ice. Stir well. Pour into wine glasses and then float the brandy.

Where in the World?

Here you will find the suppliers and purveyors of products
that will make life a little more pleasant.

Cherry Balsamic Vinegar by Lulu
> Find it at
> www.restaurantlulugourmet.com
> or
> www.foodzar.com

D'Artagnan Duck Confit is marvelous.
> Along with many hard-to-find gourmet items, it is to be had at
> www.eurogrocer.com

Dende Oil, a red palm oil originally from Africa.
> Used in Brazilian cooking. Available in Brazilian shops or at
> store.amigofoods.com
> the African version is at
> www.safarioil.com

Digestive Biscuits
> Delicious British-made McVities Wholemeal Biscuits (crackers)
> Can be found in British shops or can be delivered direct to
> your door from
> www.ukgoods.com
> or
> www.britishdelights.com

Dried Mushrooms
> For a wonderful selection of gourmet dried mushrooms, try
> www.pistolrivermushrooms.com
> or for mushrooms and much more that is rare go to
> www.jrmushroomsandspecialties.com

Duck Confit
> Duck leg is seasoned and slowly cooked in duck fat. Enjoy cold
> or reheat on the grill or in the oven. It, along with many hard-
> to-find gourmet items, can be found at

www.eurogrocer.com

or

www.igourmet.com

Fleur de Sel, Alaea Hawaiian Red Salt, and **Bolivian Rose Salt**
These are just some of the amazing salts of the world nestled among the gourmet items you will find at
www.earthy.com

French Hermetic Jars
These, along with other containers, can be found at
www.containerstore.com

Ghee (Indian Clarified Butter)
You will find this at health food stores and gourmet markets. Also online at
www.store.ethnicfoodsco.com

or

www.spicesgalore.stores.yahoo.net/ghee.html

Jamon Serrano
This and many fine Spanish products can be obtained at
www.latienda.com

Kewpie Mayonnaise
It comes in a squeeze bottle. Available from Asian markets or online, oddly enough, at
www.amazon.com

or get it from
www.veryasia.com

or

www.yollieoriental.com

Lambanog

Unfortunately, if you want to try Lambanog you will probably have to do so in the Phillippines as it is not imported into the States yet. Most of the Lambanog distilleries are in the Quezon province of Luzon, but it is available all over the islands.

Macapuno Coconut

and other Philippine and oriental mysteries are at www.yollieoriental.com

Madagascar Green Peppercorns

If you can't find this in your local grocery store, go to www.gourmetfoodstore.com

Mandoline

This cuts, slices and juliennes. Find it reasonably priced at www.surlatable.com
For an inexpensive V-slicer go to www.thekitchenstore.com

Manual Food Processor

Velocity Deluxe Manual Food Processor. Available from West Marine or online at
www.westmarine.com
Starfrit Manual Food Processor available from
www.amazon.com
Progressive #GFCD-50 Manual Food Processor available from
www.amazon.com

Marigold Bouillon Powder

Marigold is planning a U.S. launch to major health food store chains. Until then, it is readily available from Marigold distributors in the U.K. You can also find it online at
www.aroracreations.com

Microplane Grater
You can buy these almost everywhere now or else shop online at
www.thekitchenstore.com

Miso Paste can be purchased from
www.earthy.com, who also have a huge selection of rare
wonders for the table.

Mori-Nu Tofu
can be obtained at many health food stores and supermarkets
around the country. Or purchase online direct from the
company at
www.morinu.com

Pasilla or Ancho Chilis
are readily available in the Mexican section of most
supermarkets. Or online, a convenient powder or paste form
can be found at
www.mexgrocer.com

Potato Ricer
Find this little miracle at
www.surlatable.com
or
www.williams-sonoma.com

Prosciutto di Parma
(whole or sliced) and other of the world's divine dried meats are
among the many gourmet items at
www.igourmet.com
or
www.eurogrocer.com

Silica Gel Pak
Order from
www.veritemp.com
Packaged desiccants come in all sizes. 0.5g Silica Gel Paks are perfect for spices. Order 1-gram packets for larger items
or
www.preservesmart.com/products.htm
which carries a 50-gram microwave rechargeable silica pak as well as lavender sachets for use as bug repellent.

SilPat
A silicone mat to keep everything from sticking. Buy it from
www.surlatable.com
or
www.macys.com

Smoked Paprika comes in three flavors:
Dulce (Sweet), Agri-Dulce (Bittersweet), and Picante (Hot)
The best Spanish supermarket online is
www.latienda.com

Sriracha Hot Chili Sauce
Available at Asian Markets
www.huyfong.com
or
www.heavenlyheathotsauce.com
has a collection of hot sauces that will make your mouth water.

Tamari Soy Sauce
This wonderful soy sauce is now carried in any health food store and some supermarkets. Otherwise, purchase online at
www.organickingdom.com

Textured Vegetable Protein (TVP)
Can be found at most health food stores.
Or to buy the flavored kind in cans, go to
www.usaemergencysupply.com
Also, dry in bags at
www.iherb.com

$\mathcal{I}$ndex

Here, to help you find what you seek,
is a copious manual search engine . . .
on paper, the way they used to be.

Vegan Dishes

Vegetarian Dishes

Listings by Sea State

Vegetable Dishes Under Way (Cont'd)

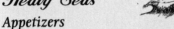
Heavy Seas

Appetizers

Desserts

Drinks

Eggs

Pasta

Potatoes

Sandwiches

Seafood Dishes